STAR ning Resources OL

D0353677

STARTING SCHOOL
Young children
learning cultures

LIZ BROOKER

OPEN UNIVERSITY PRESS
Buckingham • Philadelphia

Open University Press
Celtic Court
22 Ballmoor
Buckingham
MK18 1XW

email: enquiries@openup.co.uk
world wide web: www.openup.co.uk

and
325 Chestnut Street
Philadelphia, PA 19106, USA

First Published 2002

A catalogue record of this book is available from the British Library

ISBN   0 335 20932 7 (pb)   0 335 20933 5 (hb)

Library of Congress Cataloging-in-Publication Data
Brooker, Liz, 1946–
    Starting school: young children learning cultures / Liz Brooker.
      p. cm.
    Includes bibliographical references (p.) and index.
    ISBN 0-335-20933-5 (hardcover) – ISBN 0-335-20932-7 (pbk.)
    1. Readiness for school – England – London – Case studies.   2. Working class – Education – England – London – Case studies.   I. Title.
LB1132.B72   2002
372.21–dc21   2001054510

Typeset by Graphicraft Limited, Hong Kong
Printed in Great Britain by St Edmundsbury Press, Bury St Edmunds, Suffolk

This book is for my parents

CONTENTS

PREFACE

I used to be a Reception teacher, and for twenty years or so I thought of myself, with some reservations, as a good one. The reservations were there because although I managed, on the whole, to help 4-year-olds from a variety of backgrounds to adapt successfully to school learning, there were always a few children for whom my professional practice didn't seem to work. These children – looking back, they tended to be mostly either from the Bangladeshi community, or from the poorest white families – spent two years in my class without noticeably latching on to learning. Perhaps all teachers have this experience. But I never felt satisfied with the explanations offered by research for these children's inability to succeed, and remained frustrated by my own failure to get to grips with it. The research described in this book is the product of my dissatisfaction, and writing the book has been the means of bringing some of these experiences full circle.

At times, my own transition from teacher to researcher has seemed as developmentally dramatic as the transition children make on starting school. It required a cognitive shift from 'lived' and 'experienced' knowledge to abstraction; from common-sense practical and professional knowledge to 'higher order thinking' of the kind described by Vygotsky and Bruner (whose work I had read, but forgotten). Above all, it required a critical reflection on the beliefs and values I had acquired in my teaching career. While the ethnographic fieldwork at the heart of the study plunged me for a year into the lives of young children and their families, the analysis of the data required a shift towards conceptual models of a quite abstract kind – those of Bernstein, Bourdieu and Bronfenbrenner, among others. The explanatory power of such theory, when applied to the daily lives of the 4-year-olds in the study, seemed to me thrilling, but the thrill had a more depressing aftermath. Now that I felt I had some understanding of the ways that children from certain groups tend to fail at school, how was I to make proper use of this insight?

This question has dominated the period since the research was completed. It has been discussed with many audiences, including research groups, students of all kinds, and members of the Bangladeshi community in London. On each occasion, what started out as a 'transmission' of knowledge from me to my listeners has ended as a co-construction of knowledge, as each audience has contributed its own perspective on the processes at the heart of the study. These sessions have helped me to see that it is possible to down-shift again from theory to practice (without in the least dumbing-down); to use the theoretical understanding gained from the study to think hard about school and classroom beliefs and practices; to think like a teacher, while retaining the knowledge acquired as a researcher.

This book attempts to re-create this process: to show both how observations of children in their homes and classroom can be illuminated by theory, and how such theoretical understanding can return to inform practice. As a class teacher, I not only believed that I was acting in the best interests of the children in my care, I also assumed that if any of those children failed to make good progress, the fault could not be mine. Observing the children at All Saints' Primary – a welcoming multicultural school with a positive ethos and an exceptionally committed staff – enabled me to see that the structures of schooling may lead us to treat children unequally, even in the most well-intentioned classrooms. In describing these findings I hope to suggest how we can better understand, and combat, these tendencies.

It goes without saying that I am indebted, for everything I have learned about the interactions of culture and pedagogy, to the teachers and families of All Saints'. Their generosity and goodwill in allowing their own lives, beliefs and practices to be scrutinized and recorded was astonishing. I hope they will understand that, even where their practices are implicitly or explicitly critiqued, their dedication to the children they jointly cared for is never in question. I am deeply grateful to them all.

This is an appropriate moment to acknowledge other debts. First to my research supervisors, Iram Siraj-Blatchford and Angela Hobsbaum, who responded generously and expertly to my ideas and theories and my constant difficulties, and commented on my drafts and working documents with thought and care. In retrospect, I can see that they offered an exemplary model of 'scaffolding' learning, leading me on step by step until I was able to take on the expert role, and 'instruct' them in turn. Second, to the doctoral and post-doctoral researchers who have read and discussed my work with me: especial thanks to Charmian Kenner,

Ester Rosa, Renee Reed, Judy Lever-Chain and Andrew Burrell, who cheered the book on (critically) in its final stages.

First and last, my greatest debt is to Peter Brooker, whose critical eye has improved almost everything I've ever written. Without his urging, the project would never have begun, and without his support it would certainly never have been finished.

Sixteen children and their family and household members

Child	Mothers/Other adults	Siblings
Abu Bokkar	Rahena and her husband	Saeed 18 Abdul Motin 15 Rubina 13 Shabana 12 Abdul Rakib 11 Abdul Hasan 8
Abdul Rahman	Sabina and her husband	Abdul Motin 9 Abdul Rasul 7
Amadur	Asima and her husband	Bokkar 2 Hasina 1
Cameron	Alison and her partner	Joseph 7
Jelika	Reba and her husband and his parents	Rasul 3 Rubel 1
Jemma	June and her partner	Mary 16 Tina 13 Laura 5
Sonia and Jason	Kath	Liam 12 Nita 11 Gary 10 Terry 8
Joshua	Maisie and her husband	Jenny 8 Kirsty 6
Katy	Maxine and her husband	Charlie 8 Alice (1 month)
Kelly	Gaynor and her partner	Adam 7
Khiernssa	Minara and her husband	Salek 8 Layla 6
Mohammed	Shazna and her husband	Nasima 16 Onjona 14 Bassan 2
Rufia	Majida and her husband	Lipa 15 Abdul Hasan 13 Meera 10 Salma 9 Abdus Samad 7 Halima 1 Naseem (3 months)
Tuhura	Jamila and her husband	Abdul Rakib 6 Tahmina 5 Asim 1
Troy	Charlotte and her husband	Jerome 3 Lara (5 months)

Names and other details of all individuals and families have been disguised to ensure anonymity.

LEARNING CULTURES IN ALL SAINTS' END

This is the story of 16 children, all 4 years old, who started school together in a single Reception class in a poor and rather rundown inner urban neighbourhood. In their first four years of life, each of them had learned more than they would ever again learn in such a short space of time. For each, their home environment was a 'learning culture', in which their earliest observations and interactions had been the means of acquiring and constructing knowledge: facts, skills, beliefs and values. All of them now possessed a rich and detailed knowledge of the culture of their own family and community. All were successful members of their own intricate social worlds. The task now ahead of them was to learn, as rapidly as possible, the culture of their first classroom, and the rules for being a member of it.

The culture of the home is not hard for a child to 'learn', because it represents the only, and therefore the natural and inevitable, way to be. It consists of all of the ways of living, and systems of meaning, which prevail in each child's family. It is present in each child's experience and expectations of how people look and talk and think and act: the ways people behave, the things that are allowed and encouraged, and the things you are not supposed to do. Early lessons about the ways people act with small babies develop into discoveries for the child about the ways the household is organized (who eats when, who sleeps where, who does what), the ways different people talk to each other and feel about each other, and the things that families do together. At some point the child receives messages about what people do *outside* the family, in other places (nursery, school, work, mosque) and discovers that in time he or she is going to be experiencing those other places too. At around this time, the child may begin to receive deliberate preparation for these future forays outside the home: 'I won't be able to do your buttons up for you when you're at school'; 'You'll have to listen out for when the teacher says your name.' In this way the child becomes aware that there is a specialist knowledge to be acquired in relation to this future world: the rules of another culture, and the knowledge and skills that are needed to succeed in it.

This book describes the different, sometimes difficult, experiences of the 16 children as they attempt the transition from 'child in the family' to 'pupil in the school': a transition which for some was anticipated during their earliest socialization, but for others had barely got under way before they entered the classroom. But first, this chapter performs two kinds of introduction: first to the subjects of the research – the children and families, their school and neighbourhood, and the educational journey which lay ahead of them – and secondly to the ways in which the study was undertaken, involving the researcher too in learning new cultures.

Sixteen children and their families

The 16 children whose stories are told in this book started school together at All Saints' Primary in September 1997. All of them lived within walking distance of the school, and many of their families had lived in the area for years, but their lives differed from each other in important ways. In fact, it is probably true to say that walking through the school gate in the morning was almost the only experience all the children and families shared.

Half of the children were 'Anglo': their parents were born and educated in the UK (many of them in this town, some of them in this school). Although three of the eight children – Troy, Cameron and Kelly – were of dual Anglo and African-Caribbean heritage, it emerged that none had relatives or connections beyond the UK. For this group, their home language was English, and their home culture was that of the English working class. Their parents, if they were employed outside the home, were lorry drivers or warehouse men, factory workers or childminders. All the children lived with their mothers, but four of the children were not living with their natural father. The families rarely travelled outside the town, where some had lived all their lives. The eight children were all born in the maternity hospital in town.

The remaining eight children were from Bangladeshi homes. All of their parents were born in the province of Sylhet, although some of their fathers had arrived in the UK in time to experience a few years of English schooling. Their mothers had either 'come over' as brides for men already living here, or had arrived in the early years of their marriage. Their home and work lives were almost entirely within the Bangladeshi community in the neighbourhood. Fathers, if they worked, worked within Bangladeshi businesses. Mothers, who did not work outside the home, lived a life largely cut off from their English-speaking neighbours. The language of their homes was Sylheti, although the parents, and now their children, learned to read and write Bengali for cultural use, and Arabic for religious purposes. The families' links with the wider world were with relatives in other parts of the UK, and lengthy but infrequent visits 'abroad' (to Bangladesh). Six of the children were also born in the maternity hospital in town, but two were born in Bangladesh and had made the move to England during their second year.

Two of the Anglo children were twins. **Sonia** and **Jason** were the fifth and sixth children of Kath, and part of a close-knit extended family. The family had returned to All Saints' End (near to where Kath's own parents live) after several attempts to settle down in other parts of town, but were forced to leave their home after problems with neighbours, and Kath's former partners, during the twins' Reception year. Despite Kath's devoted attention to her children, the three older boys were also already in serious trouble, at school and with the police.

Joshua and **Katy** had mothers who were good friends and neighbours. Joshua's mother Maisie was a childminder and part-time play leader, and was energetic in organizing activities for Joshua and his two older sisters while their father, a long-distance lorry driver, was away on trips. Katy's mother Maxine (who did bar work as well as playgroup work) and her father, a factory worker, were similarly active in family pursuits and hobbies with Katy, her older brother and baby sister. Both families were well established in the neighbourhood.

Cameron's mother Alison worked evenings in a local factory, and made sure her partner was home to care for Cameron and his older brother Joseph on the evenings she was out. Alison came from an army family, and had got as far as the sixth form before dropping out of school. Her partner, who was of African-Caribbean heritage, was born locally and worked for the council. This family's life revolved around friends, rather than relatives.

Kelly's mother Gaynor (herself part African-Caribbean) had been a pupil at All Saints' at the start of her somewhat chequered school career. Kelly and her mother and her older brother Adam shared a home with Gaynor's new partner, but spent a lot of their time back with Kelly's grandparents. Gaynor's sisters and their children also congregated here for much of the day. No one in the family had regular work, so resources were shared among members of the family.

Jemma's family were more isolated. Her mother June, her father and her three sisters shared a life marked by recurrent financial and social stress. June had attended school locally but truanted from an early age. She had had difficulty finding and holding down jobs, and her partner had until recently been unemployed for three years. The unpredictable behaviour of their teenage daughters added to the family's anxieties, and Jemma grew up amid considerable domestic upheaval.

Troy was the oldest child of Charlotte, a mother who was taking her life into her own hands and refashioning it. Charlotte had spent her childhood in a series of foster homes, with frequent changes of school. After separating from her first partner, the father of Troy and his brother Jerome, she had met and married Bob, and set out to attain a life of respectability and esteem. Her ambition was to give her children a 'perfect life', to compensate for her own childhood unhappiness.

Abdul Rahman shared a birthday, but little else, with Troy. He was the third son of Sabina, who was brought up and educated in a town in Sylhet. The family had a network of relatives in Midlands towns, and Rahman's father, a cook in a family-owned restaurant, had some standing among the men in the local community. The family shared a house with in-laws, and visited other relatives regularly.

Tuhura was Rahman's first cousin: her mother Jamila was also town-educated, and her father was a waiter in the restaurant where Rahman's father cooked. The family moved out of a shared house into a home of their own when Tuhura was four, but stayed in close contact with the aunts and uncles and cousins. Tuhura, the third of four children, had been for a long visit to Bangladesh as a small child.

Rufia and **Khiernssa** not only shared a birthday but first 'met' when their mothers were in adjacent beds in the maternity ward, and had become friends since. Rufia's father was unemployed, and spent a lot of time helping at home, cooking and caring for his wife and children. His wife Majida had eight children and was often unwell, but her husband washed and dressed the little ones and was always available to pass the time with them. Like Rahman's father he was something of an authority in the neighbourhood. Khiernssa's father, also unemployed, devoted his time to his house and his allotment, as well as to the local mosque committee. The family grew large quantities of vegetables and herbs, a project which also involved Khiernssa's mother Minara and her older brother and sister. Minara too was frequently unwell, a trait which Khiernssa seemed to have inherited.

Abu Bokkar lived across the street from Khiernssa, and his mother Rahena was friends with Minara. Bokkar was the seventh and youngest child in the family, and was seen as special by his parents, who nicknamed him 'little prince'. His father, who was unemployed, was an educated man, involved in the Bangladeshi community at many levels, and very conscious of his children's educational progress. Their family life appeared to revolve around the children's schooling, and the requirements of mosque school; all their hopes were tied up in their children's future.

Jelika's family, like Jemma's, were rather isolated. Unusually, they appeared to receive little support from their relatives around the town, and were on the verge of homelessness. When we first met they were living with Jelika's grandparents, and her father was employed in a family-run business. Subsequently the whole family moved into a single room in an already overcrowded house belonging to another family. Jelika's mother Reba, an educated woman in Sylhet, was clearly distressed by the family's plight, but the cause of it remained unclear. Jelika 'disappeared' from school after one term.

Amadur and **Mohammed** were first cousins, both born in Sylhet and transported to England in their infancy. Their fathers were brothers but their mothers were from very different backgrounds and were not friends. Amadur's mother Asima, an educated woman with an interest in literature, felt quite isolated in her new home: with three children under 5, and a husband working seven days a week in a restaurant, she seemed unsupported and unhappy. Mohammed's mother Shazna, an older woman from a rural background, was more content. She chose to emphasize her new acquisitions – a fridge, a washing machine and a large TV set – rather than to lament the loss of society and neighbourliness which was the price both women had paid for their transition to England. Shazna, whose husband worked in a restaurant in the Eastern Counties, allowed her two teenage daughters to negotiate the daily routines of life in the UK, including sorting out schooling for Mohammed and his little brother.

These were the families who took their children to Mrs Goode's Reception class in the first week of September. They were about to share a classroom, but until now they had simply shared life in All Saints' End.

Daily life in All Saints' End

The All Saints' district lies about a mile from the centre of a prosperous county town, whose older craft industries have recently been replaced by an influx of new international companies. As is the case in similar towns and cities, most of the ethnic minority population who arrived in the postwar years have settled into the dense red-brick terraces closest to the centre, while the majority population, with increasing prosperity, has gradually moved towards the outer suburbs. While African-Caribbean families are dispersed across the town, most Asian families (Indian, Pakistani and Bangladeshi) have remained in the poorer central areas, where the Sikh gurdwara, the Hindu temple and the mosque are located.

All Saints' End, which has housed a Bangladeshi community since the 1950s, still has a majority English-speaking population, many of whom have been in the area for generations. Except among children of school age, there is no apparent contact between the two communities, on the streets, in the shops, or around the school. Bengali women, who appear silent on the streets, stop to chat in community shops like the Bangla Bazaar and the Bismillah Stores, or shop at local cut-price supermarkets on their way home from school in the morning. In this particular neighbourhood community, none are employed outside the home. Anglo mothers can be seen talking in groups around the local shopping centre, but also often make weekly shopping trips by car to the larger stores on the edge of town. Many, even those with young babies, have part-time work in shops, factories, warehouses or pubs. Bengali men, both old and young, are employed entirely in community or family businesses, and sometimes travel to distant towns to work, while Anglo men, if employed, work in factories or warehouses within a short drive of their homes. On the whole, it is possible for members of both local groups to carry on their daily lives without ever speaking to each other.

The separateness of the two communities is social rather than physical: neighbours from minority and majority groups seem not to see each other, and mothers from the two groups squeeze past each other without acknowledgement on the narrow pavement in front of the school gate. There are no indications that either group is aware of the barriers between them, or finds the situation odd.

The 1991 census indicates that both groups share a common low socioeconomic status, and poor 'quality of life' indicators: the neighbourhood suffers from poor housing, overcrowding, high levels of unemployment and little open space. A local park maintained by the council has hazardous access to a river and an intercity railway line, and is frequented by rough sleepers, substance abusers and roaming dogs. Few mothers allow their children to go there except under the strictest supervision.

The local school: All Saints' Primary

All Saints' Primary is the epitome of the 'local' school: a small school in low buildings, in a distinctive neighbourhood of narrow streets and alleys, cut off from other areas by the main roads, river and railway lines. No one travels to this school from outside the area but it is well known to local families: parents of English children (and some fathers of the Bangladeshi children) attended the school themselves. Its red-brick Victorian classrooms and windswept playground are sheltered by a red-brick Victorian church, a local landmark.

All Saints', like every other English school, was experiencing a good deal of external pressure, both local and national, at the time this study began. The 16 children started their school careers at the end of an 18-year period of Conservative government which had, apparently irreversibly, transformed educational discourse and practices. The reforms of the Thatcher and Major administrations (1979–97) had simultaneously centralized and dispersed the powers which had previously been distributed through the system, from government departments down to class teachers. Detailed control of the curriculum, after acrimonious and public disputes between academics and politicians in subject working parties, had ended up in governmental hands, and had crept downwards to include the curriculum for 3- to 5-year-olds in pre-school settings, the
. *Desirable Outcomes* (SCAA 1996). Control of finances, buildings, hiring and firing teachers, and recruiting children, on the other hand, had passed to head teachers and governing bodies, while a Parents' Charter encouraged parents to shop around for good schooling as they might

shop for other goods and services, but with school performance tables ('league tables') in place of the *Which?* Report. The combined effects of external control of the curriculum, the more formal pedagogy adopted in anticipation of Ofsted inspections, and media criticism of teachers and their methods, had resulted in low morale and reduced job satisfaction among teachers (Pollard *et al.* 1994), with no appreciable improvements for parents (Hughes *et al.* 1994). Children's attainments in core subjects, measured by standardized tests, were increasingly seen as the only worthwhile 'performance indicator' for schools and teachers.

At this moment (September 1997) a 'slimmed-down' National Curriculum for 5- to 16-year-olds was in place, national tests at 7, 11 and 14 were compulsory, and the Baseline Assessment of Reception children was being piloted prior to statutory use in the following year; Ofsted inspections had become a regular if unwelcome feature of teachers' lives, and performance-related pay (an echo of the Victorian 'payment by results' system) was back on the agenda.

At the same time, it was evident that the Education Reform Act (1988) had sidelined the multicultural and equal opportunities initiatives which had informed many of the educational practices of the 1970s and 1980s. The threat to educational equity took two forms: first, the earlier commitment to provide additional resources and appropriate support for children from low-achieving groups had been replaced by an official argument that the National Curriculum ensured *all* children equal 'entitlement'. Secondly, the National Curriculum itself constituted a narrowly Anglocentric or Eurocentric body of knowledge which left very little room at any level for multicultural curriculum content.

All Saints', like other inner-urban schools serving poor multi-ethnic populations, felt particularly threatened in this climate. The strong pastoral and multicultural ethos on which they prided themselves now earned them little credit, while the relatively low educational outcomes achieved by their pupils attracted public censure. Teachers whose sense of themselves as individuals and as professionals was deeply involved with their caring, inclusive and nurturing support for children from stressful backgrounds were beginning to feel that this aspect of their role was no longer valued. Instead, they were being compared, competitively and unfavourably, with teachers from less disadvantaged neighbourhoods, whose professional role was to teach, rather than nurture, and whose 'results' put their own to shame.

Education and expectations

What could the 16 All Saints' children be expected to achieve, in their school careers and in their lives? Certain general tendencies could be predicted from the research on children's educational outcomes, which by now was as familiar to readers of the Sunday papers as to those professionally involved in education. Some of these findings are outlined here.

Since the 1960s, studies comparing the attainments of children from different backgrounds had established clear trends. Early concerns over structural inequalities focused on the social class divide evidenced by 11+ passes, which was found to persist and worsen as children moved into secondary and tertiary education, and eventually became parents themselves (Rutter and Madge 1976). School ethnographies had described the processes whereby 'working-class pupils tend to percolate downwards in the processes of academic and behavioural differentiation' (Ball 1981: 108). By the 1980s, concern over the unequal achievements of ethnic minority groups, and of girls, had prompted national and local interventions; by the 1990s, paradoxically, the poor outcomes of boys had become a matter of concern.

The ways in which children's school careers developed in primary schools were reported by the Junior School Project (Mortimore *et al.* 1988), which systematically documented the school experiences and attainments of 7- to 11-year-olds in London schools. After controlling statistically for large numbers of variables, these authors established a strong relationship between social class (defined by parental occupation) and reading scores, *even after* eliminating the effects of minority ethnic status, family size, birth order, free school meals, nursery education, and other well-known 'disadvantaging' variables. They found too that social class differentials widened from age 7 to age 11: far from equalizing children's chances, schooling appeared to be further disadvantaging children from already disadvantaged groups. In particular, the study reported, 'evidence of underachievement by children of some ethnic minority backgrounds is a cause for serious concern' (1988: 117).

These findings, together with those from a parallel study of infant schools (Tizard *et al.* 1988) reinforced the national concern aroused by the Rampton and Swann reports (1981, 1985), which had publicized the educational disadvantage experienced by black and Asian pupils. Nevertheless, despite the equal opportunities initiatives of many local authorities, at a national level affirmative action policies were rejected in favour of a National Curriculum designed to raise the achievement of *all* children through equal entitlement to education (DES 1988) and the promotion of a 'common culture'. While Ofsted commissioned a review of ethnic minority achievement in the 1990s (Gillborn and Gipps 1996), and national concern was expressed about the low achievement of some groups of boys, concern over social class as a cause of school disadvantage was no longer on the political agenda.

In practice it has proved impossible, when researching children's achievement, to separate social class from ethnicity, and to distinguish different aspects of minority background, such as bilingualism. Reports on ethnic minority family incomes (Berthoud 1998) and on poverty and social exclusion (Howarth *et al.* 1998) indicate that minority groups, particularly those concentrated in inner urban areas, are 'easily the poorest groups in the country', and that as a result of larger family size in low-income groups, a third of children in the UK live in poverty. Those minority communities whose children are making good progress in school tend to be from slightly higher socioeconomic groups. Thus, an overall improvement in attainment for all ethnic minority children masks both the exceptionally high achievement of certain groups such as Chinese and Black African pupils, and the continuing poor outcomes of larger groups such as pupils of Pakistani and Bangladeshi origin. Gillborn and Gipps conclude that 'The gap is growing between the highest and lowest achieving ethnic groups in many LEAs' (1996: 78).

The introduction of national Baseline Assessment has provided evidence of the group differences in attainment found among 4-year-olds starting school (Strand 1999a). Together with follow-up studies across the infant school years (Strand 1999b) these assessments confirm not only that the traditional inequalities still persist, but that the differential between some groups at age 4 sometimes widens by age 7.

All of this suggests that All Saints' Primary, which serves a poor multiracial neighbourhood, was already subject to low expectations of its children, and especially of its Bangladeshi pupils.

Explaining the differences in expectations and achievement

The kinds of differentials described above have become so familiar as to risk seeming 'normal', and acceptable. But *why* should children from poor or minority communities have poorer educational outcomes? The debate about the effects of social class, ethnicity and gender has focused by turn on the specific practices of parents and teachers, the incompatibility of home and school values, and the structural inequalities in society as a whole. None of these explanations, which are sketched below, accounts adequately for the failures, or the successes, of children from different class and cultural groups.

Home practices

Explanations attributing children's poor school achievement to factors in their homes, families and cultural background have focused on three key areas: language and literacy practices, cultural and childrearing practices, and parents' interest in their children's education.

The well-publicized findings of studies which have demonstrated the richness of children's home language experience (Tizard and Hughes 1984; Wells 1986) have not entirely eliminated a persistent earlier supposition that children from lower social groups 'lack language'. Children from different social groups, as we have known since the early work of Basil Bernstein (1971) may talk in *different* ways, but they have the whole range of communicative skills available to them within their habitual speech repertoire. Whether teachers (who themselves very often originate from different social and cultural groups from the children's) can respond to children's home language patterns is another matter entirely.

Similar folk beliefs have obtained with respect to family literacy practices, where the *differences* from mainstream (middle-class, school-like) practices which in fact influence children's school progress in literacy may have been misread as an *absence* of literacy in the home. The social class basis of such differences was identified early on by the Newsons: 'attitudes to literacy vary so much from one social group to another that a child's progress through school is significantly predetermined before he ever sets foot in the place' (1976: 445). This effect has been attributed both to the overall 'expectancy' of middle-class children, their 'air of entitlement' (Heath 1983: 242), and to specific 'middle-class' practices which have been associated with school success in reading and writing: 'books in the home', bedtime stories, parents who model literacy habits by their own frequent reading and writing.

Efforts to improve the literacy prospects of educationally 'disadvantaged' children, such as Bookstart (Wade and Moore 1993) and many home–school reading schemes (Hannon 1987), have focused with some success on encouraging parents to share books with their children. Meanwhile, a good deal of research supports the view that high-quality 'literacy events' occur in households where children share in the family's spontaneous literacy practices (paying bills, writing rosters of household duties, making shopping lists or reading magazines), and where appropriate forms of literacy are an integral part of family life. Parental efforts to teach children to read and write according to their expectations of 'school learning', rather than in accordance with their everyday family and cultural practices, tend to be less likely to benefit the children; while the 'quantity of books', as opposed to the ways they are used, is no guide to the child's future success (Heath 1983; Harste *et al.* 1984).

Arguments about the influence of family class and cultural preferences on the ways parents choose to rear their children received strong support from the Newsons' longitudinal study of English provincial families (1963, 1968, 1976). This study explored the relation of parents' beliefs to specific patterns of childrearing, and the consequences of such patterns for children's school behaviour and progress, and drew some disturbing conclusions about the outcomes of social class-related practices. The analysis revealed innumerable small but ultimately influential class differences in socialization, all of which favoured middle-class children on entry to formal schooling: play routines, problem solving, the resolution of disputes; the tolerance of messiness and emergent sexuality and 'imaginary friends'; the emphasis on reciprocity and shared responsibilities, all carried a social class component. The authors conclude that:

privileged parents, by using the methods that they prefer, produce children who expect as of right to be privileged and who are very well equipped to realize those expectations; while deprived parents, *also by using the methods that they prefer,* will probably produce children who expect nothing and are not equipped to do anything about it.

(1976: 445, emphasis in original)

The methods in question lay in the detail of day-to-day parenting decisions – on bedtimes, children's chores, discipline and punishment, and the use of praise. In almost all cases, a social class aspect to parenting decisions was found, which had consequences for children's adaptation to school.

As this tells us, parents bring up their children in accordance with their own culturally appropriate rules. The disadvantaging effects of these 'rules' when the child from a working-class or minority background enters a middle-class or majority educational setting have been demonstrated in a number of subsequent studies (Heath 1983). In many cases, the culturally valued practices of the minority group may be in direct opposition to those of the majority culture within which children are educated and set on the path to future success or failure.

Finally, parents' 'lack of interest' in their children's education has been a persistent explanation for low achievement among some groups. Teachers who are unaware of parents' actual views may retain stereotypical views about such interest. The effects of teachers' perceptions of parental views on children's experiences in the classroom have been convincingly demonstrated (Huss-Keeler 1997; Reay 1998) and are discussed in greater detail in Chapter 6 below.

School practices

Explanations of the role played by school policies, and classroom practices, in influencing young children's achievement have focused on two areas: the mismatch or discontinuity experienced by children from certain groups on entry to school, and the unintended effects of teacher expectations of children, which influence the curriculum, and the level of control, experienced by individual children within the same classroom. Research into the early years of schooling suggests that a discrepancy often exists between teachers' beliefs and intentions, and their actual classroom practice (Sharp and Green 1975; Biggs and Edwards 1992), and that such practices may unintentionally disadvantage certain children or groups. In Early Years settings, teachers' professional practices are closely entwined with their views of childhood, and their developmental expectations of young children (Bennett *et al.* 1997). These 'common-sense' assumptions are the basis both for practitioners' preferred pedagogic methods, and for their early typifications of children.

As the age of entry to school drops, the importance of children's experience of transition to school looms larger. Even for 'mainstream' children, the move from home or pre-school to school has been shown to be fraught with misunderstandings (Barrett 1986). Children's confusion about why they were at school, and what they should be achieving, is often matched by their parents' misconceptions. Ethnographic studies have highlighted the additional difficulties experienced by children from minority backgrounds (Jackson 1979; Gregory and Biarnes 1994; Woods *et al.* 1999). Both bilingual and bicultural children *and* their families may experience not only language difficulties, but a range of frustrations in their dealings with the educational establishment.

Individual children in one classroom can also have highly differentiated experiences from the start of their school careers. As Pollard points out,

> each child experiences the classroom in the light of their particular structural position, learning stance, interests, strategies, identity and cultural background. The ways in which each child interprets the classroom setting, acts and learns is bound to reflect this differential positioning and to lead, in consequence, to differential experiences and outcomes.
>
> (Pollard 1996: 281)

Teacher expectations and typifications of children account for many of the classroom practices associated with children's differential achievement. Social background and ethnicity are particularly implicated in teachers' unconscious and unintentional stratification of children's learning (Blatchford *et al.* 1989; Biggs and Edwards 1992). Teachers' own accounts of the differences in the educability of ethnic groups, even where sympathetic, may reveal a 'deficit' view of minority communities. Stereotyping of ethnic minority children, with adverse effects on their educational experience, emerges strongly in Wright's (1992) ethnography of primary schooling, and in Ogilvy *et al.*'s (1990) observation study in nursery schools. The additional impact of gendered behaviour, and gender expectations, on teachers' practices and children's outcomes are revealed in the study by Tizard and colleagues (1988) in London infant schools. They show how a four-way split in educational experience and outcomes occurs when white and black boys and girls of similar social class and entry attainments enrol in the same classrooms and schools.

One of the principal ways in which 'low-expectation' individuals or groups are maintained as low achievers is through unequal curriculum provision. Teachers' judgements of children's needs, as well as their ability, may restrict the quantity and quality of learning experiences offered to children. Teachers who are particularly sympathetic to minority children tend to offer a caring social and pastoral environment for their pupils, to compensate for the perceived racism and hostility of the society outside the school, rather than the academically challenging environment which many minority parents would prefer for their children (Tomlinson 1984).

Teacher expectations and beliefs also influence the degree of autonomy and independence granted to children, and in consequence their ability to become independent and confident learners. Rogers (1989) reports on the demotivating effects of high levels of control on children, with the result that the experience of schooling actually reduces children's intrinsic motivation: 'Pupils for whom teachers have low expectations will be held for longer at the lower levels of control than will pupils for whom teachers have high expectations.' Systematic studies of classroom discourse have shown which children are most frequently subject to controlling behaviour by teachers. Any of these factors in children's early school experience may become self-perpetuating through forms of classroom organization which keep children semi-permanently at their 'entry level'.

Evaluating the explanations

There are several obvious problems with the above 'explanations' for children's differential ability to thrive and succeed in school, all of which tend to ignore the ability of individuals – children, parents and also teachers – to exercise their own agency and overturn the expectations created by general, structural accounts.

The first, then, is the fact that, while 'group differences' of the kind described are clearly evident, at a local and national level, there are also *individuals* whose school experience runs counter to all the evidence: children from poor and disadvantaged communities who achieve outstandingly in their school and later lives. Such individuals are not even all that unusual (at All Saints', two older siblings of the previous year's Reception intake were now studying at Oxford and at Nottingham: both were from poor Bangladeshi families with ten or more children, and both had started school at All Saints' themselves). Successful pupils from poor communities are not unknown, that is to say – they are simply less usual. What makes these children succeed in circumstances where their siblings and classmates, on the whole, do not?

The second problem is that identifying 'disadvantaging' factors does little to explain how these factors construct their effect on children's lives and learning. *Why* should the child of a lorry driver or a waiter or a warehouseman be slower to learn to read and write, for instance, than the child of a barrister or a dentist? *Why* should membership of a black community make transition to school more difficult for a child than membership of a white community? *Why* should 'number of books in the home' (counted in Tizard's study) make a direct difference to the school progress of a 4-year-old? Particularly since, as suggested above, substantial numbers of children from lower achieving groups do achieve at the highest levels, in spite of predictions to the contrary.

Third, if we accept the evidence for large differences in the predicted achievement of children from different social and cultural groups, must we accept that there is little to be done about it? If teachers are aware, for instance, that being the third or subsequent child in a large family lessens a child's chances of school success (Osborn and Milbank 1987), how are they to respond when a high proportion of their intake belong to this 'low-achieving' group? Is it unrealistic for the teacher who receives a new intake of children from poor, minority, bilingual communities to hold high expectations for them at all? In the 1970s and 1980s, teachers, schools and LEAs worked hard to reduce the educational inequalities which they believed were derived from factors of 'race, sex and class' (ILEA 1981). By the 1990s, they could be forgiven for thinking that their efforts – in anti-racist, anti-sexist and multicultural education – had had little impact on the inequalities identified decades before, and that their task now was simply to get on with the job of providing all children with access to the National Curriculum.

As the Preface has indicated, I was until recently one of these teachers, and the present study is the direct result of my continuing concern over some children's poor progress, and over the apparent inadequacy of the explanations for it. The story of the All Saints' children, then, is the story not only of children learning cultures, but also of my own learning. This has meant learning to step outside the safe perspective of the 'successful Early Years teacher' and view the process of starting school from other angles; learning that the rich and inviting environment of a well-planned Reception classroom looks different to children and families from different traditions; and learning that teachers' good intentions do not always, necessarily, have good outcomes.

This process involved acquiring, with some difficulty, an 'insider' view of the Early Years experience from the perspective of the children starting school, and their families. While my admiration for the staff of All Saints' was as great at the end of the study as at the beginning, it was balanced by an increasingly strong sense of the difficulties and inequalities experienced by some of the children and families in their encounter with the school. Learning to see from *their* perspective meant learning to question my own deeply held and long-standing assumptions about children's learning, and the role of the teacher.

Learning through ethnography

The All Saints' study was an ethnographic investigation of the learning experiences *offered* in a Reception classroom and in children's homes, and *experienced* by 16 children in the class. To go beyond the familiar explanations for children's progress, and predictions of their outcomes, required observing and working with the children, and talking to their teachers and families, for the whole of a school year. Only by knitting together the threads of evidence and ideas from the year's work – children's drawings and what they said while they did them; teachers' plans and daily practices; close observations of classroom interactions; interviews with parents and visits to families – was I able to make sense of the way the system was working for each of the individuals concerned.

Ethnographic research, usually understood as 'living with' the research subjects, and sharing and reporting their daily lives and experience, makes a special claim which other research strategies do not: to represent the culture of the research setting from the point of view of the participants (see for instance Fetterman 1989). This I have tried to do, but with some qualifications as to 'culture' and 'setting'. Each child, as suggested above, experienced not one culture and one setting, but many – a series of nested contexts, unique to each individual, above all that of the family (nested in the community, and in the neighbourhood), and that of the classroom (nested in the school, and in the local and national education system). In representing the 'insider' view of these cultures and contexts, therefore, it was necessary to interpret each perspective in relation to others. Each child's encounter with the school, and school learning, for instance, was shaped by that child's understanding of learning in the home. Without connecting and associating these two experiences in the life of a 4-year-old, it was impossible to comprehend the meaning they gave to them. (The relation of this research strategy to an overall understanding of the children's development is made clear by Bronfenbrenner's ecological model of development (1979), discussed in Chapter 5.)

So how was the evidence gained? Educational ethnographers, unlike traditional anthropologists, cannot hope to pick up insider knowledge simply by 'hanging out' in school, although that's a good place to start. The research evidence for this study was collected according to a timetable and design planned before I ever met the families. (A brief summary of the research design, and data sources, appears in the Appendix.) Over a period of eighteen months in all, families were contacted, children observed, teachers interviewed, policies scrutinized, families revisited, teachers reinterviewed, questions asked, and answers puzzled over. The analysis and interpretation of the findings, at a formal and informal level, was ongoing and sometimes feverish.

By far the hardest task came afterwards: thinking about, and making sense of, the data that resulted; untangling the contradictions and surprises, the multiple versions and descriptions of reality, until a consistent and theoretical explanation emerged which fitted *all* the evidence. (The role of theory in supporting and extending and generalizing a multiplicity of small-scale explanations is referred to in the chapters which follow.) By the end of a further eighteen months, the pieces of evidence had at last fallen into a pattern which seemed to account for all the facts, and all the anomalies, I had recorded and puzzled over. This book tries to show how that pattern not only 'explains' the children's experiences and outcomes, but suggests how we might make them more profitable and productive.

The role of the researcher: respecting cultures

How can an outsider – in my case, a middle-aged, middle-class white re-searcher – become an insider to the cultures of children and families from working-class communities? Some have argued, persuasively, that this is simply impossible: that members of privileged and 'dominant' groups in society can never shake off their own social conditioning sufficiently to understand what it is like to be a member of an *under*privileged, domin-ated, group. In other words, white people researching black experiences, men researching female experiences, prosperous professionals researching poor communities, are presuming to inhabit a point of view from which they are by definition excluded.

The debate over insider and outsider perspectives in research has been carried on since the 1960s and 1970s, when Robert Merton's classic essay (1972) challenged the view that only 'insiders' to a group or subculture could adequately report on it. More recently, feminist, anti-racist and critical researchers have suggested complex criteria for the researcher's appropriateness and authenticity. They argue too that it is up to the researcher to make the intellectual and moral effort to enter the culture of other groups than their own: Lois Weis suggests, 'It is our job as re-searchers to become an insider in these settings, much as we are insiders . . . within our own class cultural locations' (1992: 52). With time and integrity, she claims, 'outsiders' may be better able to represent a com-munity to those outside it than its own members.

The issue is clarified by Iram Siraj-Blatchford, who points out that 'what is important here is not whether one is *outside* or *inside* a particu-lar group, but rather whether one is a party to, "inside" or "outside" a particular political discourse' (1994: 33). What is more, such discourses can be viewed as open and permeable, so that 'individuals and groups may enter or leave according to their understanding and inclination' (1994: 35). In other words, if the researcher makes a commitment to the research subjects, whether professional, personal, or political, her or his efforts should be judged by their results rather than rejected in advance.

How can the researcher engage with this debate in the process of conducting the research? The answer to this question must be different in every case. For me, the largest challenge was to enter and investigate the homes and lives of people who in terms of education and status were recognizably 'worse off' than myself. Once 'inside', my task was to pose questions about their personal lives, note down their family practices, and ask them to think hard about their own beliefs, and why they held them – without myself becoming an additional burden in the daily lives of people who already had burdens enough. An additional challenge was to conduct part of this work with a group – the British Bangladeshi community – with whom I shared, it seemed, neither language, beliefs or life experiences.

There were many grounds then for recognizing that the research relationship I was entering required careful monitoring: the *ethical* responsibility to do no harm to my respondents – neither to add to the difficulties of their daily lives, nor to prompt negative feelings about these lives; the *research* responsibility to set my own beliefs and views to one side and allow my respondents' understanding of their own, and their children's, situation to come through.

Many of my anxieties about conducting the research appropriately were dissipated after a few meetings with the families, in which it became clear that my relationship with their children was the only token of good faith and good intentions they required. A shared affection for the children, a fascination with their progress and development, and a concern for their welfare, quickly overcame linguistic and social barriers and minimized the differences between parent and 'professional'. My status with the families combined the assets of trusted friend to the children, and authority in educational matters. Although it was I who had, for my own purposes, initiated the relationship, it was the family members themselves, for *their* own purposes, who chose to come and find me at school to report bits of news, to ask how their child had coped with the day, or to request that I speak to the class teacher on their behalf.

Once the bond of our common concern for the children had been established, therefore, the matter of 'recognizing and respecting cultural differences' became more of an academic one. It was irrelevant to the families, who were understandably more interested in exploiting the relationship for their children's benefit. For me, however, in the long process of analysis and interpretation, such differences remained in the forefront of the explanations I was discovering, as will be seen as the story of the 16 children unfolds.

How the book is constructed

The following chapters present the learning contexts and cultures of the 16 children in the sequence in which they themselves experienced them – first the home, then the school. At the same time, each chapter acknowledges that both contexts are continually present for the child: that the 'idea' of school is present in the home in the child's early years, and helps to shape parenting and preparing work, just as the idea of home is present in the child's consciousness, and intrudes at some level into the consciousness of teachers, throughout his or her school life. The relationship between home and school is therefore of paramount importance.

Chapter 2, 'Family values, and the value of families', fulfils two functions. It outlines the circumstances of the individual families in the study, and introduces some of the theoretical concepts which help to explain the influence of family life on children's learning. In this chapter, these include the theories of Pierre Bourdieu, whose explanations of the effects of economic and symbolic capital run through the experiences of the families.

This theme continues in Chapter 3, 'Learning how to learn at home', which discusses the children's preparation for school. Each of the families is shown to hold clear views on the appropriate curriculum and pedagogy of children's learning *before* school; each family, to the best of its ability, attempts to provide such learning. Even where families succeed in carrying out their intentions, the appropriateness of their work to the official educational world their children are about to enter remains an issue. Basil Bernstein's theories of pedagogy are introduced to illustrate the hidden differences in pedagogic principles on which children's home learning experiences are based. Bernstein's claims about the crucial work of mothers, in particular, in shaping their children's future chances, underlie the account of each child's early experiences.

Chapter 4, 'School culture at All Saints' Primary, shows the reader how early learning is viewed, and provided, by the school staff. The biographies and training of the class teacher, head teacher and classroom assistants have produced views about teaching and learning which contradict, in many respects, the theories and beliefs of the children's families. The school has a culture all its own, and a pedagogy and curriculum which are unique (while strongly resembling those of other schools of its type) and, to many parents and children, initially incomprehensible. The overall pedagogy of the school and classroom are illustrated through examples of the 'pedagogic discourse' in practice – the register session, the home–school reading scheme, the conduct of school outings, the balance of work and play in the classroom. Bernstein's concepts are used, again, to explain the origins and effects of such practices.

Chapter 5, 'Learning to be a pupil', describes the different ways in which the 16 children adapt to their new learning environment, and acquire the means of succeeding in a new learning culture. The process of transition for each child is understood in part through the ecological model of development devised by Bronfenbrenner (1979), many of whose theoretical 'propositions' are borne out by the children's experiences. Factors which favour some children, and disadvantage others, become clear as the children are observed, and assessed, in their early weeks of school. Baseline assessment measures throw such factors into sharp relief, as children who have appeared competent and skilled and well-adapted in their home settings are recorded as lacking in the cognitive and social skills required by school. As the year goes on, the dedicated efforts of the teaching staff enable some children to adapt smoothly to the expectations of school learning, and make the transition to being a 'proper pupil'. In the process, however, others seemingly inevitably fall further and further below expectations.

The continuing relation between the adults in the two cultures is discussed in Chapter 6, 'Linking home and school: learning to be a parent.'

The gulf between the school's good intentions towards parents, and the parents' actual experience of school, is shown to have many causes: not just the differences in experience and perspective discussed above, but also the constraints within which schools and teachers have operated in recent years. The consequences for the case study children of their parents' relationship with the school become graphically evident as the year proceeds.

Children's end-of-year achievements can be measured, and viewed, in a variety of ways. The forms of evaluation practised by parents and teachers differ as widely as the forms of instruction they employ with their children. But in the end it is the school's evaluation of children which counts, influencing both the child's experience, and the expectations held by subsequent teachers. Chapter 7, 'Outcomes: children's progress and achievements', reports the children's progress – both the social and cognitive gains which define their success as 'pupils' and as 'learners', and the learning dispositions which they have acquired during their adaptation to school. Disappointingly, the pedagogic discourse of the classroom, which aims to be inclusive and egalitarian, has already allowed some children to experience disaffection and failure.

The final chapter, 'Understanding outcomes; changing practice', is in two parts. The first reviews more systematically the factors which have been identified as contributing to children's differential progress in Reception. A minority of the children – children of normal health and intelligence and cheerful good humour – despite their parents' best efforts and the unceasing professionalism and hard work of their teachers seem already set to fail academically after their first year of school. Weighing the contributions of 'structural' and 'cultural' factors to children's progress does lead however to optimistic conclusions. The second part of the chapter indicates some ways of rethinking practice to help more children from diverse backgrounds to access the learning culture of schools.

Because readers would have difficulty getting to know all 16 of the children at once, a smaller group of children and families has been introduced in brief case studies in each chapter, against the background of the larger group's experiences; and a table of family members appears at the beginning of the book (page xii). By these means I have tried to build up a picture of the learning cultures of all the All Saints' children.

FAMILY VALUES, AND THE VALUE OF FAMILIES

Family values: what parents want for their children

What would you like them to be, when they grow up – any idea? [Parent interviews, September]

> I'd want him to be happy in whatever he did . . . if you've got a good education behind you, that's great, but I wouldn't want to force it on him . . . it's better to learn a trade than leave with nothing.
> (Alison, mother of Cameron)

> He will never get anywhere in life if he works in a restaurant.
> (Mr Ali, father of Abu Bokkar)

> Perhaps an engineering job, solicitor, lawyer, barrister . . . we would like to give them a chance to go to Higher Education . . . but we can't know the future.
> (Minara, mother of Khiernssa)

> I think he'll be a hairdresser – he loves playing hairdressers!
> (Maisie, mother of Joshua)

> I don't have any plans for her, except for her to be happy.
> (Maxine, mother of Katy)

> He might become a chippy – he'll put a pencil behind his ear, to be like Bob – or a milkman, he's always counting the milk bottles when he walks past people's houses.
> (Charlotte, mother of Troy)

Parents' aspirations for their children tell us a lot about their personal and cultural beliefs and values, and about the reasons why they bring their children up as they do. Children may not always turn out the way their parents wish them to, but parents' conceptions of their children's future underpin every aspect of family life and values: basically, families behave in ways calculated (consciously or unconsciously) to bring about the ends they desire, and rear their children in the light of their own views on what a good outcome for the child might be. Such 'desirable outcomes', to borrow the government phrase, are shaped by parents' cultural belief systems – by their idea of what a good life, and a good person, is like.

The 16 children in this study, as their parents' responses indicate, were subject to very varied expectations. The goals their parents had in mind for them reflected class, cultural and family differences, and were not always those which their teachers (or a researcher, or policy maker) might prioritize. However, when parents tell researchers or other outsiders what they want for their children, several layers of misinterpretation may creep in: the views they express have to be understood in the context of their actual behaviour, and the patterns of their family and community lives.

There can be no doubt that all the families in the study wanted 'the best' for their children. But what was that 'best'? Was it to be measured in terms of economic or social status, in wealth or in happiness, in duty or in fulfilment? Was school achievement a prerequisite for these goals? Did the same criteria apply for boys as for girls, for first as for last children in the family? And how did these criteria translate into childrearing practices with a lasting influence on the child's knowledge, skills and dispositions?

This chapter refers to two kinds of *value*: the 'values' held by families, and the 'value', or *capital*, possessed by each family and handed on to its children in their early years. The first consists of the beliefs, conscious and unconscious, which inform family goals, and shape parenting practices and children's development. The second is a more calculating assessment of the capital the child was able to bring with it to school. Both forms of 'value' have been theorized, in recent decades, in ways which help us understand their impact on children's school outcomes. Aspects of these theories, particularly the concepts of Pierre Bourdieu, are used in this chapter to explore the lives of the families in All Saints' End. But before this, we begin with a visit to Khiernssa's family.

Case study: Khiernssa's family and their values

My first visit to Khiernssa's home was made in the company of Mrs Khan, the classroom assistant who made regular home visits to All Saints' families, and acted as interpreter for the study. The visit created a lasting image of this organized and purposeful household. It was a Friday morning, and Khiernssa's older brother and sister were at school, but she and her mother and father were busily occupied on a domestic project of their own. Khiernssa (then aged under 4) was 'helping' her father to hang new wallpaper in the living room: pulling up the end of the roll, fetching and carrying, listening carefully and following instructions, while her mother Minara looked proudly on, and her father checked that I was noting every example of his daughter's precocious skills.

Subsequent visits and conversations confirmed these first impressions. The family was always engaged in some useful or productive task. In the day, this might be cleaning the house, preparing the vegetables, or cleaning out the back-yard pigeon lofts. In the evening, it was playing chess or *karrom* together, reading the children's school books, or practising the Bengali and Arabic alphabets. Only when Khiernssa or Minara was 'feeling poorly', which happened quite frequently, were they found together on the sofa watching Hindi films. At such times, Mr Khan might be busy with his own projects: preparing the minutes or agenda (in two languages) for the local mosque committee, or sending off for text books for the Bengali Saturday school.

Minara Begum was less confident and extrovert than her husband. She was brought up in a remote part of Sylhet, where she attended a village primary school for about six years, and might have attended high school but it was considered too far away. Instead she learned embroidery with her mother, and helped in the home, throughout her teenage years. She was 20 when she married her much older 'cousin brother', who had lived in her family household in Bangladesh, but had also spent many years in England. She had her first child Salek at 22, her daughter Layla one year later and Khiernssa at 26. The couple have deliberately limited their family to three children – 'How we supposed to look after any more?' demands her husband – and appear to live comfortably although Mr Khan is 'not working' and the children qualify for free school meals.

Mr Khan's energy permeates the family. He is active in the local Islamic association, is well known in the community, and is one of a group of fathers who meet to talk in the school playground or the Bismillah Stores. His wife is diffident about her own education, but on one of my visits was encouraged by him to join in reciting the Bengali and Arabic alphabets, and in teaching me simple words from a children's ABC. Mr Khan is proud of his own command of four languages, of his wife's and children's accomplishments, and of the family's strength and stability. He has made a deliberate investment of time and effort in maintaining the family culture: reading in Bengali and Arabic in the evenings, taking the children to mosque and Bengali school, studying the Qur'an at home, buying the children English and Bengali books, and reading Bengali newspapers together.

Aside from their domestic chores, the family's greatest project is growing vegetables on an allotment, supplying their own needs and providing a surplus which is given to friends and neighbours. In September, Minara proudly displays the harvest: runner beans, spinach, tomatoes, cabbages, marrows and squash, coriander, onions, potatoes and plums. Khiernssa meanwhile demonstrates the odd-shaped gourds and heads of coloured corn which are grown for decorative purposes and hang in the house. Family discussion of the work on the allotment, which includes the children, is evidence of their purposeful planning for the future, and of the inclusive, close-knit ethos of the home.

The family's well-being seems hampered, however, by its limited access to information on healthcare and education. Minara suffers from chronic tiredness and infections, and her frailty is reappearing in Khiernssa, whose frequent bouts of asthma and eczema, poor appetite and lack of energy are a constant concern to her parents. Since she 'never wants to eat' when at home, she drinks baby-bottles of milk and has 'lots of little sleeps' on the sofa, which appear to sap rather than conserve her strength. The family seems to have received no advice on her physical development.

The ways of the school system also seem hard to access, even for this articulate and well-established family. In September, with all three children now in school, Khiernssa's parents still claim to be mystified as to what is taught, and how their children are learning, though they are more than willing for their children to engage with English culture: 'You have to learn when you're living in this country, and going out, you have to learn, or you will have a problem' says Minara. Both parents are anxious for their children to do well at school – as Minara puts it, 'Without education there is nothing, not only in this country, everywhere.' They firmly believe that parents play an important role in their children's school progress: even if they are not able to *teach* them, they can urge the child constantly to listen and learn at school, to obey their teachers and work hard. In this household, whereas Mr Khan reads and writes with the children, and drills them in their alphabets and spellings, Minara's self-appointed role is to keep the children on task, switch off the television and tell them to get their books out. Like her husband, she claims high hopes for Khiernssa's future in the professions ('perhaps engineer . . . solicitor, lawyer, barrister') but reminds herself that 'we can't know the future'.

The family's 'values' then are clear: they have a high esteem for both English (school) education and for moral education, and are motivated to maintain their own language, culture and religion while accepting and adapting to the new social environment they find themselves in. They believe in the family as an institution, and in the duties and responsibilities of parents in all aspects of their children's upbringing – physical and social, intellectual and moral. They respect, and defer to, the social hierarchy their children are growing up in, and wish them to succeed within it, although they are not sure how it operates. For this reason they devote themselves to their children's development, and seek to give them advantages. But what 'value' in the wider society will the family's efforts secure for Khiernssa and her brother and sister?

'Values' and 'value': forms of family capital

Khiernssa, we might judge, has been given a very promising start in life by her parents. Their strong family commitment, their interest in education and respect for hard work, their energy and organization, and their high expectations for their children, seem likely to produce pupils who thrive at school and achieve good academic outcomes. The family values are in many respects recognizably those of the traditional middle classes. In putting these values into practice, and working together towards family goals, they are employing what Bourdieu calls the **habitus*** (discussed later in this chapter), which marks them out as a potentially high-achieving family.

The 'value' of this family background, however, can only be reckoned within the contexts the family inhabits – the local contexts (the Bangladeshi and the Anglo communities of All Saints' End, and the school community of All Saints' Primary) and the national context of a class-divided multiracial Britain. In order to describe the variability in this value – the family's *capital* – we turn to the formulations of capital, and its uses, offered by Bourdieu.

Forms of capital

Bourdieu's most significant contribution to social theory was his transformation of the Marxist theory of capital. Capital is power acquired through labour, and ultimately forms the basis of the class system and social structure, but in Bourdieu's formulation it is *symbolic* as well as *economic*. Though economic capital is the underlying force which shapes the lives of individuals, groups and societies, **symbolic capital** – cultural, social, linguistic – meshes with it in complex ways to confirm or transform their life chances. Each form of capital, Bourdieu suggests, can be converted into any of the other forms, and is theoretically transposable across '**fields**' (from home to school, for instance), but economic capital is the easiest to convert: it is simpler to buy an 'education' for one's children (encyclopaedias, piano lessons, private tuition) than to convert educational qualifications into cash for them to inherit. Educational achievement is a major contributor to an individual's or family's **cultural capital**.

The value of an individual's *cultural capital* ('what you know') may be enhanced by the ownership of **social capital** ('who you know'), which does not independently benefit the individual but 'exerts a multiplier effect on the capital he possesses in his own right' (Bourdieu 1997: 48). Social capital is described by Bourdieu and Passeron (1977) as the means by which individuals can vicariously exploit, through their relationships with others, all the economic and symbolic capital those others possess.

---

* A glossary of theoretical terms appears on page 177. Each of these terms is shown in **bold** in the text when it is first used.

Bourdieu's own examples are of dinner parties with the mayor, or drinks with the president of the golf club, but it is not difficult to imagine an equivalent hierarchy of social connections within local communities, and within the social world of the school. In a social context in which *no one* dines with the mayor or drinks at the golf club, different but equally important indicators of distinction obtain.

In the field of education, cultural capital is the most effective form of capital, the one which for Bourdieu 'made it possible to explain the un-equal scholastic achievement of children originating from the different social classes' (1997: 47). By calculating cultural capital, he claimed he could break with 'the commonsense view, which sees academic success or failure as an effect of natural aptitudes', and reveal instead a more potent factor: 'the best hidden and socially most determinant educational investment, namely, the domestic transmission of cultural capital' (1997: 48). In other words, the work of mothers and other caregivers in bringing up young children.

This hidden investment is the reason, Bourdieu suggests, why it is difficult for children from poorer homes to 'catch up' at school on middle-class children who were given an educational 'head start' at home. Middle-class children's early acquisition of cultural capital, he believes, derives its effect from 'the amount of time devoted to acquiring it', which depends in part on the family's financial ability to contribute that time to the child's early education. Families from lower social groups, though not providing the same cultural environment as the dominant classes, can nevertheless prioritize the effort to give their child 'a gain in time, a head start' by transmitting what knowledge they have to the child in the years before school. Cultural capital requires above all a lengthy period of acquisition, and it is too late to catch up when the child begins statutory schooling.

Bourdieu's account of the workings of the various forms of capital helps to explain the experiences and outcomes of Khiernssa and her classmates at All Saints' Primary. We consider below, in turn, the families' *economic capital*, and their strategies for maximizing it; their *social capital*, and their efforts for social esteem; and their *cultural capital*, and the ways they seek to enhance it.

Economic capital and the All Saints' families

All Saints' End is a poor neighbourhood, and 'on paper' there may be little to differentiate one family from another in terms of their income and its sources. No effort was made to discover actual family income for the purposes of the study, because the ways in which families *experienced* and managed their income seemed more important than the actual figures. At a national level, however, reports on ethnic minority family incomes (Berthoud 1998) confirm high levels of poverty among Bangladeshi families, and indicate that 60 per cent of Bangladeshi households are 'poor' by the conventional criterion of having an income less than half that of the national average. Only 16 per cent of white and 20 per cent of Caribbean families fall into this category, but census data suggests that the Anglo families in the All Saints' area, and in this sample, are probably among them.

When individual families are studied 'in the flesh' rather than as 'cardboard cut-outs' (Gewirtz *et al.* 1994), it soon becomes clear that conventional indicators of family income and occupational status are problematic within this sample. 'Free school meals', the most common index of child poverty, is unreliable for two reasons. First, because it relies on families receiving Income Support or Jobseeker's Allowance, which itself depends on a lengthy engagement with the Department of Social Security (DSS), now the Department for Work and Pensions, and a consistent period of unemployment or low-paid work: it therefore tends to exclude families who are frequently in and out of temporary, part-time or 'unofficial' jobs (as many of these families are). Second, because the Bangladeshi families, who prefer their children to return home for lunch, rarely request free school meals.

Occupational status is similarly hard to interpret. Most Bangladeshi fathers, for instance, defined themselves as 'not working', though some went on to describe their long working hours in shops and restaurants. At some point, many also claimed to own or co-own these businesses, only to retract when I showed an interest, and point out that they were actually in their father-in-law's, or cousin's, name. Two things are clear: first that, despite working long and extremely unsocial hours, these fathers are in poor housing in a poor neighbourhood, with little to spend on their own or their families' needs. Second, that much of the income that *is* acquired is either sent back to Sylhet, where it is needed by elderly relatives and extended families, or used to support other relatives in the UK. None of the Bangladeshi mothers has worked outside the home.

Anglo mothers, in contrast, have all been economically active. Most have worked, or are working, in shops and factories, packing and despatching, or in office jobs requiring no educational qualifications. Most take up, and leave, temporary and part-time jobs, when the opportunity offers itself or when acute financial problems dictate. During the year this included bar work and poorly paid piecework at home: as Jemma's mother explained one morning, 'I've got to get off, I've got a hundred and fifty "101 Dalmatians" brush sets to put in their boxes, and he'll be round to get them at tea-time.' The partial exceptions to this pattern are two mothers (Joshua's and Katy's) who have taken some play leadership courses.

Anglo heads of household have no consistent pattern of employment. The present partners of the Anglo mothers include men who are unemployed, a long-distance lorry driver, a factory storesman, a glazier and a council maintenance man. Only the last of these was felt by his partner to be in a secure and permanent post. Five of the eight Anglo children

(Jemma, Sonia, Kelly, Jason, Troy) had a 'dad' who had been out of work during the last year.

Position in the housing market is also an unreliable guide to affluence among these families. Home ownership is the norm in the Bangladeshi community in this town as elsewhere (cf. Bhatti 1999). Rather than signifying social and financial success, it reflects the difficulty minority families experience in securing council housing, and their willingness to pool resources within the neighbourhood or wider network to provide accommodation for relatives, even distant ones. Most newly married couples live with their in-laws or other relatives, in crowded conditions, until the money is accumulated or loaned to buy another of the small rundown houses in the streets around the school. Money from restaurants and businesses is invested in buying up these houses so that families with several children can eventually move into their own homes close by. Five of the eight Bangladeshi children who started the year (Amadur, Abdul Rahman, Jelika, Mohammed and Tuhura) had lived in houses shared with other families until a few months previously.

The Anglo families are housed in properties ranging from similar small terraced houses close to the school to council accommodation on nearby estates. All are in single-family households. The area has no high-rise housing, so all families have a small fenced yard behind, if not a garden. All front doors in the area give straight on to the pavement, which is where most children play.

Thus, while fluctuations in the family fortunes do sometimes have a dramatic impact on the children's daily lives, their basic economic situation is fairly similar. Differences in their actual disposable incomes were not superficially evident. While a family might, in an emergency, find the money to leave at short notice for Bangladesh, none of the 16 children had a family holiday, or a trip to Alton Towers or Legoland, or even London, in the year I knew them. Most never left the neighbourhood except to shop in the town centre, or visit relatives. The experience they all share is that of being hard up. The major difference between them is the way they respond to this experience: in Bourdieu's term, their **strategies**.

Economic strategies

None of the families in this group experiences extreme poverty. All had a TV and video, fridge and phone, and many had access to a car at some time in the year. Nevertheless for some families the shortage of money is such a central, energy-consuming issue in their lives that it constrains all their options. Jemma's family provides the clearest illustration of this.

Jemma's father is a fitter who now works full-time after three years of unemployment. But with a backlog of debts to clear, the family teeters on the brink of financial disaster all year: June's response is to get a part-time job, but her attendance and work rate are so poor that she is offered piecework at home instead, packing Christmas gift sets. After Christmas the family's finances worsen rapidly, and a great deal of June's week is spent appeasing or avoiding the housing department, the rent collector and various other debtors. By the middle of the summer term the family is fearful of eviction, and when their (uninsured) fridge freezer breaks down during a brief hot spell, they are unable to retrieve their deteriorating food supply, and are obliged to shop for every meal in turn. Lacking both a supportive network, and the skills to handle their debts, June has to devote all her energies to patching up one financial mishap after another. Even this task is not tackled energetically or efficiently: appointments, deadlines and final demands, it appears, are 'forgotten' or 'lost in the post' until each situation is almost beyond retrieval.

No other family's money problems reached this stage. Among Anglo families where the father was employed (such as Cameron's, Joshua's, Katy's), the mothers organized their lives so they could take part-time jobs, from childminding to bar work or telesales, to patch the gaps in the family's income. Other mothers living on benefit (Kath, Gaynor) were heavily reliant on their own parents to offer meals, clothes and childcare as well as emotional support, while Charlotte energetically and successfully committed herself to the task of helping her husband write off for jobs. Among Bangladeshi families, where only the men worked, the response to difficulty was to work longer and longer hours as waiters, at the same time as learning to cook, which was better paid. Amadur's father sometimes worked lunchtimes and night-times seven days a week, so that the only time he was home with his family was from 3.00 to 5.00 in the afternoon; the family paid the price when Asima, who by then had four children under 5, became ill and unable to cope. But all these parents showed ingenuity and determination, as well as practical organizing skills, in keeping their families out of serious financial trouble.

The indirect and complex ways in which financial hardship shaped the academic careers of the 16 4-year-olds become more clear when other aspects of their family capital, and family strategies, are taken into account.

Social capital and the All Saints' families

The social capital of the All Saints' families is low when viewed from outside the neighbourhood, but contains its own internal hierarchy, in terms of which some families are much more highly ranked than others. Though none of them has 'connections' of the kind Bourdieu envisages (old-boy networks and the like), some have easier access to what is arguably the most influential institution locally – the school itself.

Within this local hierarchy, the All Saints' families vary, not simply in the *amount* of social capital they can muster, but also in the value such capital holds for their children when they start school. Some families, like Khiernssa's, are held in considerable esteem within their own (minority) community in the (white majority) neighbourhood: Mr Khan's

Figure 2.1 The effectiveness of family practices in creating social and cultural capital, and supporting children's school learning

	Field of education [E]	Field of local community [S]
Anglo sphere [A]	[A/E] *highly effective* Family educational practices which create social and cultural capital for the child in school.	[A/S] *probably effective* Family social practices which create social capital which can be converted to cultural capital in A/E.
Bangla-deshi sphere [B]	[B/E] *possibly effective* Family educational practices create (minority) cultural capital which might be transposed to A/E.	[B/S] *probably ineffective* Family social practices create (minority) social capital which is unlikely to be recognized in A/E.

position in local Islamic organizations gives him authority and prestige, particularly among Bangladeshi men. It is hard to see, however, what benefits this high status can confer on Khiernssa as she starts her first term in Reception. It does not, in Bourdieu's terms, convert into social or cultural capital in the 'field of education'. In comparison with other Bangladeshi families in the area, the Khans enjoy social esteem; viewed from the school perspective, however, their success and influence are invisible. They carry no weight, therefore, in shaping teachers' expectations of Khiernssa.

An important way of reckoning the social capital of the families, then, is to look at how effective it is in creating social and cultural capital for their children at the point of transition to school. In this way the types of capital possessed by parents, and inherited by their children, can be measured by the yardstick which really counts: the children's status and achievements on entry to mainstream education. The model shown in Figure 2.1, which sorts family practices into different spheres and types, illustrates how this yardstick discriminates between those which count, and those which do not.

The model locates family practices according to two intersecting axes, or boundaries. The vertical axis separates the school from the out-of-school world (the fields of Education [E] and Society [S]), while the horizontal axis divides the minority (Bangladeshi) from the majority (Anglo) community. The location where family practices 'count' the most for children's social and cultural capital, it is clear, is the area A/E: the intersection of the field of education with the majority community – in other words, the school. For although Bourdieu claims that *all* capital is transposable and transferable (across boundaries, into new fields, taking new forms), we can see that in reality this is not always true. For many families, and particularly for minority families, there are barriers to transposing and investing the capital they have worked to accumulate.

In All Saints' End, social capital becomes effective through a range of roles and relationships within the field of education, or within the broader social field, and in forms which characterize the practices of the majority (Anglo) or the minority (Bangladeshi) community. The boundaries between the four fields defined by these two dimensions are permeable to differing degrees: as the model suggests, some admit the transfer of family capital into the school setting, and some do not.

The upper left segment of this model (A/E: activities in the field of education within the Anglo community) includes practices which carry social prestige within the majority community, *and* are effective in a child's schooling, creating social and cultural capital for the child. Examples of such useful capital in this setting are the activities of Joshua's mother, Maisie, whose occasional work in the local playgroup and active support of school fund-raising events put her on first-name terms with the teaching staff, and give her easy access to the classrooms, as well as confident relationships with the mothers of past and present playgroup children. Maisie's sense of ease on school premises and with school personnel is communicated to Joshua and his sisters, who are similarly relaxed and confident in their relationship to the school. While Maisie (a childminder married to a long-distance lorry driver) would carry little social capital in the wider community, within the local field of education constituted by this particular school she is socially affluent.

The same is true of Katy's mother Maxine, who in the course of the year trained as an after-school club organizer. Katy's family experience many difficulties over the year which characterize them as powerless in their dealings with the world outside the family. Nevertheless, Maxine's initiative in entering the field of education on her own behalf brings her into regular contact with the staff at All Saints', and thereby raises the family's and Katy's profile in the school, and gives them greater access to school knowledge of all kinds.

The upper-right segment (A/S) shows the intersection of the majority community with socially valued activities *outside* the field of education. It includes the efforts of those parents whose work in local businesses enables them to donate goods to the school: three families in the class, for example, are market traders and make regular donations for school fund-raising events. Parents with connections in local residents' associations and community groups are similarly 'visible' to the staff, and are welcomed as partners in promoting the interests of school and community. The social capital this brings – first-name chats with teachers, and purposeful activity on school premises in school time – enhances their children's cultural capital. Below the horizontal axis, in the minority community, parental activities, though equally energetic and purposeful, are less effective in securing social capital within the school, or cultural capital for children.

In *the lower left segment* (B/E), minority families' investments in the field of education may include recruiting children for the local mosque school, or appointing a teacher for the Bengali Saturday school, roles taken on by Abu Bokkar's father. *The lower right segment* (B/S) represents other forms of social action which carry prestige within the minority community, such as those undertaken by Mr Khan. Both these fields of activity, however, are hidden from the mainstream educational arena (A/E). None of the All Saints' teachers is aware of the activities of minority parents within their own community, or of the esteem in which they are held. Their children, therefore, gain no social or cultural enhancement in the field of education from the family's work in the community. To be effective in this way, Bangladeshi parents' work would have to take place in the visible world of the majority community: becoming a classroom assistant in the school, or a local councillor, for instance. None of the parents in this group has made that step as yet.

Those activities which fall within the majority community's orbit, both within and outside the field of education, are effective in securing cultural capital for children because they are recognized by the school. Those which are carried out in the minority community, *even* those directly related to educational ends, remain invisible and ineffective within the school setting. Within this particular community, in consequence, a Bangladeshi identity allocates a low social status to families, whatever their differences in capital and strategies.

One other aspect of family life might be called 'negative social capital': the problems and misfortunes which sometimes reduce families' effectiveness in supporting their children's learning, and reduce their standing in the eyes of teachers, as well as damaging the parents' sense of their own efficacy in managing their lives. During the year, some families experienced multiple difficulties. Serious medical problems affected the families of Katy and Jemma, Mohammed, Tuhura, Abdul Rahman, Amadur, Rufia and Khiernssa. Social or relational problems were experienced by both Jemma's and Sonia and Jason's (the twins) families, and involved disputes with neighbours and police as well as family members. The anti-social and sometimes criminal behaviour of older siblings overshadowed several families, but particularly these two.

Social strategies

Families with pressing financial problems, even if they deal with them successfully, have little time to spare in cultivating social esteem, though they do what they can. One means of doing so is through attending to their young children's physical appearance on starting school. Most Anglo and many Bangladeshi parents consistently brought their child to school in the wholly optional 'school uniform' of white shirt, red sweatshirt and grey skirt or trousers. The 'uniform' seemed to reinforce the view of All Saints' as a 'good school', though some mothers complained about having to boil the shirts, and scolded their children severely for failing to keep them clean.

Not all parents recognized this route to respectability. Tuhura's mother, unaware of mainstream expectations, sent her daughters to school in the gorgeous finery of satin-frilled party dresses, bright nail varnish and *mendhi* (henna decorations). Kath's strategy for giving the twins a good start in school was equally anomalous, and involved conspicuous consumption of a sort the family could ill afford.

At the time of my second visit to her, two of Kath's older sons had been excluded from school, and the 12-year-old, missing all weekend, had just been brought home by the police, who had found him with a teenage gang on empty industrial premises. Kath herself, though she did not tell me this, had recently been restrained by the police during a drunken attack on a neighbour. It is hard to imagine what opportunities remained to the family to acquire respectability in the neighbourhood. Nevertheless, like many parents who have few available routes to social recognition, Kath saw the start of school for the 4-year-olds as a fresh start for herself: a chance to be seen as a good parent, and for the twins to be seen as well-reared children.

In place of school uniform, the twins were frequently dressed in new and 'fashionable' clothes from the market: fatigues, camouflage trousers and leather flying jackets for Jason, fake fur and impractical heeled sandals for Sonia. They were the first to own Barbie lunchboxes, Sonic backpacks and all the other pre-teen paraphernalia of the majority culture; they frequently brought new toys to school to 'show'. Their appearance suggested an effort to appear as model pupils – an image from a mail-order catalogue, however, rather than an educational one. Neither the clothes nor the toys could be described as 'school approved'. In their first term the twins also behaved as model pupils: they were punctual and quiet and polite, and never forgot their book bags. Though the family fortunes subsequently worsened, Kath's overtly conscientious parenting at the start of school probably gave the twins more confidence and more strategies than their older siblings had enjoyed.

The Bangladeshi community displayed a range of social strategies. Well-established families, despite their lack of recognition in the majority community, committed time and effort to maintaining their position in the self-contained hierarchy of their own community. Abu Bokkar's and Khiernssa's fathers, because of their involvement with the mosque and Saturday school, were consulted by other families on community matters, while the ranking of Abdul Rahman's father was enhanced by his two sisters. The younger, Milou, who was educated locally and has native-like English, dispenses advice and opinions over the counter of a small family grocer's. The older, Jamila, is Tuhura's mother: highly educated in Bangladesh, she shares some of the influence wielded by Milou. On one occasion, the sisters jointly persuaded Bangladeshi parents not to allow their children to go on a three-day school trip. Another child in the extended family had been homesick and unhappy on the previous year's trip, and Milou in particular mounted an effective campaign to have the next school journey boycotted by Bangladeshi parents. This resistance to the authority of the majority community, which earned them the respect of their own community, did not enhance their children's interests or their own standing with the school, where Milou was seen as a 'troublemaker', and Jamila's habit of keeping her children home from school provoked annoyance rather than sympathy.

At the other end of the scale are the families of Amadur and Mohammed, whose recent arrival has assigned them to the lowest ranks of the Bangladeshi community. The two mothers, now sisters-in-law, would have very different social standing in Sylhet: Shazna had no schooling at all, while Asima had extensive private tutoring. Both, however, have been uprooted from the culture in which they were socially competent; both find themselves isolated, unsupported, and lacking in social recognition. Both, in consequence, find it hard to fight against their present circumstances.

Families' strategies for maintaining and enhancing their social capital were a measure of their overall resilience to hardship, which depended in part on the family's stability and self-concept, and in part on the strength of their supportive network. The non-prestigious social capital of family, neighbourhood, and community support is not included in Bourdieu's reckoning, but it proves an important factor in the lives of these small children. For whereas Katy's mother confesses, in a difficult period, 'She's a bit stressy at the moment . . . we've not been handling them well, given all this going on, we've not given them the time', Mohammed's family can only cope with unexpected problems by taking off, without warning, to their home village in Sylhet.

Cultural capital and the All Saints' families

Family ownership of cultural capital is accumulated over time. It is the product of the life experiences of parents and grandparents, including the historical and geographical contexts which shaped them. Unlike other forms of 'inheritance' it is not simply passed on to the child as a gift, but must be earned in each generation by the investment of time and effort. Once acquired, however, it is immediately effective in the field of education, giving children a head start when they commence the long and competitive process of acquiring school knowledge.

While all aspects of family life – religious observance, sporting activities, tastes in entertainment – may be imbued with cultural capital, the three aspects described here are those most commonly associated in research with the prediction of children's school achievements: they are mothers' educational experiences; family language and communicative skills; and family literacy practices.

Mothers' education

Maternal education is a major constituent in Bourdieu's definition of cultural capital: it makes possible the 'domestic transmission' of useful

Table 2.1 Mothers' educational experience

Child	Mother's education and training	Years of education
Abu Bokkar	Primary, village school in Sylhet	5
Abdul Rahman	Primary and secondary, town school in Sylhet	9
Amadur	Primary and secondary, village school in Sylhet, private tutor	7
Cameron	Primary and secondary, UK (town schools and FE college)	12
Jelika	Primary and secondary, village schools in Sylhet	10
Jemma	Primary and secondary (town schools, then truanted)	9
Joshua	Primary and secondary, town schools, FE, YTS	11
Katy	Primary and secondary, town schools, YTS	11
Kelly	Primary and secondary (excluded), town schools	10
Khiernssa	Primary, village school and mosque school in Sylhet	6
Mohammed	–	–
Rufia	Primary, village school and mosque school in Sylhet	5
Sonia and Jason	Primary and secondary (intermittent), (town schools)	10
Tuhura	Primary and secondary, in large town school in Sylhet	12
Troy	Primary and secondary, frequent moves (in care) UK	11

knowledge which is such a strong predictor of children's early attainments (Tizard *et al.* 1988). Mothers in this study were asked about their educational *experiences* as well as their eventual attainment, and in particular their recall of literacy learning.

The extent of mothers' schooling is shown in Table 2.1. Only Shazna (Mohammed's mother) has never attended: there was no school in her village, and as the oldest girl in the family she stayed at home learning to cook and sew, while her younger siblings went to school in the next village. Nevertheless she acquired enough Arabic to be able to decipher the Qur'an.

Other Bangladeshi mothers have detailed and happy memories of school learning. Most grew up in villages, and typically attended a village Model School from Class 1 to Class 5; some spent additional years in the preparatory classes, or stayed on for a year or two of high school or mosque school. The two mothers (sisters-in-law) who grew up in towns had an extended education: Tuhura's mother Jamila, some of whose relatives taught in schools and colleges, attended school from 4 to 16 and describes herself as an accomplished pupil. Bangladeshi mothers' learning in the home, which continued until they married, focused on traditional embroidery, and studying the Qur'an.

The Anglo mothers had very varied experiences of schooling. The most 'successful' was Cameron's mother Alison, who enjoyed school, worked hard and began three 'A' level courses; she gave up after a year, she says, because 'when I talked about leaving, nobody said anything, no one tried to stop me'. She alone among the mothers regrets not achieving more. At the other extreme are mothers whose educational failure began early: Kelly's mother Gaynor, who was 'in trouble for being naughty' throughout her school career and was eventually 'thrown out for messing about'; Troy's mother Charlotte, who was in care from an early age and attended numerous schools; the twins' mother Kath, who was in hospital so often as a child that she never settled at school or made friends, and left when she became pregnant at 15; and Jemma's mother June, who 'got picked on' because they couldn't afford the uniform, and was in a day centre for truants from the age of 14. Only four of the mothers (Cameron's, Joshua's, Katy's and Troy's) passed any exams.

All the mothers were sufficiently educated to provide their children with early literacy and numeracy experiences, and to furnish them with some degree of school-like knowledge about the world. Many, however, from both communities, were vague in their conceptions of the kind of knowledge taught and valued in school, and most had little understanding themselves of what it meant to be a successful secondary pupil or college student. From the start therefore there were to be barriers in their relationship to their own child's learning and schooling.

Language and communication

Language is an important component of cultural, as well as social, capital. It may be the single factor which most disadvantages Bangladeshi mothers and children, as well as being a major factor in disadvantaging working-class families from all groups in school (Bernstein 1970). While every child's home language endows her or him with the necessary tools for thinking and communicating, competence in the majority language counts more in influencing the status of families, in school and in the community. But the ability of parents to communicate, whether orally or in writing, with their children's schools depends not simply on their language use or educational level, but also on their confidence, and their knowledge of the school system. Parents who have skills in this area are able to intervene in the education market to their child's advantage (Lareau 1987; Reay 1998).

For Bangladeshi families with limited English, the potential benefits of bilingualism (Cummins 1989; Levine 1996) are outweighed by the constraints they currently experience. The ability to read and write in Bengali, and often in Arabic and English too, and to understand Hindi, does not confer social status, or grant access to the field of education. Some Bangladeshi fathers' considerable fluency in spoken English still leaves them at a disadvantage in participating in their children's *mainstream* education: though many are knowledgeable within the minority community's own educational arena, this capital is not transposable. None of the Bangladeshi mothers had more than a few words of spoken English.

Within the Anglo group the hierarchy of communicative skills largely reflects mothers' own educational success or failure. This is reinforced by the experience of re-encountering school as parents, and being vulnerable to the judgements of teachers all over again (notwithstanding the reassuring welcome offered to parents at All Saints'). In particular, many monolingual parents are disadvantaged by their poor writing skills once their child enters school, a disadvantage which becomes more acute as their child proceeds through the school system, and contacts between home and school become more formal. This is already evident in Reception, when parents are asked to contribute to the home–school reading folder. Few parents managed to write a 'comment' at any time in the school year, and their obligatory 'absence notes' demonstrated the difficulties many experienced with writing.

Family literacy practices

Family literacy practices are another significant and influential aspect of family culture (Teale 1986). The frequency, purpose and visibility of family members' reading and writing activities, as well as the actual presence of reading and writing materials, comprise the context for the child's acquisition of capital in this essential area of school knowledge.

Conventional indicators such as 'number of books in the home' give no hint of the rich variety of literacy environments experienced by the children in their first four years. The home with the most books (Troy's, discussed below) is the one in which the adults 'hate reading', as Troy confirms when interviewed:

Does your mum or dad have a favourite book?
They hate books, they both hate books, they do read with me but they do hate books.

Children's responses to this question were important, not so much to verify their parents' claims but in discovering whether the child was aware of its family's habits. As Joshua's mother, Maisie, advised me, she can only read the history books which she finds so enjoyable after the children are in bed, 'So it's not as if he sees me reading, except magazines.' A questionnaire I issued to all parents in the class asked, *Is anyone in the home a keen reader? Who? What do they read?* On the whole the responses were confirmed by the children. Perhaps few 4-year-olds can pronounce confidently on their parents' tastes, but Joshua and Jemma both got it right: *Does your mum or dad have a favourite book?* 'My dad's got a Star Trek book' (Joshua); 'My dad's got Playstation books' (Jemma), just as their wives reported. Cameron however assured me, 'They don't have books', whereas his mother Alison writes 'I read light novels and magazines.'

Bangladeshi children are generally aware that their parents read in Bengali and Arabic. Khiernssa's response is typical:

My dad hasn't got a book; my mum's got a Bengali book.
What about the Qur'an?
Yeah, they both got that.

All the Bangladeshi parents cite daily reading of the Qur'an and other religious texts or books of prayers, while some read extensively beyond this. Four families buy Bengali newspapers locally, and read and discuss them in the family group, while several mothers use the local library, or read their older children's school books with enjoyment and interest. Most families' evening routines are built around the comings and goings of the older children who attend mosque school, or have Arabic tuition at home, and the hour or so set aside for homework, as well as around family prayers and reading the Qur'an.

The reading habits of the Anglo family members are more spontaneous and irregular. Most treat reading as an optional pastime, used to complement TV viewing or the occasional hobby. Jemma's mum June answers the question, *Does anyone in the family like reading?*, 'No, I don't read, but I like knitting when I've got time', while Gaynor enthuses about Catherine Cookson (but hasn't 'had much time lately'), Maisie recalls history and non-fiction she has enjoyed in the past, and Maxine is nostalgic about being introduced to Steinbeck at school. Other mothers (Charlotte, Kath, Alison) equate reading with the parental duty of 'hearing them read'. Nevertheless there is no family in which reading of some kind does not figure regularly.

Writing, though less frequent, occurs in every home. All the households with older children describe homework sessions, and many families (including all the Bangladeshi group) write and receive letters from time to time. All the households had some form of paper and pens, though they were not always for children's use.

Cultural strategies

Most families seem to regard their own cultural capital – their existing accomplishments in education, language and literacy – as natural and appropriate, if not entirely satisfactory. On the whole, mothers who made an early exit from school accept this as a fitting end to an unsuccessful school career. Among the Anglo families, Maxine might be an exception: she wanted to be a pathologist when she was young, but learned that 'it took till you're about 40 to qualify!' so she became a YTS trainee in a shoe shop instead. When I asked if she had any regrets she was astonished – 'No, no, everything I've done, I've loved it, I wouldn't change any of it.' She and Maisie both seem to regard their courses in playgroup management and play leadership as an extension of their mothering skills, rather than as educational qualifications. These two mothers, while accepting their limited school credentials, are in fact investing in a field which brings financial, social and cultural ('school-related') benefits for their families.

Some Bangladeshi mothers are depressed, not by their lack of qualifications, but by their feelings of inadequacy in supporting their children's learning. Sabina is convinced that her lack of English prevents her from assisting Abdul Rahman and his brothers in any way, and feels she is letting them down badly: this is one reason why she defers to her sister-in-law Milou in all matters relating to the boys' education. All the Bangladeshi mothers expressed their regrets at being unable to read with their children, or teach them at home, through lack of English. None however considered joining local English classes: their time was fully occupied with traditional household chores, and they were grateful that their husbands and older children could speak for them and act on their behalf. This resignation is combined with some sadness, as Abu Bokkar's and Rufia's mothers pointed out: everyone else in the family was speaking English in the evenings, and the mothers were becoming isolated within their own families.

Rufia's father, however, expresses the pride felt by many Bangladeshi parents in their faithful adherence to Islamic family practices, and in their stability and security as a family unit. During a discussion of Bangladeshi children's maintenance of their home culture in English schools, he proudly asserts that 'some of them may change, but some of them – *we* look after them properly, *our* children don't change'. He and his wife devote an hour every evening to teaching their children Arabic, as well as sending them all to Bengali school and mosque school. The respect of his own community helps to offset the majority community's ignorance, or disapproval, of his family values. There is an active resistance, rather than a passive acceptance, in holding on to prized (minority) capital when it is at odds with the dominant culture. Not all the Bangladeshi families have the resilience and resources to maintain this struggle. Those who do may not find their efforts appreciated by their children's teachers.

Family habitus: exercising agency

Capital, particularly cultural capital, is one important explanatory concept for Bourdieu. Another is *habitus*, which we turn to now.

Several of the factors influencing the ways families respond to their circumstances have been referred to above. Extended family networks and neighbourhood support (available to all the Anglo families except

Jemma's and Troy's; and to all the Bangladeshi families except Amadur's and Mohammed's) help some families both to survive difficult times and to fight back when their external problems threaten their internal cohesion. The stoicism and acceptance of certain types of religious faith, which also sustains some of the families in hostile circumstances, may result in a more resigned and passive response. But the resilience and resistance some families display is a complex and durable quality which, rather than being the effect of a single cause, is an attitude or disposition derived from accumulated experience. It is this quality which Bourdieu calls the *habitus*.

Habitus, like symbolic capital, is a concept devised to explain social and educational inequalities, the different life chances which open up to individuals from differing social and cultural groups. But it also, as in the present case, provides a means of describing *within-group* differences between individuals and families. Before going on to discuss Troy's family, where the role of the habitus in shaping individual fortunes is particularly evident, we consider the features Bourdieu ascribes to the concept.

Habitus is defined as a system of dispositions – towards life, and in childhood especially towards learning – which is acquired, by individuals and families, through experience. It is the product (in the present), of the past history of the individual/family, and of their class and cultural context: 'The habitus – embodied history, internalised as second nature and so forgotten as history – is the active presence of the whole past of which it is the product' (1990a: 56). Family habitus, Bourdieu argues, partakes to a large extent of the collective habituses of the family's class (and ethnic group) membership. Families who experience domination as a result of their poverty, low occupational classification and/or ethnic minority status may have many characteristics in common, including the prospect of relatively low educational achievement for their children. Yet, *within* dominated groups, the different strategies which individual families adopt in response to their disadvantages can create entirely different physical as well as psychological environments for the small children growing up within the family. These environments in turn generate different ranges of strategies for children to select from when they enter formal schooling, and make possible differing chances of success.

Accounts of family habitus, therefore, must include both their response to their present circumstances, and their expectations for the future. Their response, as we see, may lie somewhere along a continuum from apathy, through acceptance, to active resistance, and their expectations may bear more or less resemblance to what Bourdieu calls the 'objective probabilities' of their situation. Families who share similar structural constraints, in other words, may differ in the amount of agency they can exercise.

The child growing up within the family acquires not only aspects of the family habitus, but also a unique and specialized habitus of its own

– for every child's experience, in the home as in the classroom, is different. Within a single family, older and younger children, boys and girls, and children with different characteristics, are subject to different experiences, expectations and aspirations, which help to structure their own individual *primary habitus:* 'I am talking about dispositions *acquired through experience*, thus variable from place to place and time to time' (Bourdieu 1990b: 9, emphasis in original). This system of dispositions, Bourdieu claims, *influences* rather than *determines* the child's future actions, since these are the product not of 'rules' but of 'strategies'. At one point Bourdieu likens the concept of the habitus to Chomsky's generative grammar, a system which can generate an infinite range of possibilities.

In the course of its early socialization, the child develops a 'practical mastery' of the skills and knowledge needed to move within and beyond the family circle, as well as the cultural capital (educational knowledge) to invest in the new setting of school. The child's unconscious mastery of the rules gives a 'feel for the game' which enables her or him to improvise successfully in new settings or situations: 'mastery' acquired in one field can be imaginatively exploited in another, throughout a lifetime.

So, in the case of the family, the habitus describes not what capital the family owns, but what it decides to do with it: how it chooses to 'play its cards', as Bourdieu describes the process of investment and accumulation. The differences in the ways families 'play their cards' is evident when we consider Troy's family.

Case study: Troy's family

Charlotte is the first to admit that she, and not Bob, is the force behind the family environment in which Troy is growing up. She recognizes too that her determination to create an 'ideal family' and rear 'perfect children' derives from the anger she feels over her own unhappy early life – she was in local authority care from an early age. The birth of her first two children (Troy and Jerome) and the subsequent split with their father galvanized her into reinventing herself. With her new husband Bob she pursues social and cultural capital by every means available, determined to make a success of her children's lives.

When Troy starts school, Charlotte's efforts start to bear fruit. She has acted purposefully to acquire respectability and social esteem, which she associates with marriage and motherhood, religion and manners. This is why she chose a church wedding for herself and Bob, and had the boys and their baby sister christened, and insists that the whole family goes to church every Sunday. She has no interest in religion ('I tried to tell Troy about what God was but I got it wrong, what they told him at church contradicted me!') but sees churchgoing as both training in good behaviour and an opportunity to show off her children's good manners in public. One of her reasons for choosing All Saints' Primary, which is not her nearest school, is 'because if someone says it's a Christian church or a Christian school that's going to come across better to somebody'. Another reason is that she learned from her health visitor (the source of much of her information) that All Saints' had 'lots of Indians and mixed kids', so that Troy and Jerome would not be so conspicuous as in a mostly white school. At the same time Charlotte symbolically denies the boys' Jamaican origin: when I referred to Troy's 'natural father' she disputed the term, claiming there was 'nothing natural about him'.

It is because Charlotte is aware of the status and importance of books that she has bought Troy 'literally hundreds of books', which he is not allowed to touch, in case he tears them. The possession of all those books therefore (which are kept in a glass-fronted cupboard) does not confer on Troy any 'practical mastery' in the traditional middle-class skills of browsing and sharing stories. Charlotte likewise knows the official value of play in early learning, and has bought Troy 'every toy from the Early Learning Centre possible', claiming that his favourite occupation is Duplo. (Troy begs to differ, naming his main occupations as 'playing football and watching telly'.)

Charlotte holds strong views too on the relative status of other families, and on the effects of parenting on children's outcomes:

> If you've got a bad home life, or they're allowed to do things which I know kids are allowed to do which I wouldn't allow my kids to do . . . I know for a fact some children talk about 'my dad's in jail', I hear children say it, or 'the police were round my house last night' . . . And for instance if a child's swearing you know that's probably what they're allowed to get away with, and you gather from that what their home is, all the little clues . . .

Though she is inclined to disparage the 'Indians' ('they don't talk to anyone, I wonder if they ever talk to their children'), her greatest scorn is reserved for white parents who fail to regulate their children's home environment.

Though Charlotte and Bob, as Troy reported, 'hate books' and only buy them as a down payment on their children's future, both are habitual writers:

> I write and write, I'm always writing something, like a shopping list, or a letter . . . I suppose he sees me always writing, and Bob's always writing, letters for jobs, letters for this, letters for that, we do do a lot of writing in our house, the paper and the trees we get through is actually amazing . . .

This continual writing, in other words, is instrumental rather than expressive: job applications, letters to the council and Social Services, and once Troy starts school, a stream of letters to his teachers. Charlotte's written skills are matched by her oral skills. She is extremely forceful in presenting her views on the roles and responsibilities of parents and teachers. In the absence of a family supportive network (Charlotte is an orphan and Bob's family are in Scotland), she has established links with the professionals who can supply her need for information and access – the GP, the health visitor, the social worker, and latterly the school staff and governors.

Perhaps the most important aspect of Troy's family habitus is that it includes conscious planning and projection, and a calculation of effects and consequences, efforts and profits. The propensity to invest in the future is visible in Troy's preparation for school and his classroom behaviour, as well as in the relationships his parents develop with the school. Nevertheless, the constraints on Charlotte's conception of the future for her children are evident when she discusses her hopes for them: Troy, though expected to be a star in the classroom, will probably become 'a chippy . . . or a milkman' when he grows up.

Summary: family capital and family habitus

Small and hidden differences between families, as we have seen, provide children with very different early environments, which equip them very differently for the start of school. In All Saint's End, each family's economic and symbolic capital is a unique blend of culturally disparate bits and pieces, which will only be 'valued' when their children are exposed to the education market. How families choose to invest and exploit their various forms of capital counts equally for their children, who in their earliest years are learning ways of behaving which they will take with them into the classroom. The ways in which parents prepare their children for school, and endow them with educational capital, and an individual habitus, are discussed in Chapter 3.

LEARNING HOW TO LEARN AT HOME

$$\left(3\right)$$

Kinds of knowledge: what do children learn at home?

Can you think of anything you learned to do at home when you were little, before you started in Mrs Goode's class? [Child interviews, December]

Tuhura: I eat ice cream.
          Eat ice cream?
          Yes . . . I eat white ice cream.

Katy: Doing letters on paper – I got a new pencil.
          How did you learn to do letters on paper?
          Mummy showed me.

Amadur: Drink a cup of tea with a biscuit.
          Who showed you how to do that?
          All by myself. If the tea is too hot, you dip the biscuit in
          and eat the biscuit. Then it's not too hot.

Joshua: Drawing.
          How did you learn that?
          I just learnded and learnded from my mum.

Khiernssa: Reading.
          How do you think you learned that?
          My sister just read it all and I just knowed it.

Children learn all kinds of things at home, and all the children quoted above had 'learned' to work with pencils and paper, *and* of course to eat and drink, as well as a whole range of other kinds of knowledge, before they started school. All of this knowledge was either useful to them in their home (learning which enabled them to become a member of their home culture) or was intended to be useful to them at school (learning which would enable them to succeed within the school culture). Some was acquired unconsciously through their daily experiences, and some was imparted to them deliberately, by explicit or disguised instruction. One of the most important things they had learned, additionally, was about learning itself: what counts as knowledge, and how you get it. The responses quoted above show that children understand this key concept in different ways.

Since families are the major source of children's early learning, the 'curriculum' of their home is an amalgam of parents' own school learning, passed on in some form to the child, and the learning which is acquired through daily life in the culture. The former is often consciously taught by parents to children, and is a version of an imagined 'school' curriculum. The latter is the 'natural' curriculum learned (but also taught) by all members of the family and community.

So these two kinds of knowledge may be acquired in different ways. When Khiernssa helps her father and mother with the wallpaper or the allotment, she is learning, through apprenticeship, her own family's customary practices. When she goes with her father to mosque, or to the Bengali class, she is absorbing the ways of her cultural community. However, when she sits at the table with Salek and Layla, reading school books and copying the ABC, she is learning, *and* being taught, 'school knowledge'. Mr Khan is keen to ensure that his children can access both kinds of knowledge: the cultural capital which counts in the children's own community, and (he hopes) that of the mainstream community, and the field of education.

One factor which differentiates some families from others, of course, is the degree of overlap between their home and their school knowledge, or, as Bernstein calls it, their 'local' and 'official' knowledge. Bernstein's terminology should not be seen as a mere pedantic renaming: it usefully distinguishes not what is learned at home from what is learned at school, but what is *valued* in the home from what is *valued* in the school setting. **'Official knowledge'** (which can lead, via school success, to power and status in society) is taught in many homes (Bernstein would say, mainly in middle-class homes), and the children who have learned it there adapt smoothly to the classroom, where they meet the same expectations as to what *counts*. In Bourdieu's terminology, it is the cultural capital of the 'field of education'. **'Local knowledge'**, though undoubtedly useful within the context in which it is learned (home or community), is not necessarily of much use to the child in the wider society, and specifically in the child's first non-family setting, the Early Years classroom. Much of the research evidence referred to in Chapter 1, such as studies of family and community literacy practices, discloses the difference between what we might call 'official' and 'local' understandings of literacy (Teale 1986; Gregory and Williams 1998).

All of children's early experience – from being picked up and cuddled, fed and changed, rocked and soothed, to being taken to the library or shown how to count – is a form of learning, and all the All Saints' children had acquired an incalculable amount of knowledge before starting school. This chapter looks not just at *what* was taught and learned in the children's homes, but also at *how* such learning took place: in other words, at both the curriculum and the pedagogy of children's early learning. It introduces the simple concepts devised by Bernstein to describe different forms of pedagogy, and the consequences these have for children's adaptation to life outside the home. It describes both the origin of these differences in parents' own cultural and educational experience, and the effect of parental beliefs and knowledge on children's expectations of school.

Ways of learning: visible and invisible pedagogies

Khiernssa's home learning, as we saw, took at least two distinct forms: what we can call the *implicit* socialization she received into her own culture, and the *explicit* instruction she received in the formal knowledge associated with both her mainstream schooling, and her religious and cultural traditions. These two ways of learning, found in all the children's homes, correspond to the two main types of pedagogy identified by Bernstein (1975, 1990, 1996): the visible and the invisible.

Bernstein's theorizing about forms of pedagogy depends in turn on two key concepts developed early in his work: *classification* and *framing*. **Classification** defines the strength of the boundaries which exist between categories: between schools and homes, between teachers and pupils, between curriculum subjects, between classroom groups. Where classification is strong, we can envisage a school which is strict about uniform (maintaining the boundary between home and school styles), formal in its teaching methods (maintaining the boundary between school and non-school discourse) and precise about assessment arrangements (maintaining the boundaries between success and failure). **Framing** regulates the forms of behaviour and communication which are permitted within and between the categories which classification creates. Where framing is strong, expectations about all aspects of the school and classroom – work, behaviour, relationships – will be explicit and unambiguous.

Where strong classification and strong framing are combined, a traditional, formal mode of schooling (such as a grammar school or prep school) results. The pedagogy is fully explicit, and is said to be *visible* (VP). Where both classification and framing are weak, a very informal or progressive mode of schooling results (in practice, somewhere like Summerhill, but some liberal–progressive infant classes might resemble the mode). The pedagogy is very implicit, and is described as *invisible* (IP).

Three things make Bernstein's concepts important and helpful in explaining the learning experiences of the All Saints' children. First, they permit a description not just of the two rather simplified modes suggested above, but of an infinite range of 'modalities' created by different degrees of strength and weakness of classification and framing, in combination. Thus, an apparently informal infant classroom of the 1970s (weak classification and framing; an integrated day; teachers addressed by their first names; free choice of activities) may have turned out to contain some elements of strong framing (aspects of the hidden curriculum which are immutable, for instance). Only an analysis of the classification *and* the framing of an educational setting allows a good description of the pedagogy, and hence of the children's experience.

Second, the concepts can be applied to all pedagogic settings and not only to schools: hence, in this study, they are applied to the children's homes as well as their classroom. Third, the concepts have, in Bernstein's account, clear and significant consequences for the learning and success of children from different social groups. This important claim is explored in the home and school pedagogies discussed below. We begin with Jemma's story.

Case study: Jemma at home

June's daughter Jemma is the youngest of four sisters – teenagers Mary and Tina, and Laura, just a year older than Jemma herself. Her family had suffered financially during the girls' father's lengthy unemployment, and June was still finding it hard to maintain orderly routines. Managing the recalcitrant teenagers and the household finances often seemed too much for her, and she gave up on other priorities (such as paying the rent, organizing meals and bedtimes, and bringing the little girls to school on time). All of them suffered from poor health (the younger girls had frequent diarrhoea and permanent head lice), and all four girls had unsatisfactory records of school attendance and punctuality. Nevertheless Jemma herself had been conscientiously prepared for school.

Jemma was born prematurely and had a precarious early infancy, as a result of which June believes she has been spoiled and has serious temper problems ('but she's like her father, if he can't have his own way'). Her mother and sisters are wary of taking her out in case she has tantrums. But in many respects they are a closely bonded unit, and Mary and Tina (now 17 and 14) have always played with, and taught, Laura and Jemma. Jemma's favourite activities, the sisters agree, were bricks and Lego, and playdough and painting – a 'school' agenda not unlike that of the All Saints' classroom. June reports, 'They all used to sit down and draw, so the bigger girls were learning them; she's got on really good with her drawing.' Jemma names 'building with bricks' (a valued school skill) as the thing she has learned at home before coming to school.

Tina also had a particular 'school' agenda in mind, and a very explicit instructional method. She attempted to teach Jemma letters and numbers by drawing dots for her to trace over, and writing 'whole pages for her to copy', as well as 'testing' her on colours, shapes and numbers, and marking the results with ticks and crosses. Jemma regularly brought to school a scribble pad full of the 'sums and writing' Tina had done with her, and June reported proudly that Tina 'writes her own little stories when she's got nothing else to do at home'. Jemma also encounters a wide variety of print at home: June's magazines and knitting patterns, her father's Playstation magazine, Tina's Mills and Boon books, comics and the odd newspaper, and a stock of cheap children's books, mostly Disney stories. Both June and Tina enjoy reading to her.

In this very gendered household, Jemma patterns herself on her mother and sisters: 'She makes her own toast, and she does like to wash up if she gets the chance.' Jemma reports confidently that 'I can read a story to mum . . . I can help with cooking . . . tidy my toys . . . chase my cat.' Many aspects of her pre-school experience appear to be appropriate preparation for school, despite the constraints on the family's resources and expectations. The home curriculum has included the 'core skills' of early schooling, as well as a range of play opportunities. However, Jemma's ability to invest her pre-school learning in the classroom depends, both on whether the *capital* she has acquired at home is of the approved kind, and on whether her *habitus* enables her to make good use of it. As she starts school there are indications that her family's low self-esteem, and their helpless and defeated stance towards outside agencies, may hinder her chances of doing so.

Family socialization: local knowledge

For most families, their children's early socialization into ways of behaving appropriately occurs by means of apprenticeship – the child alongside other children and adults, first observing and imitating, then taking over, the behaviours and activities of others in the social group (Rogoff 1990). In this way the child acquires a 'practical mastery' of all the knowledge and skills needed for membership of the household, while the parents may not be fully aware themselves of having passed these on.

So, although some aspects of children's early socialization may be explicit – learning the rules about respectful ways of speaking to elders, or about washing and eating, tidying and bedtimes, obedience and sanctions – much of this learning may be invisible, to both child and parent. It is a matter of learning to do *what comes naturally* within the setting – the rules of the culture, which may be more visible to 'outsiders' than to those within the setting. Two examples of this kind of learning are discussed here because of their effect on the children's adaptation to school. They are learning how the family understands the uses of time and space, and learning to take responsibility.

Time and space

Learning the rules governing the use of time and space may be seen as an essential part of the social training required for school, but in All Saints' End the rules are very different for different families. Some are individual, but many are shaped by the family's cultural background.

All the Anglo mothers share a 'common-sense' belief that children require firm and regular routines from earliest infancy. These include being 'put down' to sleep in the day and at bedtime, and if necessary left to cry alone in the interest of acquiring regular habits. Such practices are taken for granted by this group: Cameron's mother actually complains that as a baby he failed to observe them, 'He could never work out where this hour between feeds came.' As they grow up, daily diaries for the Anglo children confirm that regular routines for eating and sleeping exist in most households. Once they start school, the children mostly eat breakfast as a family, survive the day without naps, and begin their bedtime routine around seven o'clock. The exceptions are the twins, who have a nap after school, and then stay up until 9 o'clock, and Jemma, who has few routines in her life.

The eating and sleeping routines of the Bangladeshi children bear little resemblance to mainstream expectations. Unlike the Anglo families, Bangladeshi parents do not require their little children to vanish from sight at a certain hour of the evening, but expect them both to be a part of family life at all hours, and to sleep and to some extent eat when they are sufficiently tired or hungry. Until the children start school, as their diaries show, they are left to wake naturally, and eat breakfast when they are hungry. In Mohammed's case (disastrously for his school attendance) his normal waking time is between 11.00 and noon. Since male family members are often at work in the evening, the children eventually go to bed, and co-sleep, with their mothers and siblings – often at 11.00 or 12.00 at night.

The 4-year-olds who rise early on school days, but go to bed with the rest of the household, manage by napping after school, and then joining in a family meal late in the evening. For some of these children, changing from their pre-school sleeping and waking routines to those required by school is a difficult process. The consequences for their understanding of how time is organized in school (cf. Heath 1983; Lubeck 1985) may depend on how explicit teachers are about their own expectations.

A similar clash between home and classroom habits can be seen in the children's spatial routines, and their understanding of order. Individual families vary in their housekeeping arrangements, but there is also a group difference, between the parents whose upbringing was in a Sylheti village, and all the others. The two Bangladeshi 'town-dwelling' families, like the majority of the mainstream Anglo families, compartmentalize their domestic activities and locate them in different areas of their homes. Both Abdul Rahman and Tuhura are used to a 'tidy' and toy-free sitting room, a more lived-in back room or family kitchen, and bedrooms for sleeping. Like the Anglo children, they know there is a time and a place for toys and children's clutter, as well as a time for tidying them (*all* the Anglo mothers spoke of expecting, or requiring, children to tidy their own toys and their own room, and Troy has to 'take every single toy off his floor' before he goes to bed).

The six 'village' families, by contrast, use their living space flexibly for eating and sleeping, juxtaposing their children's bikes and their babies' cots with large-scale food preparation, while male family members sleep on during the day under quilts on sofas. This easy and unself-conscious mingling of family activities, however, is poor preparation for the more formal organization of school spaces. Like Heath's 'Trackton' children (1983), the 'village' children in this study have to adjust to a classroom where there is a time and a place for *everything*: where the sand and water may not be taken into the home corner, or indoor toys taken outside, and where 'tidy up time' punctuates the day's activities.

Most fortunate in their home experience are children like Joshua (whose mother Maisie is a childminder), who enjoys a school-style home environment in which all the toys are stored, tidily but accessibly, in brightly coloured crates. Joshua understands that a proliferation of toys, and children's disordering activities, are welcome during the day but unacceptable at bedtime. Mothers at opposite ends of the tidiness scale are Charlotte and Rahena. The former boasted of her high standards of housekeeping ('there is not one single cobweb on my Lilliput Lane figures') and was unapologetic about taking away Troy's paints 'because they made a mess'. The latter is relaxed about sofas piled with half-eaten plates of food, and bottles of ketchup. Each mother socializes her children according to her own requirements for domestic order. The children's teachers, how-ever, provide a physical environment – outwardly informal, but inwardly orderly – run along rather different lines.

Responsibilities

An equally powerful aspect of early learning derives (as the Newsons suggested: 1968, 1976) from the family view of children's household responsibilities. For the All Saints' children, there were very different expectations as to how they would be involved in helping at home.

For some parents, children's involvement in household tasks was clearly so 'natural' as to be invisible. Among the Bangladeshi children, Khiernssa's participation in such projects is noteworthy: yet her mother responds when questioned, 'She's not expected to help, she's only a little girl.' Similarly Rufia looks after her two younger siblings 'in the afternoon, every day, my mum's too tired', and has the job of taking the family rubbish out (as well as being an interested spectator at the butchering of chickens in the back yard); but her mother reports, 'No, she has no responsibilities, she will have those when she's married.' Abdul Rahman, whose mother reports that he 'doesn't have any jobs to do', helps the whole family to hoover, clean and 'fix things', as well as joining in the family's food preparation. In other Bangladeshi families, where the mother takes sole responsibility for cooking and childcare, some 4-year-olds may be required to do no more than fetch a nappy or tissues for the baby. They were, however, observed to respond spontaneously to babies' crying by looking for a bottle or dummy, or tucking in blankets.

In contrast, most of the Anglo families claim that their children help and take responsibility in the house, while their children on the whole are unaware of this! Within these families, 'helping' appears to mean another kind of play, an activity which parents permit to please their children, or reluctantly encourage because they believe it is good for them. Kelly, for instance, tries to help her mother, but 'she's such a nuisance really, she gets in the way', so she is banned from the kitchen; Jemma 'does like to wash up, if she gets the chance – but I have to make sure I wash up all the knives first'; while Maxine says of Katy, 'Yes, she's very helpful, a bit too helpful at times.' The inference is that the children's 'helping' is for the child's pleasure rather than for the benefit of the household. Only the twins perform 'real' household work: in their family, the children rotate household chores every evening after their meal, and the twins join in as well as performing their own task of putting the milk bottles out.

Child interview responses confirm that gender plays an important role in the extent to which most children 'help', or have responsibilities. A majority of girls prefer to assist their mother in household tasks, including childcare, while a majority of boys prefer not to. Among the boys in particular, 'helping' may be a euphemism, used by parents but unrecognized by children. While Amadur confirms his father's questionnaire response: 'No, I'm not big enough; mummy works, I don't work', Troy blithely contradicts Charlotte's claims that he tidies, shares in childcare, and lays the table: 'No, I don't help: I don't like helping.'

What children actually *do* to help may be less important than their sense of responsibility for the maintenance of the household. Children whose 'cooking' and 'washing-up' is seen as a nuisance are unlikely to acquire this sense, while children whose duties, however small, contribute in some way to the running of the family, may be learning to be accountable. A Saturday morning call at Khiernssa's house offers an example:

> There was a knock at the door and mum murmured to the girls, who rushed into the kitchen and returned bearing a cheque between them (holding one corner each), which they carefully carried to the front door. They chatted for several minutes, in English, to the milkman, and came back into the room beaming.

> [Field notes]

For some Bangladeshi children, the responsibility for mediating between their mothers and the mainstream culture is a genuine contribution to the running of the household, and has nothing to do with play. In a similar way, some children's participation in childcare, cleaning and food preparation forms part of a natural apprenticeship to the life of the family and community. While western-educated parents, like Early Years teachers, may encourage their children to *role-play* the occupations of adults in their culture, Bangladeshi children often seem to have embarked on a real-world experience of adult roles. In consequence, the emphasis on explicitly child-related 'jobs' in the Reception class (tidying toys, hanging up coats) may appear confusing.

One example may serve to illustrate the difference in expectations. Several Anglo mothers referred to the 'dangers' of children being in the kitchen, or near the stove, handling knives, or dropping plates ('they're not plastic, you know!'). Their homes were 'child-proofed' for children's safety, in accordance with western social expectations. In many Bangladeshi households, however, a razor-sharp *dar* stood on the kitchen floor for slicing food, and children knew to make their way carefully past it. In Jelika's house, I came across her standing on a chair using a heavy knife to chop onions: as I moved towards her to intervene, her grandmother mildly stepped forward and tidied the chopped onions, leaving Jelika to continue chopping. On another occasion I found Abdul Rahman, under his father's instruction, using two hands to manipulate a large meat cleaver.

As Rogoff (1990) observes, *all* children are 'apprenticed', but to different things. The Anglo children in this study (with the possible exception of the twins) seem principally apprenticed to childhood, and to play; the Bangladeshi children, however, seem to be apprenticed to the life of the family and community. This difference in the curriculum of the home clearly has implications for the ways the children adapt to the culture of the school, with its overwhelming emphasis on childhood and play.

Family beliefs and parental roles

Children's play

One of the largest influences on children's early experience of 'school learning' was their parents' beliefs about childhood and play. On the whole, mothers brought up in the UK, with some experience themselves of a child-centred, play-based early education (whether or not this had made them successful pupils), claimed to believe that play was important in children's early lives and learning – the natural thing for a child to do, and for a parent to encourage. Those brought up outside this tradition found such views both novel and naïve.

Most consciously child-centred of the mothers were Maisie and Maxine. Maisie talked with enthusiasm about Joshua's early years:

He liked his Lego, and anything to do with Thomas the Tank – and now of course it's Action Man . . . he *can* play on his own, but most of the time I'm there on the floor with him anyway; but he's got his own bedroom and he'll spend time up there on his own on the odd occasion.

Maxine offered a similar account of Katy, detailing her early enthusiasm for bricks and construction toys – 'she was never into dolls very much' – and her love of books, recalling precisely which were her favourite books as a toddler. Both these mothers organized their day around their pre-school children, regarding them as pleasant companions when they were home together.

Other Anglo mothers showed equal interest in their child's enthusiasms and activities. Alison describes Cameron's early 'obsessions' for toys:

He's always been obsessive about one thing or another, one of the first things he said was 'Popo Pat', and he wanted to watch Joseph's videos all the time and look at his Postman Pat books . . . then it was Buzz Lightyear, now it's Teletubbies . . .

Kath, the twins' mother, believes they always had distinct and gendered preferences: Sonia 'always liked dolls, changing them and feeding them', whereas Jason 'liked cars and trains, right from the start, that's all he ever really played with'. Gaynor offered graphic accounts of Kelly's preference for getting muddy in the garden, 'on her bike, in all weathers'.

All the Anglo parents had funds of anecdotes about their children's involvement with favourite toys and pastimes. It is clear that their children have all, to some extent, shared their play and imaginative lives with their mothers, and that their 'childish' interests have become part of the family's collective history. Only Charlotte (who can give the fullest account of any mother of her child's pre-school years) seems to have regarded Troy's early activities principally as a vehicle for learning: asked what she remembers about his babyhood, she cites the 'educational' toys, books and tapes she supplied for Troy, rather than his actual interests or enthusiasms.

Bangladeshi mothers' accounts of their children's pre-school years depict children as self-reliant, if occasionally bored. Abu Bokkar's mother Rahena reported, 'In the morning he plays on his own or draws or watches TV: he has always watched Cartoon Network and now he likes *Teletubbies*, *Neighbours*, *EastEnders*, even the news . . .' Sabina paints a similar picture of Abdul Rahman's day: he 'always keeps a small car in his pocket, and plays near his mum, nice quiet games with cars on his own'. Amadur, like his cousin Mohammed, is reported as mostly 'fighting with his little brother' or watching television, all day, though both boys have small cars and toddler-size bikes or cars to ride on. Neither of their mothers is sure how they pass their time in the long hours at home, though

Mohammed's mother reports, 'He does his own work, on the sofa, I don't know what it is.'

The Bangladeshi girls have generally had more company. Jelika 'never spent time on her own' because her schoolgirl aunties (whose own school attendance was very irregular) liked to draw and colour with her, or watch TV with her, while mum looked after the house and babies; Khiernssa intermittently chats with her mother in the course of lying on the sofa, playing with dolls and watching TV or Hindi films; Rufia, in addition to visiting next door to chat and play, goes upstairs to play with her older siblings' electronic toys, or watches TV (as Majida says, 'She would like to live inside the television, she loves it so much!'). Only Tuhura, according to Jamila, 'likes to do nothing' until the older children return from school.

'Learning through play'

Parents' views about play are closely entwined with their beliefs about learning, with consequences for their children's experience of learning at home. Among the Anglo mothers in All Saints', all of whom recall 'playing' rather than 'learning' in their own early years at school, there is general agreement that this is the tried and tested method for fostering young children's learning. Two assumptions follow from this: that play is the appropriate means for children to acquire 'school' knowledge at home, and that attendance at playgroup or nursery benefits early learning. The fact that the mothers might have difficulty explaining just how and why children learn through play does not lessen their attachment to this common-sense belief, which dovetails with their other beliefs about childhood. Nevertheless, the belief is maintained rather half-heartedly, and many indicate that they will be relieved to see some evidence that their children really are learning. Even Maxine, with her playgroup training, asserts that 'children should be allowed to play a lot at first, and then learn more, bit by bit', rather than implying that they are learning *while* they are playing. Other Anglo mothers feel the same:

> Yeah, the school's fine: even if they play now, you know they're going to learn in the end.
>
> (Gaynor)

> I think the school's OK, they have to learn to play before they learn to work.
>
> (Maisie)

Seven of the eight Anglo children have experienced some kind of pre-school provision: only Jemma's mother reports that she 'couldn't get the girls in'. The twins attended two nurseries in succession for two days a week, but Kath recalls that 'they were never happy there so I kept them home a lot'. Of the remainder, both Katy and Joshua had five half-days at the nearby playgroup where their mothers sometimes worked, while Kelly, Cameron and Troy had all attended part-time nurseries.

Mothers' understanding of the benefits of pre-school learning varies. Maxine volunteers that Katy 'gained a lot in her drawing and writing, and her cutting and sticking, that came on a lot', as well as 'learning to mix'. Maisie describes playgroup as the place where Joshua extended his social network, while Gaynor and Kath have no view on what their children gained from nursery. Several mothers were relieved that their children were introduced to letters, numbers, nursery rhymes and 'writing their name' by pre-school professionals, since they 'didn't want to know' or 'refused to sit down and do it' at home.

Charlotte is unusual, both in stressing the importance of academic learning in Troy's pre-school experience, and expressing her dissatisfaction with his nursery on this count. Troy had previously attended a Social Services facility, at which 'they *taught* them, one shape, one colour, one letter, one something else, every week he learnt far more there than he did at nursery!' Despite the systematic learning programme she and Bob implemented at home, Charlotte believes Troy 'forgot a lot of what he'd learned, in that year'. She is not persuaded that play has educational outcomes, a scepticism shared by the Bangladeshi parents.

Within the Bangladeshi community in the All Saints' neighbourhood, take-up of pre-school provision is almost non-existent. Only Abdul Rahman and Tuhura have tried the local playgroup or a Bengali drop-in session. In their mothers' view, neither was happy, and only Abdul Rahman persisted for a few visits. Most parents offered reasons why their child had *not* attended, ranging from the cost (Rufia's father) or the inconvenience of taking and collecting little ones (Amadur's father) to the admission that the children are 'only playing there, sand, water, not learning' (Khiernssa's father). Recent efforts to persuade parents of the benefits of playgroup have met with little success.

Parents' beliefs about the relevance of play for children's learning is reflected in their provision of toys and activities for their own children. Once again, the continuum in the group stretches from the didactic extreme of Charlotte's provision for Troy, to the *ad hoc* and unplanned provision in Amadur's and Mohammed's families. Troy, who has 'had every toy from the Early Learning Centre possible', is reported as preferring Duplo to 'all his other toys'. By contrast, Asima and Shazna were both rather perplexed to be asked about their children's play. Shazna explained that in Bangladesh, Mohammed 'didn't have anything to play with, only the mud', although he now enjoys a trundle-car to ride on, two toy cars with flashing lights, and the television.

Most Anglo parents, having themselves grown up with a play pedagogy, have consciously or unconsciously selected some of the 'educational' toys which their children were to meet in playgroup, nursery or Reception. Unlike the Bangladeshi families, all their households feature Lego or similar construction toys, train sets or other small-world toys, tape-stories and jigsaws, and the Anglo children evidently know what to do with these items in the classroom. Bangladeshi children on the whole sidestep these 'educational' toys (cf. Drury 1997) and move directly from ownership of a doll or car or bike to playing with computer games and electronic toys, as well as watching hours of satellite TV. As Troy's response reveals, there may be some disparity between parents' perceptions of their children's activities, and the children's own view. Nevertheless it is evident that all the Anglo children have acquired considerable expertise with the 'learning tools' they will be using when they start school, which the Bangladeshi children's home experience has not provided. As we will see, this experience combines with Bangladeshi parents' *explicit* instructional efforts to give them very different expectations about learning in the classroom.

Beliefs and practices: the pedagogy of the home

In keeping with their culturally differing views of childhood and play, the Anglo and Bangladeshi families in All Saints' End have generally contrasting attitudes to instruction. For most Anglo families, their stated belief in the importance of young children's play, and their knowledge that little children are supposed to learn through play and 'discovery' rather than through direct instruction, gives rise to considerable unease when it comes to teaching them at home. The majority of Bangladeshi parents, on the other hand, are confident in their parental duty to instruct their children in a culturally appropriate curriculum at the appropriate time. So while some Anglo mothers admit to a sense of guilt and subterfuge about their instructional efforts, the Bangladeshi parents (fathers as well as mothers) are far more assured in this activity, and are only 'guilty' if they feel they have neglected it. In this respect, despite their own backgrounds, the Anglo parents appear to have acquired views formerly associated with middle-class parenting (Newsons 1968, 1976; Bernstein and Young 1973). The Bangladeshi parents, however, like other ethnic minority groups within western societies, remain committed to more explicit *teaching*, and a view of learning as transmission (Tizard *et al.* 1988; Stevenson *et al.* 1990).

Among the Anglo mothers, only Charlotte is assertive and unapologetic about 'working constantly' with her child. The others imply that learning needs to be sneaked in through play, or without the child noticing. They seem to recognize that if they 'believe' that children learn through play, they should not interfere with this process by direct teaching. Their views support the findings of Lightfoot and Valsiner's study: 'The prevailing belief . . . is that the success of educational efforts lies in how well they are disguised as play' (1992: 407).

Joshua's mother in particular expresses a cultural assumption that young children's learning is 'caught' rather than taught. Like many Anglo parents, she distinguishes 'sitting down' teaching and learning from knowledge acquired informally: 'If I was to say to him, let's get the paper and pens out, here's a book, let's sit down, he'd say no!', whereas Joshua 'picked up shapes and colours, just normally'. Maisie completed her questionnaire thoughtfully, writing in:

> Sometimes it can be difficult for parents to 'teach' children as they don't always know how to – or the normal process doesn't apply to a child, i.e. what worked with one child won't with another, so the parents don't know what they are doing, 'right or wrong'.

Maisie confidently describes her own family's activities as 'all the things *normal* families do', unaware that what is normal in her own family would be quite abnormal among some of her neighbours. At the same time she expresses a view of children as individuals, with differing learning styles, which fits the child-centred approach her children experience at All Saints'.

Some of the Anglo mothers who express ambivalence about direct teaching may have communicated this anxiety to their children. Alison describes Cameron as 'suspicious' that she is 'trying to teach him something', while Gaynor describes Kelly as 'not a sit-down sort of person', which explains why she 'won't look at books if I'm in the room, she knows I'll be watching her'. None of this anxiety afflicts Troy's parents, who 'work with him constantly on letters and numbers' on the grounds that he 'just thrives on learning things'. But for Kath, as for many of the Bangladeshi families, the issue is circumvented by the active instructional role taken by the twins' older siblings (cf. Rashid and Gregory 1997; Volk 1998).

The majority of Bangladeshi parents are not only confident of their instructional role, but also have an explicit curriculum in mind: inculcating religious knowledge, teaching the alphabets and counting systems of English, Bengali and Arabic, and conveying appropriate messages about school and study. They make no apology for utilizing their children's evenings and weekends in pursuit of this curriculum, which requires 'sit-down' tasks with a regular timetable as well as ongoing instruction. Home visits, and daily diaries completed with the mothers, show children aged 4 to 17 sitting together round the dining table, reading, writing and reciting under the supervision of a parent, or a visiting teacher. None of these parents would sympathize with the Anglo perspective of sneaking in learning without the child's noticing: like Charlotte, they are proud of fulfilling their own duties, and explicit with their children about *their* duty to learn. Unfortunately, their dedicated teaching does not always result in the kinds of knowledge, or cultural capital, which can be usefully invested in the Reception class.

Family teaching: the 'school' curriculum at home

For all the differences in 'home knowledge' acquired by the children through their early apprenticeship, there was a broad consensus among

Table 3.1 Parental teaching: 'should parents try to teach this item?'

Item	Yes	No	Blank
ABC names	30	3	2
ABC sounds	25	7	3
Counting	31	2	2
Adding	22	10	3
Write name	28	5	2
Nursery rhymes	28	4	3

parents as to what counts as 'school knowledge'. Almost all the families expressed the view that parents should instruct their children in certain types of knowledge before they start school.

Parent questionnaires issued to the whole class asked, *Should parents try to teach their children any of these skills before they start school? Did you try?*, and specified ABC letters and sounds, counting and adding, writing the child's name, and nursery rhymes. Fifteen parents from 35 answered 'yes' to all six items, a further eight answered 'yes' to five items, and five answered 'yes' to four items. Of the remainder, Mohammed's family ticked three items, and Amadur's father simply wrote in 'no'. Of those responding, almost all believed the ABC should be taught (names of letters, rather than sounds) and almost all claimed to teach counting. While these responses, shown in Table 3.1, may not reflect parents' actual practices, they presumably give an accurate picture of what the group as a whole believe constitutes good parenting.

The range of children's experiences and accomplishments in the home is nevertheless very wide.

Literacy learning

Within the group, some Bangladeshi children (Khiernssa, Tuhura and Abdul Rahman) have been exposed to three alphabets (English, Bengali, Arabic) before starting school, while a few Anglo children have started to learn letter sounds as well as letter names. Others have not been told any letters, or shown their own name written down. Some (Cameron, Rufia) have used the local library since they were little, or have shared school reading books with older siblings (the twins, Abu Bokkar and Abdul Rahman), while others have rarely seen a children's book before starting school. Some of the Anglo children, but none of the Bangladeshi group, have a nightly bedtime-story routine, with all that entails (Heath 1982). On the whole, however, the variation in children's experiences reflects not ethnic background, but the complex combination of family circumstances, past and present, which have contributed to each family's cultural capital.

Research on family literacy practices (Teale 1986; Taylor and Dorsey-Gaines 1993; Gregory 1997) emphasizes the *uses* rather than the *mechanics* of literacy. All the All Saints' children observed *some* reading and writing activities in their homes, but the more privileged inhabit households where literacy practices permeate every aspect of daily life (parents who write letters and lists, read magazines, fill in job applications, share children's homework, use knitting patterns and cookery books, take evening classes). These children may also experience literacy events which are targeted at their age group, and foster literacy learning through play and pleasure. The less privileged, whatever their cultural background, have to scratch around for a piece of scrap paper to draw or write on.

For the more advantaged – in differing degrees, Troy, Cameron, Katy, the twins and Joshua – both the content and the methods of their pre-school literacy learning (the curriculum and the pedagogy) would be replicated in school: picture books and ABC books, tape-stories and nursery-rhyme videos, letter-matching games based on lotto, dominos or 'snap'. The school-related *content* of their home literacy, and of their pre-school settings, has been conveyed by school-approved *means*. Where such means are used, the benefits are seen in children's school reading progress, as demonstrated by Stuart *et al.* (1998), who found them predominantly in middle-class children.

Similar *content* is presented, according to their parents, to Abu Bokkar and Abdul Rahman, Khiernssa and Tuhura, but is taught by the didactic 'sit-down' method of the children reciting and copying at the dining table, which many Anglo parents would be embarrassed about attempting. This explicit teaching of alphabets and scripts, including Qur'anic recitation (and the subsequent memorizing of school reading books) is unlikely to produce cultural capital for the child on entering school (Luke and Cale 1997; Rashid and Gregory 1997). Learning which is valued in the community is only valued in school if it can be used, and displayed, in classroom activities. While some of the children are acquiring 'home' knowledge which does not match the official currency of the classroom, still others acquire little literacy knowledge of any kind. The most privileged group, however, have literacy knowledge and skills which can be displayed to good effect during their early school assessments: they can discuss, 'read' and interpret illustrations, invent and predict stories, and utilize story-book language in their own improvizations (Gregory 1993).

Mathematical learning

Most children entering this Reception class have learned to recite the sequence of counting numbers in their homes, even if they are unable to recognize or apply them (or tell them apart from letters). All the parents value the skill of counting, and many Bengali parents have tried to teach their children to count in Bengali too. Most of the children have practised counting at home, and some have counting books and videos. There is less of a gulf between the 'play' and 'instructional' methods used by parents in teaching this skill, though the more knowledgeable parents (Maisie, Maxine, Charlotte) are aware of the need for one-to-one matching while counting: Troy is encouraged to practise his skills all the time, counting front doors and milk bottles as he walks down the street, and playing board games at bedtime. None of the parents seems aware that in school children are assessed mathematically on their sorting, classifying, ordering and patterning skills, rather than on their recitation and recognition of numbers. It seems likely that the mathematical skills which some Anglo children demonstrate on starting school are the result of the educational toys and games they have used, rather than of their parents' teaching.

The one culturally marked aspect of mathematical knowledge for children of this age is the learning of colour names (discussed by Woods and colleagues, 1999: 43). This is seen by the Anglo parents as an essential skill. Kath's account is typical: 'I taught them to say their colours, I always said, "a blue car, a red bus", saying the colour first, so they learned it.' While some of the children (Jemma, Kelly, Joshua) learned colours from older siblings, all the Anglo mothers named this area of knowledge. By contrast, none of the Bangladeshi children had learned colour names in their first language (a few could think of black, or white, or red), though Tuhura was expert in English. Their mothers, unaware of the value attached to this particular curriculum item when children enter school, did not prioritize it in their own teaching. They assumed that such knowledge would be acquired by the child as and when necessary, without explicit instruction.

Attitudes to oracy

Children's language socialization in the home, and its effect on their school progress, was beyond the scope of this study. We already have good evidence, both that language use in families varies in ways which can disadvantage some children on entry to school, and that the language used in 'disadvantaged' families is adequate and appropriate, rather than deficient (Tizard and Hughes 1984; Wells 1986). These findings are of particular relevance to the children's transition to school, discussed in Chapter 5. However, two aspects of the children's oracy relate to the present discussion: the evidence of bilingual children's acquisition of English, and of their parents' expectations about the relative importance of speaking and listening skills.

The range in English development found among the Bangladeshi children is as wide as every other aspect of their development, and similarly reflects both the family's history (of migration and education) and the child's position within the family. In this respect, children who are born sixth or seventh in their families are advantaged over first- or second-borns. The optimal environment for under-5s seems to be one in which teenage siblings, with native-like fluency in English, take on deliberate instructional responsibilities, while primary-age siblings provide play opportunities. Abu Bokkar and Rufia have both enjoyed this privileged situation in their early years, and a similar environment has been provided for Jelika by her teenage aunties. The mothers of these children report them as having heard both English and Bengali since infancy: Jelika's mother reports that in this respect 'she follows the person she is speaking with'. However, none of their mothers speaks English, and none of the children is fully fluent in their second language before school.

Children with primary-age siblings (Abdul Rahman, Khiernssa, Tuhura), though less fluent, have listening and understanding skills which give them some confidence in English-medium environments; while Amadur and Mohammed, whose main experience of English is their TV viewing, are at a great disadvantage. Their mothers describe all these children as fluent in Bengali, but it is evident that some have far fewer opportunities for conversation than others, and that parents have very different expectations for Sylheti or Bengali correctness.

Anglo parents describe their children as learning to talk 'early' (Katy and Kelly), or 'at the normal time' (Cameron, Jemma), and report them as 'talking constantly', 'always chatting', 'never stops', 'she's always talked'. While some mothers admit to finding such 'constant talk' bothersome, Charlotte has made a point of talking to Troy 'all the time'. From her perspective, her insensitive question to me about the 'Indian mothers' – 'they never talk to anyone, so I wonder, do they ever talk to their children?' – is pertinent. Whereas she, more explicitly than other Anglo mothers, regards 'talking to your child' as a parental duty, the Bangladeshi mothers in the group take a relaxed view of their children's linguistic and social development. They appear to trust their children to develop appropriately within the family without undue pressure or direct attention, and never refer to competitive, age-related developmental norms for children's speech. Unlike the Anglo children, the Bangladeshi children are praised by their families for listening rather than talking.

Questionnaire items on children's social learning, summarized in Table 3.2, confirm the cultural emphasis on oral language among the Anglo parents. Parents were asked to rate (as 1, 'not important', 2, 'quite important', and 3, 'very important') six social skills for children starting school: dressing, eating, sharing, playing, talking, and tying laces. While some items produce very similar average scores for 'all parents', 'Anglo sample' and 'Bangladeshi sample', 'talking confidently' is scored by 'all parents' at 2.2, by the 'Anglo sample' at 2.5 and by the 'Bangladeshi sample' at 1.4. Anglo parents appear to prize children's ability to communicate, and to recognize its value in school, while Bangladeshi parents are less concerned about children's *talk*, and prefer them, once they start school, to *listen*.

This aspect of the home curriculum is well hidden from teachers.

Table 3.2 Social behaviour to be learned before starting school

Item	Not important	Quite important	Very important	Blank
Dressing independently	3	16	12	4
Sharing sociably	1	8	22	4
Talking confidently	3	12	15	5
Eating independently	2	10	19	4
Playing sociably	1	4	26	4
Tying shoe laces	14	11	5	5

Preparation for school: what parents tell their children

One of the most important aspects of parental 'knowledge', and a vital element of the family's cultural capital, is knowledge about the school system their children are enrolled in. Several studies have shown a link between such parental cultural capital, and pupil success (Lareau 1987; Gewirtz et al. 1994; Reay 1998). Among the All Saints' families, in addition to individual variations, there are predictable group differences in this form of capital.

The most striking source of variation among the All Saints' families lies in the parents' own school experience. None of the Bangladeshi children's mothers has ever attended school in the UK, and those fathers who did had an intermittent and unsatisfactory experience, mostly at secondary level. All of the Anglo children's mothers were educated in the UK – some at All Saints' – as were all of their present partners. These parents all recollect a vaguely informal, 1970s infant school culture, which superficially resembles the classroom their children are entering, while Bangladeshi parents have no personal experience of UK primary education.

Not only do the two groups begin their 'parent' careers from quite different starting points, but there is evidence that members of the Bangladeshi group are still poorly informed after many years of sending children to school. Even the most experienced among them are constrained by an inbuilt trust in the system and the teachers: as Rufia's mother Majida reports, 'Bangladeshi schools are all right for Bangladesh, but this country's system is right for here: she will learn well enough.' Like Asian parents reported in other studies (Macleod 1985; Joly 1986), they emphasize how 'kind' English teachers are – they like the children, and never hit them; they look after them when they are unwell, come to visit when they are absent, and are always friendly towards parents. This gratitude for teachers' goodwill, and confidence in their professionalism, enables the Bangladeshi parents to turn a blind eye to classroom practices which they find quite inappropriate. None of the parents complained specifically about the informal, play-based curriculum their children were offered on entry to Reception (though some were clearly unhappy with some aspects of it, and told their children not to take part in these activities). But Tuhura's mother admitted, 'I thought, how long will they be playing, when will they learn anything?', although she seems satisfied that her children will learn, in the long run. The most disadvantaged families, in this as in other respects, are Amadur's, Mohammed's and Jelika's. Each of these families is sending a child to school in the UK for the first time, and is entirely unprepared for what awaits them.

Cultural beliefs about learning, and parental knowledge about school, as well as influencing 'home' practices, influence what parents tell their children about school. The most significant factor here, for both parents and children, is their prior relationship with the school. If parents are on good terms with school staff (Joshua, Katy and Cameron's mothers), *or* if older siblings have a successful experience of the school (Rufia, Joshua), the 4-year-old starting school is likely to be eager and positive without any parental coaching: Cameron 'couldn't wait to come', after regularly accompanying his brother; Joshua, Rufia and Katy 'always looked forward to coming'. These children could see for themselves what went on in their siblings' classrooms. Equally importantly, all their parents feel positive and relaxed about school.

Other parents felt more need to prepare and reassure their children. Jemma's mother 'sat them down and told them about school, what they'd be doing, just to let them know what it was going to be'. Gaynor told Kelly, 'If anyone starts, tell the teacher and let the teacher sort it out and not hurt or bite.' Abu Bokkar, Abdul Rahman, and Khiernssa (all of whom had accompanied siblings to school) were 'told not to worry', and taught to 'say their name' or ask for the toilet. But Bangladeshi parents, who emphasized both good behaviour and hard work in instructing their children, included messages the children may not have found encouraging. Mohammed was told he must 'study reading and writing, and not play'; Amadur that he should 'be good at school, and sit down and study, and don't do anything naughty'; Tuhura that 'you must listen to the teacher, watch what you say, don't talk too much, obey everything the teacher says'. The most fearful child, Jelika, was warned by her mother, 'You must go to school every day, behave properly, and stay there as long as you're told; if you cry, remember other children don't cry when their mothers leave them.' At the crucial moment of transition, it seems, some children were expecting school to be fun, while others were preparing to submit to hard work and even unhappiness.

Case study: Abu Bokkar and his family

Abu Bokkar is the youngest child in his family, and the seventh child to start school at All Saints' primary. His mother Rahena expresses simultaneously the utmost confidence in the school and a complete ignorance as to what her children learn there, and why and how. Her trust is based on acquaintance with the staff rather than with the curriculum or pedagogy: Rahena can remember and recite all the teachers her children have had over the years, and speaks well of them all: 'Shahena – Mrs Moore, nice lady, Mrs Johnson, nice teacher, we like . . .' She is sure they teach the children well – 'they are trained, they know what they are doing' – and assumes that the system works: now the children 'are doing a little bit of learning', later 'they will learn writing, letters, counting' and 'one day they will learn everything'. In Bokkar's case, she believes he is especially talented, and will do especially well. In any case, she asserts, 'If children don't learn, it's not the teacher's fault.'

Rahena's optimism contrasts with her husband's disquiet over his older children's poor achievements, and his pessimism over Bokkar's likely progress. Mr Ali has kept every one of the older children's school reports, and on my first visit courteously asked me to sit and read them through. The pattern he discerned in them gave him legitimate cause for concern: each child in turn had been warmly praised for their efforts and success at All Saints', and each in turn had ended up in low streams or non-examination groups at secondary school. What could he do? 'We teach them, we sit with them, we make them study, we ask their teachers, are they doing all right? We ask our children, are you working hard, they say yes.' All his children, he claims, wanted to 'be something' after leaving school; one by one they are realizing that they are not going to be good enough, that they will end up in an unskilled job. Now, he claims, the younger ones say to him, 'What's the point of working hard?' In his view they are just 'passing the time' at school, not learning.

Abu Bokkar has benefited in his pre-school years from the devoted attention of his mother and regular explicit instruction from his father and older siblings: a visible, strongly-framed pedagogy is in place for teaching 'school knowledge' at home. His siblings have taught him letters and numbers, and looked at books with him. When the older children do homework, Bokkar sits with them and copies writing out of books, or draws with them. He hears both English and Sylheti spoken indoors, and understands both quite well. 'He's very bright', Mr Ali says. But can his family's social and cultural capital be invested successfully in the classroom? Or will he too have a mediocre school career ahead of him?

Summary: preparing for school

Bernstein argues that the *way* parents teach during their children's early years – the 'domestic transmission of school knowledge' – is more influential in children's subsequent school careers than *what* is taught and learned. As we have seen, the ways in which the All Saints' families bring about learning in their homes reveal both individual and group differences. The Bangladeshi families, in general, favour a more visible pedagogy than the Anglo families, but an individual Anglo mother, like Charlotte, may simultaneously advocate explicit instruction *and* provide educational toys, in an effort to maximize her child's chances of success.

Figure 3.1 The curriculum and pedagogy of the home

	'School' knowledge (literacy + numeracy)	'Local' knowledge (hobbies, religion, language etc.)
Visible pedagogy	*Explicit instruction* in the 'school' curriculum [e.g. ABC learned by rote and recited, ABC books taught]	*Explicit instruction* in a non-school curriculum [e.g. mosque school, Sunday school, Bengali classes]
Invisible pedagogy	*Implicit instruction* in the 'school' curriculum [e.g. fridge magnets, nursery rhyme videos, story tapes]	*Implicit instruction* in a non-school curriculum [apprenticeship into home and family routines and responsibilities]

By covering both options, it seems, she has tried to ensure that Troy will both satisfy her own standards for children's early accomplishments and be seen as a successful and high-achieving pupil by his Reception teacher.

The model in Figure 3.1 suggests some of the combinations of curriculum and pedagogy offered by families to their young children, and enables their instructional practices to be compared, with each other and with the model of pedagogy which will underpin their Reception experience. It depicts, on two axes, the curriculum and the pedagogy which the child is offered at home.

The vertical axis is divided into the two principal pedagogic types described by Bernstein: the 'visible' (explicit, didactic, direct instruction) and the 'invisible' (implicit, informal, indirect). Charlotte, as we have seen, employs both forms, but most families tend to prefer one or the other, and Bangladeshi families tend to opt for a more visible version than Anglo families. But families also have a curriculum in mind: the 'natural' curriculum of the home, overshadowed in recent years by some awareness of the 'national' curriculum of statutory schooling. The content of this curriculum, as well as the way it is experienced or acquired, varies between families, as well as between homes and school. The horizontal axis, therefore, shows the two kinds of knowledge which may make up the 'home curriculum'. These are school knowledge (which all parents agree is based on letter and number knowledge), described by Bernstein as 'official' because it is the means of entry into the mainstream culture; and community knowledge (different for every family and community), which Bernstein describes as 'local knowledge'. The model therefore suggests how both the curriculum and the pedagogy of each family can be conceptualized, and compared with the mainstream culture of the classroom.

As the individual cases suggest, there is no simple formula for describing the ways children are prepared for school by their families, or for predicting the outcomes of such preparation. Any model of parenting practices which tried to assign a value to a particular pedagogy, or a specific curriculum, and so to calculate a high or low value for permutations of the two ('school knowledge imparted through an implicit pedagogy'/'community knowledge imparted by direct instruction') would rapidly encounter more exceptions than rules.

The model, however, allows us to compare both the curriculum and the pedagogy of both home and school. It enables us to see that, for some of the children, the **pedagogic discourse** of the home is quite unlike that of mainstream 'western' parenting practices (and as we shall see of 'liberal–progressive' schooling). On the whole, there is a broad consensus among all the All Saints' families as to what constitutes 'school knowledge', but a wide variation in the ways they attempt to impart it to their children before they start school. The actual 'value' of these methods, in terms of the cultural capital they make available to each child on starting school, is only seen when the children are observed in their early days in the classroom.

4

SCHOOL CULTURE AT ALL SAINTS' PRIMARY

Entering a new world

The 16 children started school as members of a large and poorly balanced Reception class: the final enrolment of 39 children consisted of 26 boys and 13 girls. They entered the care of a class teacher (Sally Goode) and a nursery nurse (Becky Weston), and had additional part-time support from a Section 11 (ethnic minority support) teacher, a bilingual assistant and a classroom assistant. For their first half term, they were to attend for half days only, unless 'invited to stay the whole day' by Mrs Goode, who carefully assessed each child's readiness for this step. Troy, Cameron and Katy were among those who 'stayed all day' for the first time in Week 3, and were soon staying two or three days a week. Other children, including Amadur and Mohammed, remained part-time pupils for much longer.

The Reception area contained one large classroom used as a quiet room, and a still larger classroom which housed more physically expansive and potentially noisy activities. The quiet room offered book and reading areas, writing and drawing areas, a computer, a listening area and space for games such as lotto or pairs to be played on low tables or units. The large room had computers at each end, sand and water and art areas arranged along one long side, and a maths and science area, as well as large spaces set up for floor play, puzzles, construction and small world toys, and a home corner. Within the classrooms a large stock of equipment – toys and games, maths and science apparatus, artefacts and posters, cooking and art utensils – was accessibly stored. The two classrooms therefore offered most of the facilities of a nursery class: the main difference, apart from the adult–child ratio, was the restricted access to outdoor play and equipment, which was only available for limited periods every day.

The classrooms were inviting and interesting. When the doors opened each morning or afternoon, children arrived to find small worlds and layouts half-built, puzzles half-completed, and sand and water implements attractively arranged, presenting an irresistible invitation to participate. This invitation to play was fundamental to the organization of the class. On entry in September children were encouraged to settle straight into self-chosen activities, supported by their parents or whichever school adults were available. When greeted, they were asked 'What would you like to do first?', and helped to choose an activity that interested them. Many mothers slipped away at this point, though they were free to remain if they chose.

Both Mrs Goode and Becky spent most of each session playing actively, modelling behaviour with the sand and water, bricks and home corner as well as with more structured games and activities. Reception children were exempted from the organizational requirements of the main school, and allowed to follow a largely flexible timetable within their own sheltered environment. In the early days and weeks, the only restrictions on children's freely chosen play were those occasioned by the need to control inappropriate behaviour, to give others turns at activities, or to 'borrow' children briefly for assessment tasks. For both morning and afternoon groups, the timetable consisted of at least an hour's activities, mostly freely chosen, followed by a half-hour of optional outdoor play (including wheeled and low climbing equipment, balls and hoops, and playground chalks), a snack and group story time, a further session of free activities and then singing and rhymes before their departure.

The timetable did not change dramatically in the second half term, when all the children attended full-time. More time was now available for children to tidy, sort and clean up in the last part of the afternoon, and this became a major activity, serving multiple pedagogic functions. Children still entered in the morning to a free choice of activities, but were soon summoned to the quiet room book corner for a registration session and other domestic business. From this session they were dismissed into groups, for adult-directed or self-directed activities, or simply invited to 'choose'. Normally, fewer than 10 of those present would have a free choice at this point, but since directed activities were sometimes of very short duration, most children were moving on, and effectively still 'choosing' for much of the day, even if they were selected for three or four adult-supervised tasks in the course of it.

During the second half term, the children become more used to leaving their freely chosen activities to work with an adult at a task. By Christmas all were going regularly to read or share books, to attempt writing or maths tasks, or to join in a group for discussion, experiment, or the acquisition of new skills. With large numbers of children, and the constant forming and re-forming of teaching groups of various sizes, they normally had to drop what they were doing and take up the adult activity at short notice: most children complied with these requests.

School culture

The ethos of All Saints'

While the town ranks at least middling in national educational performance tables, a handful of its schools (some inner urban and multi-ethnic, others on outlying white estates) have significantly poor results at every level, including at the Baseline entry level. All Saints' Primary is one of these. Far from being, in Ofsted terminology, a 'failing' school, however, it is a confident and purposeful institution, and sees its Christian basis as the rationale for welcoming children from all social, ethnic and religious backgrounds, and for expressing a particular commitment to children from poor families, and to the Muslim community. The 1997 Ofsted report praises All Saints' 'positive ethos', its 'inclusiveness', and its attention to pastoral matters, commenting that 'The school provides a caring and supportive environment and it is apparent that all staff are committed, loyal and work well together ... The staff know the pupils well.' At the same time, it acknowledges that All Saints' 'is not an easy school to work in'.

All the school's official documents bear the stamp of this positive ethos. The standard job description for teachers declares that 'Our definition of a good school is one in which all those present are seen as learners and mistakes are seen as an opportunity for improvement and not failure.' The class teacher's responsibilities towards her pupils include 'encouraging positive attitudes in the pupils to school, to their lives and to themselves'; having 'adequate knowledge of his/her home background, medical concerns, ethnic origin, home language and religion'; creating 'a safe, relaxed yet disciplined atmosphere in which a whole range of learning styles are employed'; and creating an 'environment which gives the children independence and reinforces the joy and importance of being literate'.

As this indicates, being a teacher at All Saints' does not, first and foremost, concern *teaching*, a term which does not appear in the document. Rather it concerns being a certain kind of person: a caring individual who is sensitive to the well-being of the 'whole child' in her care, but primarily to that child's social, emotional and spiritual needs. While not explicitly required to 'teach', a teacher must 'attempt to meet the educational and social needs' of pupils, and plan activities which 'take into account these needs'. Teachers are also required to take account of the curriculum, which is defined here as 'all of the experiences the children encounter during their career with us'. While this definition prioritizes pastoral care, and a holistic view of the child, a more detailed description of the academic curriculum is provided for each age phase.

The staff's concern to 'emphasize the positive' in children's behaviour and learning shapes its policy documents and organizational practices. School policies express a commitment to raising self-esteem among pupils *and* staff, and advocate a supportive and 'no-blame' response to infringements. The behaviour policy, for instance, is a set of 'principles' rather than rules or sanctions, and emphasizes the collective responsibility for behaviour of all members of the school community:

> The way in which teachers behave has the greatest effect on the way the children behave in school. They will model themselves on us.

> Children whose behaviour is unacceptable need to be shown our greatest love through the quality of our care. This has the effect of:

> - enabling us to introduce the concept of justice and the complex issues around the idea that equality does not mean identical treatment;
> - building the child's self-esteem which itself is the greatest inducement to socially acceptable behaviour . . .

Many of the school's organizational practices derive from these principles.

The Reception teacher Mrs Goode has played a large part, as Deputy Head, in shaping the culture of the school. Both she and her head teacher, Joan Mason, have worked for twenty years as nursery and infant teachers, and remain committed to the child-centred beliefs they acquired in their initial training and early school experience (the 'ideological tradition', Bennett *et al.* 1997: 14). Mrs Goode has a university diploma in Early Years education. Her core beliefs, and classroom practices, which she describes articulately and confidently, dovetail closely with the pastoral ethos of All Saints' whole-school policies.

Mrs Mason shares Mrs Goode's belief in working from 'where the individual child is at', and describes the implications for the school's curriculum and pedagogy of the All Saints' intake:

> The children come with very low baselines, very poor use of language, so obviously that has an effect on what is provided in the classroom . . . the baseline is very low, for instance, in Reception, we're going to have to look at the needs of those children coming in and make sure that what we provide is relevant for them; so we will have to have flexibility and adapt the curriculum to suit the needs of the children – and if you don't they're not going to learn anyway!

In particular, she emphasizes the pastoral aspect of the school's role as a prerequisite for the academic. Her awareness of the stress experienced by some children in their homes leads her to the view that children's emotional needs must be attended to before their learning can be considered:

> We can't actually teach a child if things from outside interfere: if you have a very angry child coming into school because of something that happened the night before, or through the night, or that morning, then you have to take that child to one side, and

give them time, and listen, and calm them, or provide whatever their need, before you can expect . . . you can't just say, 'Come on, it's Literacy Hour, sit down, you've got work to do', because they won't learn anything, they're not thinking . . .

The pedagogic discourse of All Saints' as a whole clearly prioritizes pastoral (emotional/expressive) requirements over academic (intellectual/instrumental) objectives (Power 1998).

The Reception staff: beliefs about children's learning

Mrs Goode not only advocates such 'liberal–progressive' tenets as 'learning through play', 'discovery', 'freedom to choose' and 'autonomy', she can also explain *how* and *why* provision based on them fosters children's learning. In her view, the Reception year needs to offer an Early Years environment and a curriculum built around the *Desirable Outcomes* (SCAA 1996), rather than a 'level-zero' National Curriculum. At the same time, however, she is conscious of the requirement to prepare children for the full-fledged National Curriculum experience of Year 1. She therefore attempts to combine two rather contradictory purposes: to supply, belatedly, a child-centred, exploratory experience for children whose early lives have been restricted to the cramped or overcrowded surroundings of their family home, giving them the time and space and opportunities to progress at their own pace; but at the same time to telescope this experience into a limited span of months in order to move the children on, forcibly, to a state of preparedness for the National Curriculum. She is fully aware of the conflict between these two objectives, as she indicates: 'I don't have any problem with *Desirable Outcomes*, as long as I don't take any notice in terms of "By the age of 5, a child should be able to" . . . the basic curriculum is absolutely fine . . . I have a problem with when they put expectations . . .'

Mrs Goode believes that children learn best by pursuing activities which interest and motivate them. As she explained to the handful of parents who attended an induction evening in September, she and the other staff would be observing the children closely to discover what motivated them, and would use this information to keep the children interested and active in extending their knowledge. She invited parents to keep her informed on what their child's favourite activities were, as this would enable the school to support their learning. (Unfortunately the pressures of the over-large class resulted in her cancelling her usual parent interviews that year, and few parents took up her invitation; most parents, as we shall see, were in any case expecting teachers to *teach* their children, rather than to encourage the children's individual interests.)

The Reception classroom offered a wide choice of activities and opportunities, to enable children to demonstrate their motivating interests. In addition, Mrs Goode believed, the setting must foster 'independence', 'social skills', 'freedom' and 'fun':

It has to first of all allow them to have independence, so they can actually direct their own time . . . they've got to be able to choose, they've got to make choices, and they've got to be able to maintain things independently, things that interest *them*, the sort of things that *they* will then learn from; and you have to have enough opportunity for them to develop their social skills, because that's one of the most important things; and they have to have a *wide* range of activities that they've actually experienced and explored, different experiences, different sensory things . . . they also *must* have space, and they must have freedom to move about within it . . . and they must also have fun, things must be of interest to them, there must be that kind of informality of learning . . .

'Learning', in other words, is viewed as the outcome of children's self-directed, self-motivated explorations, rather than the product of 'teaching': a Piagetian rather than Vygotskyan emphasis, and one which does not call for direct instruction. Granting children independence is an essential aspect of the Reception ethos, and Mrs Goode frequently refers to 'letting the children just be, and letting them explore'; 'allowing them to have independence'; 'the power to make choices'; 'you look for independence, how independent they can be, and again it goes back to maintaining their own activity'.

The teacher's role in this scenario is to make provision that is truly child-centred, personalized to individual children rather than general-ized to the age group. Ideally, Mrs Goode would fine-tune her provision through the observation of children's schemas: 'Again, in an ideal world you could take a child and if they'd got a specific schema you could actually educate them in the way of that, from their own interest: that's the way for children to learn!' In a class of this size, this is not an option.

A version of these beliefs is offered by Becky, who did her nursery nurse training at All Saints', and has modelled her practice closely on Mrs Goode's. Becky is given near-equal responsibilities with Mrs Goode in the day-to-day organization of the Reception rooms, and operates in a near-identical manner. However, both her understanding and the way she performs her duties are shaped by her own educational background. Becky grew up in the town, and gained her NNEB at the local college (for which 'I think you had to have one GCSE, I think it had to be English'). Though a skilled technician in the classroom, she does not share Mrs Goode's know-ledge of the theories of child development which underlie their joint pedagogic practice. She explains their provision for children's learning as a combination of play and practical activities, rather than instruction:

Practical I think is very important to learning, it's 'hands-on'; they learn by doing it, rather than being told, going in one ear and out the other . . . It's actually, the major aspect of learning for this age group is actually play, it is actually how they learn, the younger ones . . . to a certain degree.

Becky, though unable to elaborate on these views, expertly sets up intriguing and inviting play environments for the children to discover, and communicates a genuine interest in playing and experimenting to which most children respond with pleasure.

Becky's enthusiasm for play is not shared by the class's third regular adult, Mrs Khan, a bilingual assistant funded through the multicultural service, and my interpreter with the families. Mrs Khan, herself the beneficiary of a middle-class colonial education in pre-1972 Bengal, expresses mixed views and divided loyalties on the pedagogy of All Saints':

> I was feeling this kind of system was better when I came first, because nothing was hard work, child was playing – but now I'm beginning to feel that my system is not bad either, because generation after generation we're learning . . . and the standard we're learning is not terrible either because many people come in this country, for jobs, and students coming to study at Oxford, Cambridge . . . so if our standard is low that means they wouldn't get a place there . . . So, half and half: our system is bad because we don't do anything practical by hand, but we do more reading and writing . . .

Mrs Khan loyally defends the Reception practice to the Bangladeshi families: 'I tell them, often they're learning something because they're mixing freely with different children and they copy, without help, especially jigsaws, Lego, cutting, making something, playing different games . . .' Privately, however, she admits her own doubts and her sympathy with the parents' view that their children ought to 'sit down and study': 'I think half-day reading and writing, half-day playing and doing some other activities . . . because they are so young.'

Unlike Becky, Mrs Khan has had no personal experience of liberal–progressive methods, and little professional training. She is however subject to a high degree of control from Mrs Goode, who instructs her in exactly how to carry out her duties: which concepts to explore in a discussion group, which children to target, what to record about each child's contribution. She therefore attempts to suppress her own preferred pedagogic style, which is direct and didactic, and sometimes involves correcting the children quite sharply. When her instinctive discourse surfaces through the official pedagogic discourse of the classroom, Mrs Khan is aware of Mrs Goode's disapproval.

Teachers' beliefs about home and school

At All Saints', written policies explicitly recognize the importance both of parents and of home cultures in children's learning, and aim to be inclusive of both. The job description for class teachers includes the statement:

Parents are our partners in the education of their children. It is therefore the responsibility of each teacher to ensure that parents are fully informed of their child's rate of progress, achievements and special needs. To achieve this, the teacher needs to ensure that the school's 'Open Door' policy is fully implemented, that parents are made to feel important and welcome visitors, and that they are listened to and their views receive a positive response.

Mrs Mason spontaneously raises this issue when asked to describe the type of educational environment the school offers. In her view the key to the school's ethos is:

the openness: teachers being available to parents at the beginning and end of the day, on a parent level . . . able to communicate on a social level and be *friends* to the parents . . . the whole ethos of the school is of warmth and caring and understanding for the position that these parents are in . . .

In other words, home–school links support the school's pastoral, rather than its academic, purposes. Mrs Goode, however, is conscious of the need to bridge the gap in instructional styles of which she is aware. She expresses a positive attitude towards parents, and claims that her main interest in assessing parents' contribution towards their child's learning is in knowing 'what the parents' expectations of school and their learning are – and also, what input they expect to have':

I need to know, for instance, if a very structured approach to reading is happening at home, in terms of learning words, there is no point in me, here, not giving him any words – I wouldn't do that to a child and there is no point, I would try and work with the parents, and work together so we can have a balanced approach . . .

This ideal is inevitably compromised in practice. Mrs Goode is only able to 'work with' parents whose home pedagogy she is aware of, and in this busy class, with parent interviews abandoned due to pressure of time, this means only those parents with the social and cultural capital to initiate a dialogue with her. Many parents are not in this position.

Becky is less generous in her assessment of parents. She feels able to discriminate between children whose parents have 'done a bit at home' and the others: 'Some don't know anything because they're not taught it at home.' In the case of the Bangladeshi children, she has some sympathy for their parents ('some of it must be support at home – if the parents have no English, like the reading, something like that, they can't, it's difficult'). But in justifiably attributing some of these children's difficulties to their very poor attendance, she is apt to blame their parents'attitudes: 'Just shove your kids in when you feel like it, some of them!' Becky in fact has little contact with the Bangladeshi parents. This responsibility is largely delegated to Mrs Khan, who is more sympathetic:

I don't blame them because they first came from Bangladesh, and not mixing up with anything, so I specially help the Bangladeshi parents, a couple of mothers, every day something comes new and I need to tell them what's going on, even the holiday: 'Is it tomorrow holiday?', 'No, it's the day after!'

Though her own background is privileged in comparison with that of the All Saints' families, Mrs Khan recognizes the dislocation experienced by newly arrived women, saying of Amadur's mother, for instance: 'She can't suddenly jump – it takes a couple of years to settle down in this system, it's a difficulty coping: I can't blame her . . . it took me a long time to settle down in this situation.'

In practice, as Mrs Goode recognizes, *all* children may experience difficulties and discontinuities on transition to school. With regard to parents' staying on in the classroom, she explains, 'In September, in the first few weeks, I always say to parents that they're very welcome to stay if they want to – not many do.' In curriculum terms, Mrs Goode believes that the rich child-centred environment offered in Reception is appropriate for *all* children, and that catering for individual backgrounds would be problematic: 'The range of experiences that they've had, before school, is so huge: you have to give them the best environment.' She acknowledges that the 'home-like' activities such as shopping, cooking and going for local walks which feature frequently in Reception 'may only be continuity if you're a more middle-class type of child'.

Nevertheless the Reception curriculum, which aims to provide an environment in which *all* children can flourish, is built around such experiences. It could be argued that the pedagogy can only achieve these objectives by turning *all* children into 'a more middle-class type of child'.

Pedagogic discourse in the reception class

To understand the ways in which the Reception pedagogy works, we need to step back from the classroom and return to Bernstein's description of pedagogic discourse – the underlying rules of behaviour which shape the day-to-day practices of teachers, and the day-to-day experiences of children.

In Bernstein's view (1996), each classroom has its own unique 'modality' – a distinctive pedagogy shaped by the strength and weakness of the classification and framing principles of the discourse. These modalities, however, take two principal forms: the 'performance model' and the 'competence model'. The performance model is typified by the visible pedagogy of strong classification and framing, and by strict and standardized evaluation of performance or *product*. In Bernstein's view, it is founded on 'economic' principles (such as value for money). In contrast, the competence model rests on weak classification and framing, a subjective evaluation of the whole child (and of *process*), and on 'therapeutic' principles (for the good of the child). Since the introduction of the National Curriculum, 'performance modes dominate both primary and secondary levels' (Bernstein 1996: 74), and even influence provision for under-5s. Hence Mrs Goode, in describing her own child-centred pedagogy, is conscious of resisting a national trend.

Though the general *type* of organization in the Reception classroom resembles a competence model, its precise modality, as experienced by children and their parents, results from a complex mix of strong and weak classification (of home/school, adult/child, work/play, learning/fun) and framing (freedom/compulsion, autonomy/direction). In every aspect of the classroom operations, too, the strength of classification and framing varies according to the individuals or groups who are on the receiving end: some children, for instance, experience more control than others, and some parents enjoy greater access. So an account of the pedagogic discourse of the Reception classroom cannot describe the way that discourse is actually *experienced* by different groups and individuals, because it is a model which in reality treats children and families differently.

At All Saints', characteristics of the competence model include:

- a *curriculum and organization* characterized by weakly classified space, time and discourse (freedom to choose and explore);
- a *pedagogy* which emphasizes learning rather than teaching (freedom to find out);
- an *evaluation* based on the presence, rather than absence, of knowledge and skills, and on process rather than product;
- *forms of control* which are personalized (in the person of Mrs Goode) and individualized (to each child).

This explicitly child-centred, liberal–progressive model – the appropriate model for *all* children, in Mrs Goode's estimation – contains within it expectations of an 'ideal child' or 'pupil' who is able to learn appropriately from the model. This ideal type is more difficult for some children to achieve than for others. In order to examine these expectations, we consider in turn the two principal aspects of the pedagogic discourse: the **regulative discourse** and the **instructional discourse**. The first of these is termed 'RD' by Bernstein, and defined as the rules of the *social order* (the ways to behave in the classroom). The second, 'ID', is defined as the rules of the *discursive order* (the ways to learn in the classroom). But as we shall see, the instructional discourse, especially where young children are concerned, is always embedded in the regulative discourse.

The social order: the rules of the regulative discourse

Mrs Goode's Reception practice is grounded in a school discourse premised on concepts of self-esteem and pastoral care, and in a curriculum led by 'social development'. In the first weeks of school, she uses whole group sessions to induct children into particular aspects of the social order of the school: ways of speaking and listening to others, sitting, sharing, taking turns and putting your hand up; specifics like washing hands, hanging up coats, and answering the dinner register. Most children's pride in these new accomplishments made them eager to conform to these aspects of the culture of the school. Mrs Goode was asked what 'learning to be a pupil' meant to her, and how she set about it:

> Learning to be part of a social group within the school structure . . . so it's learning the social codes and etiquettes and whatnot . . . it's listening, it's respect, it's activities, it's turn-taking . . . The ways to do it are, going over things, different aspects of the situation; you're also explaining when things are acceptable, like, 'you've hurt somebody, now imagine how that feels' . . . and it's learning to be part of a group – and you have to have consistent expectations; it's all part of a society, and it's a structured society because it's a formal school.

Asked whether some *groups* adapted more easily to school behaviour, she speculated that

> some of the bilingual children learn it quicker . . . whether it's because they're keen to please, or they're more reliant . . . they haven't got the confidence, they want to be structured; but some of them do learn it quickly, and when you consider that they might not be understanding an awful lot of what happens to them . . .

Though she was unwilling to conclude that girls were better adapted to the process (both resisting the stereotype, and citing Kelly, who had *not* been amenable), she believed they might, on the whole, 'understand more of what a teacher tells them'.

Because she values autonomy in children, Mrs Goode tries to avoid imposing her own will, though she knows she has the skills and authority to do so. By the third term she expects 'most children in the room' to be both independent and compliant in undertaking adult-directed tasks: 'Some will wait to be asked but they're quite happy to go if they're asked – well, it depends who's doing the asking!' This last aside gives a hint of the invisibility of the regulative discourse. There is, as Mrs Goode admits, an element of compulsion by the third term in Reception – but it is disguised as 'asking'. Most children will respond to being 'asked', but only by certain adults – those vested with the authority that comes with control of the discourse; and some 'challenging' children, she observes, require more explicit control, and sanctions.

Some children had difficulty learning the rules of the regulative discourse. The friendly and informal relationship normally displayed between adults and children in the class implied an expectation by *staff* of instant compliance by children to any of their requests, and an assumption by *children* that such compliance was reasonable, because any requests made by adults would be reasonable. Such assumptions are consistent with the style of 'reciprocal' control identified by the Newsons (1968, 1976) as well as in Bernstein's early research as a middle-class characteristic, but now more common among working-class families. Among All Saints' families many parents, as the Newsons put it, 'wish to be friends with their children'. Inevitably the regulative discourse of children's homes influences their expectations about the reasonableness of adults in general, as well as about the respect due to teachers; a minority of children, in consequence, challenged the adult exercise of power. A weak-frame adult 'request' such as 'Would you like to leave the sand, and come and do your writing now?' required a negotiated response which some found hard to understand. Kelly, whose home experience of conflict has proved more enduring than her nursery training, was among the children described by Mrs Goode as 'very challenging' (the others were boys). But some compliant children (including some of the bilingual children) were visibly confused and wary under this 'soft' form of control. As Bernstein has argued, the apparently *weak* framing of the regulative discourse in classrooms with a competence model frequently conceals *strong* though unspoken expectations about appropriate behaviour.

The same tension is evident in the expectations for children's activity choices. On the one hand, Mrs Goode aims to offer the children freedom, 'so they can actually direct their own time'. This freedom extends, initially at least, to the weak framing of children's time and space: they may, in principle, use the two classrooms and their contents as they please, for as long as they please. On the other hand, Mrs Goode believes the children *must* be exposed to the full array of learning experiences, which are therefore compulsory and, from the children's point of view, arbitrary.

The rhetoric of independent time management is undermined in practice by the frequent summons, without warning, to an adult-directed group activity, so that it becomes progressively more difficult for a child to spend more than a few minutes at a self-chosen activity without interruption. By the second term, management of the day, though outwardly 'unstructured', was actually complex. With long lists of planned experiences and targets to achieve, there were days when Mrs Goode and Becky, classroom assistants and parent volunteers would be checking their clipboard lists and competing good-naturedly for the same children: 'Can I have him first? I've only got one more group to do'; 'I need her now because she'll be doing cooking after play.' Though most children complied readily with such summonses, they were effectively prevented from planning or implementing any projects of their own. The minority of children who resented this constraint, as indicated, were described not as 'independent' or 'self-directing' but as 'challenging'.

Thus the informality of the discourse, together with the broad curriculum offered, could actually impede children's ability to maintain autonomy. The weak framing of the organization denied children the opportunity to plan, as all 'requests' to abandon their task were, or were made to seem, spontaneous. According to Becky, most groupings were opportunistic, 'It's just, "I'll have you, quick!" – it's just as it comes.' In consequence, children had no idea, when they settled down to a self-directed activity, how soon they would be snatched up by an adult intent on offering them another learning experience. In practice, classroom observations and diaries showed that those children most likely to sustain an independent project (such as Joshua or Katy) were those most likely to be 'picked', and picked again in a hectic curriculum roundabout. Those least able to undertake tasks independently (such as Amadur and Mohammed) were more frequently left to 'choose' until late in the day. A strongly framed organization, with clear directions to children about when they would be required for adult-directed tasks, might in practice have afforded many children a greater degree of autonomy.

The regulative discourse, for all its elusiveness and intangibility, permeates every aspect of classroom life. It is present from the start in the individualized invitation to play ('What would you like to choose?') or to stay all day ('Would you like him to do the whole day next Tuesday?'); in the adult modelling of enthusiasm and interest ('Let's go and see what Becky's put in the water tray for us!'); and in the warm and personalized overture that is made to each child. Mrs Goode is a supremely skilled practitioner of this discourse: systematic observations of classroom interactions showed that over 90 per cent of her utterances could be characterized as warm, positive and approving. Not surprisingly, all the parents reported their children's liking for her and for Becky.

Cameron, however, seemed to have recognized the nature of the discourse: as Alison reported to me,

> I think he's a bit . . . not *wary* of Mrs Goode, but when he was slow getting dressed in the morning, and I said 'Are you like this at school?', he said, 'Don't tell Mrs Goode, don't tell Mrs Goode': he knows she's in charge, kind of thing!

As Cameron detected, the regulative discourse resided in the person of Mrs Goode.

The regulative discourse in action

The regulative discourse shapes both the everyday routines of the classroom – into which the children are effectively socialized as the year goes on – and the special occasions which punctuate the school year, such as outings. An example of each shows how the 'proper pupil' is framed within the discourse.

Registration

Registration is one of those 'naturally occurring' events in the classroom which appear perfectly normal to insiders, but may be seen as meaningless rituals by outsiders. In Reception, children entered the classroom informally, over a 20- or 30-minute period, and were encouraged to 'go into activities', enabling staff to chat to parents or children socially. At an undefined moment, Mrs Goode summoned the children to the carpet in the book corner to start the day formally by calling the attendance and dinner registers. There was thus an abrupt transition from the weakly framed situation of children mixing freely (and loudly) in and out of the two rooms, to the strongly framed one of children sitting together in stillness and silence waiting to respond to their teacher. Explicit training about this transition was given in the first term, though most of the ongoing regulation was implicit: 'Sonia! look how beautifully you're sitting – and you didn't take any notice of Brian's fussing, did you? *Good girl!*' This individualized praise produced, naturally, a whole class 'sitting beautifully' for a few moments at least.

Registration itself, though formally an initiation into 'pupil' status (Boyle and Woods 1998), is used to reinforce the personalized rhetoric of the classroom, and the 'fun' aspect of its pedagogy. From the first, children are told that it is fun to choose 'different kinds of register': starting from the bottom, singing, whispering, smiling ('Where's your lovely smile, Kelly? Thank you very much!'). The range of verbal responses is permissive: 'yes', 'hello', 'I'm here', 'good morning Mrs Goode' are all rewarded with warm thanks. So are appropriate responses for the next part of the session: 'home dinners', 'packed lunch' and so on. Most of the children respond to Mrs Goode's lively, friendly discourse by giving her their full attention throughout the lengthy process of registering everyone twice over. Those children who have to be 'spoken to' repeatedly are asked to leave the group. A third group, however, appears switched off for much of the session, and have to be prompted, daily, for an appropriate answer:

Jemma? What about you?
Yes Mrs Goode.
No no, we've done the register, this is dinners . . .
Yes Mrs Goode.
No Jemma, what are you doing for dinner? *Are you . . .*
[Silence]
Did you bring a lunch box? [to Becky] *Is her lunch box there?*

The session continues with routines which combine ritual and instructional purposes: counting and estimating numbers, checking the calendar, and reporting the weather. Two children go outside for a 'weather watch', and return to announce their findings and make predictions for morning and afternoon playtimes. These reports are formulaic and strongly framed, as the children respond to identical teacher prompts every day: 'What colour was the sky? . . . and did you see any clouds? . . . and were the trees moving? . . . and that means it's . . . and will we need our coats on?' By the end of Reception a few children could report independently (that is, reproduce the formula without prompts) but the majority still needed support. In July, Amadur and Mohammed could still only nod, shake their heads or repeat phrases loudly whispered to them by Mrs Khan: 'Blue sky . . . nice day', and appeared uncomfortable with being the focus of attention.

The last part of the session was used to give the children some indication of the day's tasks, and to allow adults to select their first groups before the remaining children were allocated to play activities. These latter were directed through a weakly framed discourse ('You four may play in the water') which was actually non-negotiable, though most children soon realized that they could abandon their allocated activities once the adult who has directed them was otherwise occupied.

One other regulative aspect of the session remained a mystery. *Certain* children, *most* mornings, were allowed to continue with their activities (computer games, board games, drawing) when the class gathered on the carpet. The rule for which children, and which activities, were given this dispensation never became clear: the rule was, in practice, 'what Mrs Goode decides', although Becky was similarly empowered if she so chose. Like Mrs Khan, I more than once made the mistake of shooing children to the carpet, only to be told that they could return to their activity; hence I understood the puzzlement which caused some children to hover anxiously between their tables and the assembled class group. Again, the strong frame underlying such moments was the text: Mrs Goode (or her proxy, Becky) *is* the regulative discourse.

Outings

The conduct of school outings reveals the All Saints' culture and pedagogy particularly clearly. The school's whole 'offer' to its children and families is founded in a concept of childhood, and of adult–child relations, which coincides with the cultural beliefs of some, but by no means all, parents. This concept not only affirms play, and associated ideas such as freedom, fun and discovery, as the natural characteristic of childhood experience, it also requires adults caring for children to assume children's interests as their own. In consequence, *all* the children, once they have been socialized into the school discourse, are able to participate fully, and enjoyably, in outings, while only a small minority of parents could meet the requirements for inclusion. The two traditional summer trips taken by the class – an outing to a forest park, and an end-of-year visit to Memorial Park, a large recreation area in the town – were eagerly anticipated by staff, for whom they offered a rare chance to practise their preferred pedagogy, without the restrictions of the classroom.

The same 'rules', for adults and children, applied on both occasions. The principal objective, indeed the requirement of children, is that they have fun, and play: the rule for the day, one might say, was 'you *must* have fun and play'. But there is a covert instructional discourse too. This includes learning to explore, fantasize and role-play (we run screaming from imaginary lions and tigers, jump out on each other from bushes, and wade fearlessly through 'swamps' and 'jungles'); learning about the natural world ('Which tree do you think is older? Who could have built that nest?'); and 'learning to be a child' (children like Rufia and Khiernssa who have never been on a swing or roundabout are coached in playground skills; timid children are encouraged to run, yell and tumble down hills).

Since a childlike perspective governs the social order, the first rule for accompanying adults is to model childlike behaviour: to observe frequent 'sweetie breaks', share crisps and biscuits, and provide ice creams; to play on playground equipment, to join in hide-and-seek, to chase and shout and squeal. But the discursive (instructional) order also requires adults to offer 'constant input, constant stimulation', in Mrs Goode's words. The only adults suited to this responsibility are those who have themselves been socialized into the pedagogic discourse. Adults who prefer *not* to fantasize and enthuse, question and instruct, recite and sing and chat, all the time they are with children, are excluded (or exclude themselves: they are not invited, and do not volunteer).

The staffing arrangements for Memorial Park were typical: the children were accompanied by Mrs Goode, Becky and a Section 11 teacher; four parents who volunteer in the classroom and are school employees; and Troy's father Bob, recently appointed school premises manager. Not only were no Bangladeshi parents involved in any outings, but even Mrs Khan was not invited to accompany the class to Memorial. In many ways the discourse of the school, and especially of Reception, excludes her too.

The discursive order: the rules of the instructional discourse

Mrs Goode is well aware that the *regulative* discourse of the classroom – in her terms, its informality – has implications for the children's *instructional* experience and outcomes. She acknowledges that some of her pupils' progress may appear slow in Reception, but feels she has good experiential evidence that her methods pay off in the longer term. In a more formal classroom, she argues, 'They wouldn't have learned how to learn for themselves, which is the main thing you've got to teach children . . . so they wouldn't have such a rich experience – and they learn to read, on the whole, by Year 2, *despite* what we do to them!'

In Bernstein's terms, Mrs Goode employs a weak-framed instructional discourse consistent with the competence model of pedagogic practice. Under her instructional rules, the sequencing and pacing of children's learning is slowed or slackened to suit the needs of individual children

– or of an assumed 'type' of child. For, like Mrs Mason, she works with an impression of the overall characteristics of the school's intake: she believes that children's communication skills are a guide to their potential, but comments that 'I think generally the communication skills of children in the school are low . . . children's listening skills are very very poor.'

Inevitably, the instructional discourse of the classroom, which is carried in the regulative discourse, displays similar tensions between freedom and compulsion, exploration and regulation. The *regulative* ideal is a weakly framed order of purposeful play with personalized support from adults, though in actuality the strength of the frame rapidly increases over the year. Even this increase in frame strength is viewed as, ideally, child-driven: in Mrs Goode's view, 'It's a natural thing, the children are almost asking for it, you know when they're ready for it: they require more structure to their day.' In this 'ideal' liberal–progressive scenario, the pedagogic discourse derives from the children themselves, rather than being imposed upon them. Thus the increasing formality of the Reception class organization over the year comes in response to children's readiness: a kind of liberal 'demand learning' like the 'demand feeding' of infancy, which is not however understood as a demand for *teaching*.

Mrs Goode is too much of a realist to believe that this 'natural' process can unfold for all children, because of the tension between this model and the assessment-driven model which lies ahead:

> Sometimes by the third term you do have to insist on it, because they do have to move into Year 1 . . . again, because of the constraints of the National Curriculum, and because of the constraints of schooling, you have to, by the end of the Reception year, in terms of preparing them for Key Stage 1, have made it clear that there are certain things that they have to do, in order that they learn and in order that they can acquire skills – and again, in an ideal world that wouldn't happen until Year 1 . . .

In other words, the competence model preferred by the school is in conflict with the performance model imposed by government. For most of the year, however, the *instructional* purpose of the provision (teaching and learning) remains weakly framed, invisible to the children and to most of their parents. In Mrs Goode's discourse, children learn that 'we're going to be really busy today'; 'we've got lots of jobs to do', or 'lots to choose from'. But the 'jobs' may be dressing up or painting: children are not told that they have work to do, or learning goals to achieve. Only in June or July do they hear that they are 'learners', who have worked hard in Reception and will do their 'best work', and learn even more, in their next class.

Curriculum provision for learning, which is always grounded in play activities, is planned in great detail. Weekly plans monitored over the Spring term always included:

unstructured play [free choice of e.g. sand, water, role play, construction, small worlds];

structured play [building a castle, setting up a 'birthday party', completing repeat patterns];

adult-directed group tasks [cooking, printing, experimenting, testing, observing, building];

adult-directed group discussion [sharing non-fiction books, pictures, artefacts];

adult group teaching [phonics or maths input];

adult individual teaching [instruction on letter formation, number recognition, book-sharing];

adult-directed or self-directed worksheets [handwriting, topic, maths, phonics etc.].

The constant checking of class lists is intended to ensure that all children have equal access to the full range of learning experiences, even if they cannot all derive the same benefit from them. Groups of children, *ad hoc* and pre-planned, are rotated through activities supervised by teachers, assistants and parent volunteers to maximize their exposure to the curriculum. The rationale for the discursive order is that *all* children must experience *everything* the curriculum offers: not only activities in the Core Skills, or in the areas of the Desirable Learning Outcomes, but the emotion of fantasy role-play, and the excitement of outings. When the classroom role-play area is periodically transformed (whether to a supermarket, a clinic or a haunted house), participation is obligatory. Mrs Goode explains:

> There are certain directed activities that we do expect all the children to work with . . . so after half-term we'll have a 'jungle', and we do expect all of them to come – just to have a look, they don't have to do anything – just make a noise if they want to, or give the animals a cuddle! – just to have a go!

The very weakly classified content of the curriculum, in other words (playing, growling, cuddling furry animals), is strongly framed: having fun is compulsory (even if the compulsion is expressed as an 'expectation'), and is part of the 'text' on which children are evaluated.

While all children are 'expected' to experience all activities, deliberate but invisible differentiation is progressively built into the instructional discourse associated with the core skills of literacy and numeracy. By January the class is ability-grouped for maths and writing activities, and by Easter for phonics. In the Summer term the class is visibly split, once a week, for the whole afternoon: the high achievers, in the quiet room, have a strongly framed literacy session, while the remainder of the class continue to 'choose', or sing nursery rhymes, with me and Becky. As Becky explains, 'All the top group work together so you can stretch them', but it is not clear whether the children who remain behind are also 'working'.

Mrs Goode has a clear rationale for each grouping: 'If they had an understanding of numbers 1–10'; 'Because they were assessed as being confident with their pencil skills', and so on; but, she points out, 'The differentiation, in terms of communication, is far more, because you differentiate by how you respond, and how you question, so that's individual.' This being so, the built-in disadvantage of the bilingual children, whose communication skills are scantily assessed in comparison with monolingual pupils, is unavoidable.

While the social expectations of the classroom were carefully explained to the children, what they were *not* told was that certain learning styles and behaviours were approved, while others were regarded as inappropriate. 'Making choices' and 'acting independently', which are important learning strategies for Mrs Goode, were not the sort of attributes prioritized by any of the children's parents, and some had certainly given their children clear indications to the contrary ('Sit down, study hard'; 'Just do what the teacher tells you'). Children with prior nursery or playgroup experience were again at an advantage, since their pre-school setting would have fostered autonomy, but some of those who had spent their early years in the family home were now entering a setting with radically different requirements. In the first few weeks of school, as we will see, some children's ability to 'make choices' was relatively circumscribed, while others experimented widely.

The instructional discourse in action

Literacy learning

The tensions between freedom and regulation, and between ideal and actuality, which permeate other aspects of the curriculum give a distinct shape to the teaching of reading. Initially children are observed for their interest in books, and motivation to read: ideally, they would all 'ask' to learn, or 'demand' to be taught. In this scenario, once their intrinsic and independent motivation is in place, they will choose to read alone or with friends, or request the support of school adults, thus apprenticing themselves to more experienced readers and acquiring the necessary skills through the cumulative effects of listening, sharing, observing, repeating, emulating and *enjoying* literacy events. In support of this process all children, once identified as 'interested', are given a book bag to take books home to share with family members, so that their opportunities for acquiring the skills are multiplied and reinforced. Meanwhile their reading progress is supported and extended by the wide range of language and literacy activities on offer in the classroom, as well as by the weekly individual reading input they receive from Mrs Goode, Becky, or Mrs Khan.

The terminology associated with the teaching of reading exemplifies this liberal–progressive view of the experience. Children are assessed on entry for their book-handling skills (finding the front of the book, turn-ing pages from front to back, scanning from left to right) and for their interest in discussing the pictures or predicting the story. There is no assessment of the ability to decode print, and if there were, all the children would fail, whereas some perform well on the existing criteria. Subsequent input from adults takes the form not of 'reading' but of 'book sharing': implicitly, no handover of knowledge is implied to occur (from reader to non-reader), since teacher and child are constructed as equal partners in this process. Book sharing is a relaxed, friendly session in which the participants sit on floor-cushions and join in selecting books from small arrays, choosing the pictures which make them laugh, predicting the story's outcome, and relating it to their own lives and experiences. All the children were seen to enjoy these sessions, and many come to sit alongside and listen in to each other's book-sharing times. Both Mrs Goode and Becky are skilful in eliciting enthusiastic par-ticipation from the children they are sharing with, and it is unusual for a child to try to avoid or postpone their turn when it comes.

In a weak-framed pedagogy, however, this apprenticeship into literacy may take a very long time, as Mrs Goode recognized. Some children are being introduced for the first time to practices which children in other families may have met in infancy, and may take some time to adjust to them: if these late starters are allowed to progress at their own 'natural' rate, the pacing of the pedagogy may slacken to a standstill. Other potential problems loom. The 'demand' from the child may not be met by the supply of adult hours for relaxed book sharing (an 'uneconomic' process). The demand, spoken or unspoken, from parents may not be met by the pacing offered by the school. The demands of the Year 1 curriculum may be frustrated by the stage of literacy children have reached at the end of Reception. Above all, the criterion of individual interest, motivation or 'readiness' may justify low levels of expectation, and input, into children who do not appear to meet it. The instructional discourse does not permit a strong-framed underlying text such as 'you *must* learn to read' (with its dependents, 'otherwise you won't do well at school / get a good job'). Only weak variants of the text are implied: 'You are sure to enjoy looking at books (reading is fun!)'; 'You may choose to share books'; 'We will do some reading when you have shown you want to', and so on.

The class reading records disclose some of the problems created by the pedagogy. Because of the large class, Mrs Goode and Becky each alloc-ated a day a week to individual book sharing, and Mrs Khan spent some additional time with the bilingual children. Nevertheless, weekly book-sharing sessions for all the children required more hours than were available. In consequence, priority was given to children whose book bags had been returned to school, or whose parents asked 'when they were going to be changing their books'. In practice, this meant that the more advantaged children (those whose parents were assisting with reading at home, monitoring their child's progress, and matching the school's input) had better access to school support, and to the best expertise. For when Charlotte proved demanding and insistent on Troy's behalf, Becky opted out of her turns to read with him, and Mrs Goode took sole charge of his input; while those children whose book bag never appeared in school tended to 'read' only occasionally, with Mrs Khan or with me.

Individual book sharing was only one aspect of the Reception provision for language and literacy learning. When I audited the language and literacy provision of the classroom, three levels of activity were evident:

(i)   adult input into language or literacy skills;
(ii) adult-led activities with a language / literacy element;
(iii) children's self-chosen activities with an emphasis on language or literacy.

The audit for a typical day in February showed the following range of activities:

(i)   Mrs Goode: sharing books with one or two children at a time all day; discuss the books they have brought back from home, reread the one they like best, select new ones, read them together: 15 children each had 15–20 minutes session.
(ii) (a) Becky has 'science' groups to look at still and fizzy drinks, observing bubbles, listening to them in a beaker, tasting, mixing, describing, explaining: all children.
      (b) Parent volunteers help groups to make streamers of crêpe paper on sticks and 'test' them outdoors to see effects of wind; children asked individually to predict and describe: all children.
(iii) (a) ABC matching game (children observed discussing it);
      (b) 'shopping' board game (ditto);
      (c) home corner: lively role play;
      (d) tape-story;
      (e) computer (children discussing program in twos and threes);
      (f) drawing and writing table (discussion, collaboration, copying).

The activity ranked (i) is strongly classified, and has some strength of framing: all the children understand, by now, that they are expected, in their parents' terminology, to 'read with a teacher'. Those in (ii) are weakly classified (no one knows what they are learning) but quite strongly framed (everyone does as instructed once summoned to a group). Most of those in (iii) have weak classification *and* framing: children may come and go, and make what use of the activities they see fit.

On this particular day, observations confirmed that all the children were busily occupied, and all had a range of learning experiences. Some, however, received far more active input into their learning than others. Diaries and observations for individual children suggest that the level of input is strongly associated with each child's possession of social and cultural capital, and with their ability to recognize the rules of the pedagogic discourse.

Worksheets

The use of worksheets in Reception illustrates the tension expressed in the classroom's regulative and instructional discourses. An experienced practitioner such as Mrs Goode acknowledges that 'a worksheet cannot be something that actually teaches them'; nor does she rely on them to keep children occupied, since there are abundant opportunities in the classroom's play provision for this. Most worksheets exist simply to record a child's performance on a particular day, providing low-level evidence of quite low-level skills such as tracing or colouring.

Systematic observations of the children's involvement in classroom activities suggest also a particularly low level of interest and commitment while children are occupied with worksheets. Most children treat the completion of such sheets as a self-standing task unconnected to any learning activity with which it may be associated in a teacher's mind. Rather, the sequence of actions involved in 'doing a worksheet' appears to be one of the more mysterious aspects of learning to be a pupil. It typically includes:

1 sitting down when summoned;
2 taking a sheet from a tray;
3 going to your drawer to fetch a name card;
4 copying your name, and returning the card to its drawer;
5 observing other children's efforts at drawing and colouring;
6 choosing colouring pencils;
7 comparing and swapping pencils, rubbers, crayons;
8 doing a little mark making;
9 checking other children's progress;
10 checking for any visible adult response;
11 doing lots more colouring (often until the whole sheet is obliterated);
12 handing the sheet to an adult or depositing it in a tray.

Few of the research observations describe children as involved or interested in the task, except as a colouring activity. But not all children enjoy colouring (though only Kelly responds to the question, 'Is there anything at school you *don't* like?' with 'I don't like worksheets').

The regular use of worksheets suggests a partial, reluctant surrender to the modality of the performance model, with its emphasis on product, economy and accountability. The activity is at once strongly framed as a regulative discourse (children are required to sit at a table and complete the task when summoned) and weakly framed as an instructional discourse (children have little idea what knowledge or skills they are acquiring, or demonstrating). An observer might conclude that worksheets represent the worst of both worlds: they incur the disadvantages of the performance model without realizing any of its possible advantages for children's learning.

Summary: visible and invisible pedagogies in the classroom

In describing and analysing classroom practices, this chapter provides no evidence of the effects of the school culture, and the regulative and instructional discourse of the Reception class, on individual pupils. But it does suggest that the apparently weak classification and framing of the school's curriculum and pedagogy (and, implicitly, its child-centred and family-friendly practices) conceal a strongly framed set of rules which will not be equally easy for all children to access. In particular, these rules emphasize children's learning, rather than teachers' duty to instruct. They also conceal, as the next chapter illustrates, practices which may favour some children over others from their early weeks in school, in ways which may have lasting effects on their learning.

As Bernstein argues, the effect of power is to specialize knowledge to different groups; even in a child-centred classroom, that process may begin before children are 5 years old. His own work has not attempted to describe the detailed processes and practices which 'sort' individual children, within and across their ethnic, gender and social class groups, according to the social and cultural capital they bring to school, and the habitus which enables them to invest it. In the next chapter we see the effects of these practices on each of the children as they start to learn the rules for 'being a pupil'.

5

LEARNING TO BE
A PUPIL

Becoming a pupil

Starting school, as Woods and colleagues affirm, is 'one of the great status passages of life, having profound repercussions for identity' (1999: 117). In this chapter we observe how this momentous event is experienced by the 16 children, as they start their school careers in Mrs Goode's class. We examine in particular the process of 'becoming a pupil', a task achieved with more or less success by all of them.

Earlier ethnographic studies (Jackson 1979; Pollard with Filer 1996) have highlighted important aspects of the transition from child to pupil. For children, the immediate experience includes separation from their parents and an initiation into classroom rituals (Woods *et al.* 1999), and into the formal requirements of classroom discourse (Willes 1983). At the same time, they are assessed by teachers against their own 'ideal type' pupil (Waterhouse 1991; Wright 1993) and possibly stereotyped in accordance with aspects of their background (Rist 1970; Ogilvy *et al.* 1990). Additional, if unintentional, requirements may be made of ethnic minority children: that they adopt a pupil role 'based on an anglicized model which fails to take their own background cultures fully into account' (Woods *et al.* 1999: 11), a model 'drawn primarily from the lifestyle and culture of the teacher concerned' (Wright 1993: 28). But all small children have prior notions of what it is to be a pupil: as Pollard and Filer argue, children 'cannot avoid the more pervasive influence of conceptions of the pupil role which are embedded in the wider culture' (1999: 22). Peers and parents, TV and comics carry information about the pupil–teacher relationship which contributes to children's expectations of the role they are undertaking.

Children's pre-school learning, as we have seen, includes the acquisition of both 'local knowledge' and school knowledge, and the experience of both implicit and explicit teaching. In the Reception classroom, children again encounter two kinds of knowledge, and two modes of learning. To be a successful pupil, they have to master both aspects: the regulative discourse which governs classroom behaviour, and the instructional discourse which allows them to access the curriculum. But whereas children's *primary* socialization, and the development of their primary habitus, occurs through a gradual apprenticeship into family behaviours and beliefs, their *secondary* socialization (into membership of a class) may be accomplished quite rapidly, through direct instruction. On the other hand, some children's early cognitive learning may have been accomplished through *explicit* teaching; in the Reception classroom such learning is often *implicitly* acquired. Part of a child's secondary socialization, therefore, consists very importantly in learning which *ways of learning* are used and approved in school. Some children's 'system of dispositions' (Bourdieu 1990a: 53), or habitus, has to be radically transformed in the process of becoming a pupil. This double process of learning is the focus of this chapter.

The development of the primary and secondary habitus, as described by Bourdieu, can be viewed diagrammatically:

	FAMILY			SCHOOL		
Child →	Primary socialization: *Learning to be a child* [0–4]	→	Primary habitus	→	Secondary socialization: *Learning to be a pupil* [4+]	→	Secondary habitus

A similar transformation is described by Bernstein, who argues that the process of adaptation involves children in acquiring the **recognition and realization rules** of the school's pedagogic discourse, which may differ substantially from the pedagogic discourse of their home (Bernstein 1996: 32). These rules, which Bernstein compares to learning to *understand*, and then learning to *speak*, a new foreign language, enable the child first to detect, passively, what is going on in the classroom, and then actively to produce the appropriate behaviour. We will see that these rules are an essential aspect of the social and cultural capital of a pupil.

The sections which follow examine successive phases in the process of becoming a pupil: first, the children's earliest days the classroom; next, the 'settling-in' period in which entry assessments are made; and lastly, the involvement in learning which children display as the school year proceeds. The children's own views about school and learning offer an additional perspective on their experience. But first, Khiernssa's story.

Case study: Khiernssa starts school

Day 1: Khiernssa brought in by mum who left her with Rufia and her dad and backed away. Hardly shy at all: stared mystified at Rufia who was clinging to her dad and refusing to stay. Came in to the play house for energetic games of cooking, parties, ironing etc.; found the phone and repeatedly tried to phone home and talk to her mum – eventually realized it was not connected, and held pretend conversations with her instead. When I picked up the other phone and talked to her she grinned and responded, as far as her English allowed.

Day 2: Did paintings and drawings, played in the play house and became high spirited and quite talkative; enjoyed outdoor play, experimented with balls, bikes and barrows: agile and confident, able to give other children rides in carts.

[Field notes]

Khiernssa had accompanied her older brother and sister, Salek and Layla, to school, and was known by name to Mrs Goode and Becky. Nevertheless, her immediate adaptation to the classroom from her wholly different home environment appeared miraculous. From her first day she was fully absorbed in her own chosen activities, and was active in enlisting the support of the English-speaking adults. By Day 3 she and Rufia were inseparable, and Rufia had begun to translate for her, and to prompt her in her efforts to speak English (*Day 4: Rufia has noticed that I respond faster when addressed by my name, and uses it all the time*). On Day 5, both were drawing and writing letter-like shapes on their pictures, and two days later Khiernssa was insisting that I write her whole name on drawings for her to copy ('Khiernssa Begum, B – eg –um').

When the Baseline assessment of children began, Khiernssa's early preparation seemed to show. My notes for her maths assessment include the following:

Given set of animal shapes, sorted by shape, named shapes and colours (made noises for all the animals) and mixed them up and did it all again [15 Sept.].

Matched and counted with ease, recognized all numerals without hesitation (even when they were upside down) [16 Sept.].

She is equally self-possessed in her reading assessment, recorded by Mrs Khan:

Khiernssa can hold the book correctly. She was sitting with Rufia and Rufia was holding the book upside down but Khiernssa told her, 'You are not holding the book properly.' She can follow the print from left to right and repeat the line very well.

By half-term, Khiernssa was already behaving like a motivated and successful pupil, well adapted to the learning culture of her new setting.

Several factors appeared to contribute to this success: her friendship with Rufia, her exact age-mate; the provision of a home corner where Khiernssa could replicate her favourite domestic activities; her father's careful training in English letters, numbers and sounds; and the home habitus of active and purposeful planning.

But by now certain limitations to Khiernssa's adaptation were also evident: she refused to play with sand or water (she reported that her mother said 'No, you get cold, you get cough'); she rejected all forms of role-play except the domestic (flatly refusing to play in the 'shoe shop'); and she avoided construction toys ('No: they boys'), the computer, and all the structured table-top activities intended for shape and space matching, memory, visual discrimination and so on. Despite her bright start to school, she did not conform entirely to the 'ideal-type' pupil, nor was she accessing the whole curriculum. In exercising her own agency, she was in these terms restricting her own learning.

First days

Patterns of adaptation

All the children had attended two induction sessions the previous June, and consequently had some idea of the scene that would greet them on arrival in September, but some of them had had a much more extensive preview of their new classroom. This was largely due to the presence of older siblings in the school. All the children except Amadur and Mohammed, Jelika and Troy, had accompanied brothers and sisters to school in previous years. But of these four, the three Bangladeshi children were entering a wholly strange setting, without much adult support, while Troy was entering one which was both familiar and supportive: not only had his home and pre-school contained many of the same toys and activities, but his parents had used the induction days to engage the staff in long conversations, ask a lot of searching questions, and require them to read Troy's nursery records so that they 'knew his capabilities'.

The remaining children formed two distinct groups: those who were slightly known to the staff, and those who were well known. The latter group consisted of Cameron, Joshua, Katy and Kelly, all of whose mothers were on easy terms with the Reception staff, and had brought them to 'visit' on numerous occasions. Mrs Goode and Becky displayed a good knowledge of these families' lives, and could show a friendly interest in the children by their inquiries after their brothers and sisters. The less-favoured group included Jemma (whose mother, Becky told me, 'never came up to school'), twins Sonia and Jason, and the remaining Bangladeshi children, whose families were less well known to the staff.

The children, with their differing social as well as cultural capital, adopted different strategies for coping with their first days at school. Troy's entry was managed efficiently by his mother, who brought him in early every morning and interrogated Mrs Goode and Becky about his learning. The effect of Charlotte's intervention was to guarantee Troy some individual attention from his extremely busy teachers, with whom he quickly established a friendly relationship. As the first in the classroom each day, he would chat to them, tell them his news, and then take up a position at a drawing or writing activity, or a computer, with a view of the door, so as to observe other children and parents as they entered and exchanged greetings.

The four children already familiar with the Reception staff and setting adapted to school with relative ease. Both Cameron and Joshua were very young 4-year-olds, with August birthdays, and were given to silently observing the other children in their early sessions, though they responded readily to friendly overtures from adults. Though their mothers hovered anxiously while they settled in each day, both boys had handled this separation since they were little, and coped stoically enough. Joshua was particularly chatty with Becky, whom he 'adored', according to Maisie; and Cameron, after a few days of solemn silence, identified other rather solitary children (including Jemma and her cousin Jimmy) and took to standing near them for company. Katy had overcome an initial shyness by Day 3, while Kelly had immediately thrown herself into her new setting with energy and confidence. Her struggles and screams when Gaynor dropped her off turned to cheeky grins as soon as her mother was out of sight, and she eagerly sought the company of anyone, adult or child, who looked interesting, including the rowdiest boys.

The children who were less familiar with the school took longer to settle. Abu Bokkar and Abdul Rahman, although at first timid and tearful, soon began to seek out other Bangladeshi children, but made no approaches to school adults. Rufia was sensibly 'settled' by her father, and then formed her friendship with Khiernssa. Sonia and Jason clung to each other and their mother for support: Kath had to sit and play alongside them until they allowed her to leave each day, and they spoke only to each other apart from whispered responses to adults. Both Tuhura and Jemma, meanwhile, coped with transition by isolating themselves from the busy world of the classroom. Each was absorbed in her own play and initiated few contacts. Tuhura stayed for long periods at a single occupation (feeding a doll with a plastic teaspoon from a plastic cup; stirring an imaginary meal in a plastic saucepan), while Jemma flitted rapidly from sand to water, drawing to writing, pegboards to playpeople, alone but seemingly content. Neither Jemma nor Tuhura reacted to their mother's departure.

The most difficult adaptation was that of the three 'new' Bangladeshi children. Amadur and Mohammed, who were daily ushered through the door by an anxious-looking parent, adopted a strategy of total mutual involvement: they worked alongside each other, mostly with sand and water, in silence or incessant chat, apparently oblivious to the presence of others (when addressed they avoided eye contact). Jelika overcame her initial fear and distress with great stoicism, and took on the role of mothering Tuhura.

Each child quickly established a pattern of activities. Troy spent much of his time seated at a drawing table or computer, while Kelly demonstrated an enthusiasm for mathematical activities such as matching and memory games. Amadur and Mohammed spent most of each session at the sand and water trays, unless they were outdoors with balls and bikes. Sonia and Jason divided their time inside between drawing and colouring, and small-world or construction play such as train-tracks and Duplo. Cameron and Katy were most frequently observed in the home corner, as were (but at different times) Rufia and Khiernssa. Jemma and Tuhura both continued to play alone, solitary or parallel, in the home corner, but were also drawn to art and craft activities: Tuhura visibly enjoyed painting, drawing, printing, collage and clay during her first few days.

Most children's choices seemed haphazard: they mostly reflected their evolving friendships, and the impromptu suggestions of staff and parents, rather than developed preferences or prior experience. A few had pre-existing play partners: the twins were inseparable and conferred to choose their activities, and Amadur and Mohammed gravitated towards each other, and towards the sand tray, as if obeying some inner instruction. Jemma, however, only occasionally spoke to her cousin Jimmy, and appeared to proceed by picking the activity nearest to her; while Tuhura rarely acknowledged her cousin Abdul Rahman, but allowed herself to be 'adopted' by Jelika, who led her from task to task, put her apron on and put a paintbrush in her hand. The child who experienced the most noticeable difficulty in getting acquainted, and getting involved, was Abu Bokkar, who wandered the classrooms almost silently, apparently unable to infiltrate other children's activities or their relationships.

The difficulties experienced by some children were matched by the apparent discomfort of their mothers, many of whom seemed quite unclear about the rules and expectations of the school: the place of parents in the classroom; the 'invitations' to stay for the day; the availability of staff to discuss the children, or simply to chat; and the nature of the activities being offered to their children. However, mothers interviewed around this time were not especially anxious to know more about the school. Their immediate priority was their child's happiness, and they openly expressed their relief that the milestone of transition had been safely passed. Majida's view – 'if Rufia is happy then I am happy' – was echoed by most of the mothers, and even those with reservations about the school's methods were reluctant to complain (see the discussion in Chapter 6).

Explanations from Bronfenbrenner

The children's experience of transition was shaped by factors which would continue to influence their progress. An explanation for the variation in children's adaptation and development on starting school is offered by Bronfenbrenner's account of the enabling variables in developmental change (1979). Bronfenbrenner locates the school setting or *microsystem* (the new environment for the developing child) in the *mesosystem* (the network of settings inhabited by the child). His analysis identifies in particular the importance of supportive links between the different microsystems or settings the child experiences. A number of his hypotheses clearly apply to the move from home to school, one of the major ecological changes in the child's life. He argues, for instance, that 'The developmental potential of a setting in a mesosystem is enhanced if the person's initial transition into that setting is not made alone' (*Hypothesis 27*; 1979: 211). The optimal case might be one where the child is accompanied for some time in the classroom setting by her or his mother (as occurred for Cameron, Joshua, Troy, and the twins), although some children's transition may be supported by their teachers or peers. But the children's subsequent development, Bronfenbrenner suggests, requires another form of support: 'Upon entering a new setting, the person's development is enhanced to the extent that valid information, advice and experience relevant to one setting are made available, on a continuing basis, to the other' (*Hypothesis 42*; 1979: 217). In his example, 'A child's ability to learn to read in the primary grades may depend less on how he [*sic*] is taught than on the existence and nature of ties between the school and the home' (1979: 3).

Bronfenbrenner's account makes the dual advantage of some children in the study particularly plain, for the optimum developmental context he describes is one in which two-way communication takes place. Just as 'information, advice and experience' about the home setting needs to be made available to the school, so does information about the school need to be present in the home. Where this exchange occurs (meeting Bronfenbrenner's ideal case), the result is an accumulation of capital. The *social* capital enjoyed by children like Katy and Joshua (whose mothers have close ties with their teachers), and actively created by Charlotte for Troy, legitimates and multiplies the *cultural* capital created by the child's pre-school learning. So a predictable continuum of advantage exists, from those children whose development is enhanced by the possession of both social and cultural capital, *and* who experience a connection and continuity between their home and school learning (Troy, Joshua, Katy, Cameron), to those whose school experience is in every way discontinuous with their home (Amadur, Mohammed, Jelika).

The less predictable points on this continuum are occupied by children such as Jemma and Tuhura, and Abu Bokkar, whose families' conscientious teaching is not part of any 'information exchange' between home and school, and is therefore not so easily 'invested' in the field of education. The difficulty some children experienced in transposing their home knowledge to school became clear when their first assessments began.

Settling in

Early assessments

As the children settled in, the Reception staff began to observe them, and to make a range of assessments: of their curriculum knowledge, their social skills, and implicitly of their approximation to the school's idea of a successful pupil and learner.

Mrs Goode's assessment of children's potential relied less on their existing skills than on their *approach* to learning – in Bourdieu's terms, the 'system of dispositions' which characterizes the child's primary habitus – and the Reception setting was designed to allow children to display such qualities.

> You'd look for communication skills really, and that covers non-verbal, gestures, and verbal communication . . . you'd look for confidence in different situations; you look for the ability to tackle things; you look for independence . . . and of course you look for how they relate socially . . .

Most of the early observations recorded the children's social adaptation, along with their curriculum knowledge and skills. By half-term, Mrs Goode and Becky had jointly completed a statutory Baseline in Personal and Social Development for each child, and a Social Behaviour Inventory for research purposes. The Baseline included six scales – Initiative, Relationships, Cooperation, Involvement, Independence, Behaviour – each scored from 1 (negative) to 5 (positive). Like all such ratings they are subjective, and measure not simply the child's behaviour, but the adult's interpretation of it: so the children's ranking in relation to each other indicates the degree to which their behaviour approximated to Mrs Goode's expectations at this point in the term.

The ratings (Table 5.1) show an ethnic advantage (favouring Anglo children), and an advantage for boys: no Bangladeshi child scores 5 on any item, and only one girl has a 5 (Sonia, for 'involvement'). The expected influence of 'age in the year group' is not apparent: the highest ratings are awarded to two of the oldest (Troy, Abdul Rahman) *and* the two youngest boys in the group (Joshua, Cameron).

The extent of the Bangladeshi children's *group* disadvantage varies for different items: for 'Relationships' for instance ('shows respect for others'), all except Abdul Rahman are rated at or below the midpoint, while all the Anglo children are at or above this point. For 'Behaviour' ('well adjusted') their scores range from 2 to 4, while the Anglo children are rated from 3 to 5, despite Mrs Goode's supposition that bilingual children, on the whole, adopt approved school behaviours more quickly. Bangladeshi children's status as pupils is made particularly problematic by their low ratings on the two qualities prioritized by Mrs Goode's pedagogy – 'Initiative' and 'Independence'. Since the classroom pedagogy requires children to learn *by means of* such attributes, children who lack them are

Table 5.1 Baseline assessment: children's personal and social development

Child	Initiative	Relationships	Cooperation	Involvement	Independence	Behaviour
Abu Bokkar	2	2	2	1	4	2
Abdul Rahman	3	4	4	3	4	4
Amadur	1	2	3	3	3	4
Cameron	1	5	4	3	4	5
Jason	2	3	2	5	4	3
Jelika	1	2	1	2	3	2
Jemma	3	4	3	3	4	3
Joshua	5	4	3	5	5	4
Katy	1	3	3	3	2	3
Kelly	4	3	4	3	4	3
Khiernssa	3	3	3	4	3	3
Mohammed	1	3	2	2	3	2
Rufia	2	3	2	1	2	3
Sonia	1	4	2	5	4	3
Tuhura	2	2	2	3	3	3
Troy	4	4	4	4	5	4

Table 5.2 'Involvement': Baseline personal and social development ratings (from 1 ('flits') to 5 ('concentrates'))

1	2	3	4	5
Abu Bokkar	Jelika	Abdul Rahman	Khiernssa	
Rufia	Mohammed	Amadur		
		Tuhura		
		Cameron	Troy	Sonia
		Jemma		Joshua
		Katy		Jason
		Kelly		

poorly equipped to learn in this setting, and staff may form a poor view of their potential. But the low scores of the Bangladeshi children are not surprising, since they have been explicitly instructed by their parents to behave in other ways – to sit still, say nothing, and listen to the teacher. Children's primary habitus cannot be transformed all at once.

Equally disadvantaging, potentially, are some children's low ratings for 'Involvement', illustrated in Table 5.2. As the next section describes, 'Involvement' in activities and in social interactions was to emerge as the most significant indicator of the children's learning as the year went on. By this measure, the Bangladeshi *group* seem disadvantaged from the start, although the *individuals* who are likely to succeed within this pedagogy are starting to emerge. Ratings on this scale indicate not only that certain children are less likely to benefit from the Reception pedagogy, but that Mrs Goode and Becky have already identified their disadvantage.

Overall, the staff's unwillingness to label children at this early stage can be judged from the difficulty they found in completing the Social Behaviour Inventory I had supplied. After some discussion, they declined to complete the scales for Abu Bokkar, Amadur, Tuhura, Jelika and Mohammed, on the grounds that they felt unable to interpret the children's behaviour, or judge how much they understood. This was an honest response. Nevertheless, it implied that some children were already seen as hard to 'know', as pupils.

Baseline skills

1 The Early Years Profile

The children's first half term in school was also the period in which their school knowledge, or cultural capital, was assessed. As a participant observer, I was both carrying out the assessments, and assessing the process itself. Meanwhile the children themselves were developing at a rate too rapid for measurement, making the validity of Baseline assessment even more dubious than I had anticipated. If a child (like Abdul Rahman) displayed no knowledge of colour names in Week 2, but a good knowledge by Week 4, which was the score to be, given the seven-week baseline period? Similarly, it would be surprising if some of the children who appeared unable to count to 3, or to classify objects as relatively 'big' or 'little', in Week 1, had not either acquired these skills, or acquired the ability to 'demonstrate' them, by Week 7.

The school had developed its own Early Years Profile, composed of the behaviours, knowledge and skills which constituted social and cultural capital in the classroom. Some of its content, though 'developmentally appropriate' within the Early Years tradition, was very unevenly distributed among the children, and influenced by their cultural background. While all these items would soon be essential if children were to make speedy and satisfactory progress through the school curriculum, some children's poor showing was the result of specific early learning experiences. The profile included these items:

- *Book skills; Knowledge of traditional stories*
  (School methods of 'sharing books', creating stories from illustrations, learning from tape-stories etc. were not practised by Bangladeshi parents or by Anglo parents outside the mainstream group; no non-English stories were included in the classroom planning).
- *Knowledge of nursery rhymes; Ability to hear rhyme*
  (Most Anglo children – not Jemma – had learned rhymes at playgroup or nursery; most Anglo mothers, aware of their value as 'school knowledge', had provided audio or videotapes of rhymes and songs; only

one Bangladeshi child – Abdul Rahman – was taught the family's traditional rhymes by his mother).

- *Name writing*
  (Prioritized by all the Anglo families, if not always successfully taught; older siblings made input in some instances – Rufia, Jemma; others had no input).

- *ABC letters*
  (Learned through recognition at nursery/playgroup, and through videotapes and books, by many Anglo children; taught by rote recitation, if at all, by Bangladeshi parents).

- *Colours*
  (A valued skill in the classroom, and recognized as such by Anglo parents, who had all instructed their children with reasonable success; not valued by Bangladeshi families, who saw no need to teach colour names. The maximum number of colours known in Bengali was three (white, black, red), but Tuhura had been taught all English colour names by her mother, and astonished the staff by shouting 'navy blue! light green!' as she mixed the paints).

- *Shapes*
  (Taught by most Anglo parents: all Anglo children except Jemma could name one or more; Cameron, Kelly and Tyrone named three; only Jelika and Rufia of the Bangladeshi group could name one).

- *Jigsaw skills*
  (Reflected children's pre-school experience: Joshua and Troy had learned to do 35-piece puzzles at home; other Anglo children had 'done that one at my playgroup', and could mostly work independently; Bangladeshi children, as their records noted, 'lacked experience'; Tuhura refused to attempt them).

- *Communication skills*
  (Assessments of speaking and listening reflected children's confidence and social capital, as well as their pre-school experience and English competence).

Within the classroom, additional *implicit* markers of social and cultural capital were identifiable. These included knowing your age and date of birth (a skill taught to Anglo children, but such a low priority among the Bangladeshi families that many mothers were unsure of their own and their husbands' ages and birthdays); and knowing the names and ages of siblings (while Anglo children frequently volunteered such information about their families, these Bangladeshi families' practices meant that names, nicknames, ages and relationships were blurred or seen as unimportant).

Some children in the group had evidently acquired such capital 'naturally', while others had not. School assessments, however, were loaded with aspects of the children's social and cultural capital, and the staff's evaluations of children implicitly reflected on their families. Where children were unable to respond, for instance, to inquiries on such culturally valued topics as colours, birthdays and family names, their families could be seen as deficient in their practices. But since this type of knowledge is thought to occur 'naturally' in families, it was unlikely that staff could either indicate its importance to parents, or understand why it would *not* be natural in some families and communities.

2 Baseline assessment of Core Skills

The Core Skills baseline covered the statutory minimum areas of Speaking and Listening (in English), Reading, Writing and Maths. Because of the size of the class, the assessments were shared between Mrs Goode and Becky, Mrs Khan, the Section 11 teacher and myself. Mrs Goode selected the method of each assessment with a view to intruding as little as possible into children's freely chosen play. Care was taken too not to mark children down on entry in order to increase the value-added scores when they were assessed again in Year 2: it was agreed that we must 'give children a chance to show what they are capable of'.

In spite of this, a statistical analysis of the school's outcomes in relation to other town and county scores shows All Saints' children achieving at quite a low level. In this class, 34 per cent of the Reception intake were rated zero for Speaking and Listening (compared to 9 per cent county-wide), 12 per cent for Reading (10 per cent overall), and 20 per cent for Writing (11 per cent overall). In the school as in the county, however, the *majority* of children achieved Stage 1 in all four assessed areas. The table of aggregated scores for Core Skills (the sum of all descriptors achieved, from a possible total of 41) is shown in Table 5.3.

Table 5.3 Baseline assessment of core skills, and age of child when assessed

Child	Age	Score (from 41 items)
Abu Bokkar	4.4	8
Abdul Rahman	4.11	11
Amadur	4.10	3
Cameron	4.2	8
Jason	5.1	14
Jelika	4.11	11
Jemma	4.5	11
Joshua	4.2	18
Katy	4.4	10
Kelly	4.8	19
Khiernssa	4.3	10
Mohammed	4.8	4
Rufia	4.3	9
Sonia	5.1	13
Tuhura	4.3	9
Troy	4.11	26

Table 5.4 Baseline assessment: speaking and listening (from a possible 11 items)

Items achieved	Children scoring at this level
11	–
10	Troy
9	–
8	Kelly
7	–
6	–
5	Joshua, Jason
4	Jemma, Katy
3	Cameron, Sonia, Abdul Rahman, Jelika, Khiernssa, Rufia
2	Abu Bokkar, Tuhura
1	Amadur, Mohammed

One aspect of the assessment which immediately disadvantages the Bangladeshi children is the *English* Speaking and Listening requirement, in which the highest score for Bangladeshi children (3) matches the lowest score for Anglo children (shown in Table 5.4).

Overall, most children's scores demonstrate the expected developmental effects of 'age in the year group' as well as factors in their early experience. Although Joshua scores higher than his age would predict, Katy (who is experienced in the ways of school, but 'young' in the year group) achieves lower scores for Reading and Maths than inexperienced Jelika and Abdul Rahman (who are older). Cameron's results resemble those of the younger Bangladeshi children. Only Troy, Kelly and Joshua display to the full the advantages of their pre-school preparation; Amadur and Mohammed, correspondingly, display the disadvantages (in the official 'field of education') of theirs.

3 Standardized assessments

In the same period, I assessed the 16 children on three subscales of a widely standardized cognitive assessment, the British Ability Scales (Elliot 1996): one measure of spatial awareness (Block building), one of logical and conceptual skills (Picture Similarities) and one combining both areas (Pattern Construction). Children's outcomes on these measures overturned the hierarchy of achievement produced by the school's measures. Amadur (one of the older children, but with the lowest Baseline) achieved the highest score for 'Block building', and above his chronological age for 'Picture Similarities'. His cousin Mohammed, with a Baseline almost as low, achieved average scores on all three scales. Although *group* medians for the three subscales favour the Anglo children, this may be due to the Bangladeshi children's unfamiliarity with the test items, particularly the very traditional, 'English' pictures (which included a blackboard, a ruler and a map of the world).

Results like these confirmed my suspicion that the statutory Baseline was providing a very inadequate picture of some children's achievements and abilities. But it is hard for teachers, faced with children's low scores, to avoid holding low expectations of them, which in turn may influence the curriculum offered to them.

4 Predicting literacy: phonological awareness

Finally in this period I administered a simple phoneme-segmentation test to the children. Researchers in this field (Bryant *et al.* 1989; Byrne and Fielding-Barnsley 1995) argue that children's early phonological skills are the most reliable predictor of their subsequent success in learning to read, and I anticipated that this assessment would offer further evidence of the children's home and pre-school learning, and the extent to which this 'paid off' in Reception. As Coles argues,

> phonological awareness is a marker of social and literacy experiences that promote a whole array of written language abilities – of which phonological awareness is but one – and availability of these experiences to children is strongly determined by political-economic inequities in class, race and gender.
>
> (1998: 7)

The children's scores, on a test devised for use with culturally and linguistically diverse groups (Stuart 1995), are shown in Table 5.5.

Table 5.5 Phonological awareness scores

Score (from 24)	Child [age when tested]
23	Khiernssa [4.3]
–	
18	Troy [4.11]
17	Kelly [4.8], Abdul Rahman [4.11]
–	
8	Joshua [4.2]
7	Jason [5.1]
–	
4	Jelika [4.10]
3	Tuhura [4.3]
2	Katy [4.4]
1	Sonia [5.1]
0	Cameron [4.2], Jemma [4.5], Abu Bokkar [4.6], Amadur [4.10], Mohammed [4.8], Rufia [4.3]

The children's home preparation, as well as their age, is reflected in these scores. Khiernssa's outstanding achievement is the product of her family's conscientious work on three alphabets, but other children's ranking is closer to their age ranking – the six children who, even after generous teaching examples and group games, were unable to isolate any sounds, are all summer-born except for Amadur and Mohammed. The scores bear little relation to those of the Baseline in Reading.

Interpreting the assessments

The powerful hierarchy of achievement displayed by all these assessments is in place as the children start school; or more accurately, is created *in the process of* the children becoming pupils. Anomalous outcomes such as Khiernssa's phoneme segmentation, and Amadur's block-building skills, are mere blips in a prevailing classroom profile which by and large favours the 'older', the more socially endowed, the nursery graduates and the Anglo children; and disfavours the younger, the low-status, the non-nursery and the Bangladeshi children.

It is important to remember that the form of the school assessments, like the school pedagogy as a whole, has the potential to create, or exaggerate, differences between children. Children's experience of the assessment process, like all their school experience, is influenced by both 'home' and 'school' factors. For many, their cultural or subcultural backgrounds prescribe different kinds of playing (James 1998) and different kinds of mathematical knowledge (Emblen 1988) from those employed in school assessment tasks. But additionally, children's performance reflects the explicitness – here the lack of explicitness – of the tasks, and the intentions of the assessors. 'Child-friendly' measures are only fair to children if they offer them modes of behaviour, and styles of questioning (Heath 1986), which bear some resemblance to their early experience.

The child-friendly assessment modes that were adopted at All Saints', such as inviting children to sort farm animals into fields, are quite *un*friendly to those children who have never visited an English farm, played with farm animals or encountered small-world toys of any description. Jemma's decision to assemble in one field a cat, a farmer, a chicken and some sheep offers one example:

> *Is that how you want them to go? Great. Why did you choose those ones for that field?*
> Because they friends.

Though I awarded Jemma the descriptor, 'sorts objects using one criterion' on the basis of her conscious and reasonable choice, her maths record card describes her (and Amadur and Mohammed) as 'unable to sort'. It would be surprising if any of these children were unable to sort objects in a meaningful context.

Getting involved in learning

Measuring involvement

In the second half of the term I started to monitor the ways the children were experiencing the curriculum, and accessing school knowledge. In addition to informal field notes, scribbled while working with the children, I made systematic pre-coded observations of each of them, over a four-week period. Both the 'narrative' from these structured observations and the informal field notes record not just the frequency of children's activities, but the level of interest and involvement with which they undertook them. Together they build a picture of each child's learning experiences.

All the observation data were analysed for evidence of children's choice of curriculum activities, their use of time and space, the nature of their social interactions, and the level of their involvement. The analysis took account of earlier research which suggests the most favourable contexts for children's learning in a play environment (Sylva *et al.* 1980; Hutt *et al.* 1989; Pascal and Bertram 1997), and the best ways for adults to support such learning (Wood and Attfield 1996; Anning and Edwards 1999). Evidence from these studies indicates that the All Saints' children, aged from 4.3 to 5.2 at the time of these observations, could be expected to learn both through 'solitary' explorations and experiences, and through socially interactive tasks, so long as they were actively involved in and committed to what they were doing. The interpretation, therefore, focused on

- the level of children's involvement in activities;
- the relation of involvement to the duration of activities;
- the effects on involvement of children's social interactions;
- the factors influencing different levels of social interaction.

Overall, only four of the children show consistently high levels of involvement in their activities: Jason, Joshua, Kelly and Khiernssa are almost always described in the observation narratives as 'absorbed', 'thoughtful', 'eager', 'enthusiastic', 'concentrating', 'animated'. Though all four appear purposeful, their style of commitment varies from the introspective (Jason) to the extrovert (Kelly). All but one of the remaining children display a range of responses: each is sometimes recorded as 'vague', 'undecided' or 'uninvolved', but at other times 'excited', 'eager', 'vigorous'. Only Abu Bokkar (described below) showed a consistent lack of commitment to any activities during this period.

Children's engagement with their tasks was sometimes indicated by the length of time they persisted with them: some children (including Khiernssa and Troy) habitually spent 15 or more 30 second observation intervals in one activity, while others (such as Tuhura and Abu Bokkar) rarely achieved more than three or four minutes at an activity unless being supervised by an adult. But long duration does not always imply high involvement.

Sonia, for instance, sometimes spends 15 observation intervals apparently occupied with a table-top structured task; but the narrative describes her as watching children in other parts of the room, examining her new socks and shoes, or playing at poking her tongue out with Jason. Troy similarly obtains high frequencies for categories such as 'drawing' or 'computers', but the narrative shows that he is actually watching other children organize their games (and waiting for an opportunity to join in), while absently colouring or moving a mouse about a mouse-mat.

Children also benefit in different degrees from different social contexts. Some children seem most deeply committed to their chosen activity while coded as 'solitary' or engaged in parallel play. For Abdul Rahman and Tuhura, the arrival of other children sometimes results in a loss of focus which makes them decide to abandon their play; these children's dispositions may have been influenced by their relatively solitary experience at home. For Troy, however, a solitary session often seems like a suspended state, a time of waiting for the action and interest to begin: he appears to need the stimulus of social interactions to maximize his engagement.

The aspect of children's classroom experience which varies most of all is the level of adult interaction they enjoy, and here the variation suggested by the informal observations and field notes is confirmed by the systematic records. At one extreme are the frequencies of the Bangladeshi boys: out of 90 observation intervals, Mohammed has one recorded adult interaction; Amadur, two; Abdul Rahman, four; Abu Bokkar, six. At the other extreme are those of three children who can already be seen as pupils who are learning the pedagogic discourse of the classroom: Joshua (27 interactions), Khiernssa (26) and Troy (22).

Not all interactions have an impact on 'learning'. The text for Mohammed's single adult encounter in 90 observation intervals reads, 'Mrs G: "Good boy! You may put your coat on".' Several other children experienced only 'management', or non-individualized, verbal exchanges with adults. But children who have acquired the recognition and realization rules of the pedagogic discourse know how to take the initiative, to enjoy high-quality as well as high-quantity interactions, and to turn these opportunities into learning gains. Some of their observation narratives show this process in action.

Troy, who has come to school with considerable skills in relating to adults, is able to gain the maximum benefit from the following group discussion (with a part-time assistant, Cathy) in which the other children remain silent.

1 *Troy asks Cathy why she has been absent; she responds; he loses interest.*
2 *Listens to Cathy's explanation (using picture book) of where milk comes from.*
3 *Listening; rocking chair; looking at cover of book.*
4 *Responds to questions about book, turns pages, examines pictures.*

5 *Answers questions about milk and bones; turns pages again; shuts book.*
6 *Turns all pages from front to back again.*
7 *Stands, talks eagerly and vigorously to Cathy (other three children passive).*
8 *Puts hand up eagerly to answer question although sitting next to Cathy.*
9 *Stands up again while talking, very involved.*
10 *Looking, listening, pointing; hand up again; very keen.*
11 *Examines library date-flap in front of book, asks Cathy about it, she explains.*
12 *Cathy instructing them in task (draw then write in book).*
13 *Troy sits and looks at clean page expectantly; starts to draw.*
14 *Talks to Cathy about his drawing.*
15 *Waves arms, talks, pencil in hand, reaches for book to refer to picture.*

[Systematic observation records]

Khiernssa, who is used to explicit discussions of her learning with her parents, is the only Bangladeshi pupil to 'demand' adult input into her learning. In one of her observations she persistently enlists Becky's help with her writing:

Decides to go and do handwriting with Becky: offers to show her how good she is at Ks and then at Hs . . . Listens to Becky's instructions . . . Asks questions, 'Do this one now?' and follows Becky's suggestions, oblivious to other children around.

[Field notes]

On another occasion, she demonstrates her ability to profit from adult interaction during a dialogue with Donna, a visiting 'work experience student' who actually has learning difficulties herself. Finding Donna unable to answer her questions, or help her with her activity (making leaf-rubbings), Khiernssa works it out for herself and then reverses the roles and inducts Donna into the task:

9 *Khiernssa prompts Donna: asks her to look under paper; gets new leaf and crayon.*
10 *K working on her own now, self-motivated; Donna passive.*
11 *K takes initiative: 'Shall I do another one?'; examines leaves and crayons.*
12 *Gets busy, crayoning hard, very absorbed.*
13 *Picks up leaves and talks to Donna about them; helps Donna to join in activity.*
14 *K crayoning again; explains to Donna what she is doing.*

[Systematic observation records]

Joshua is skilled in the rules which govern the pedagogic discourse. He is able to approach any adult in the classroom and initiate a conversation, enjoying a wide range of relationships and support, and receiving positive individual feedback. While being observed, he engages Becky in conversation about the water-tray; chats to a parent-helper about a computer program; shares a book with Mrs Goode; makes social chat with the Section 11 teacher as she passes; and makes overtures to Mrs Goode over construction toys, and while she is helping Jason with the computer.

There is no doubt that these three children's primary habitus, and their social capital in the classroom, give them learning opportunities which are unavailable, for example, to Mohammed, who never approaches the school adults. Overall, observations of the Bangladeshi children show they are less frequently involved in the activities and social relationships which are favourable to learning than the Anglo group, for all its variability. While being observed, they are coded as 'in transit or unoccupied' for a mean of 11.5 intervals, compared with the Anglo group mean of 4.6 intervals. In the case of Abu Bokkar, this code frequently means 'passing the time' in activities which are unenjoyable, as well as unproductive.

Some children (like Kelly and Rufia) are able to get involved in purposeful play and learning through high levels of interaction with their peers; others (like Jason and Abdul Rahman) through solitary investigations; but those with good access to adults seem multiply advantaged. The 'demand teaching' model which underlies the classroom pedagogy, combined this year with a large class size, does not offer all the children the same level of adult support, or the same access to knowledge and skills. Children who have acquired social and cultural capital, and the recognition and realization rules of the discourse, have access to regular, productive interactions with skilled adults. Children who lack these advantages are more frequently left to make their own way through the range of experiences on offer, and make what sense of them they can. What some of them seem to be learning, in the process, is that it doesn't matter if the activity doesn't make sense: all that is required of a pupil is a token encounter with the task (water-play, role-play or worksheet), and a tick on an adult's list to confirm it.

Looking back: the children's perspective

Further evidence of the children's possession of the recognition and realization rules of the classroom – what they were at school for, and how they should conduct themselves – was gathered from brief interviews conducted with them in December and April.

Children's responses reveal that most of them have acquired two strong messages about the classroom pedagogy: first that children go to school in order to play; second, that the two most important things you 'learn' there are playing, and the social rules of the classroom. Most children, in other words, have identified both the instructional and the regulative discourses of the classroom, and know how to become the kind of pupils required by this discourse. Their adaptation to school, and their acquisition of a secondary, school-approved habitus, seem to have been achieved in a few short months by the strong socializing efforts of their teachers. When this process is unpicked for individual children, however, it is clear that the transformation is only partial or superficial, and may have been achieved at some cost.

In December, the children's responses to my first question, *Why do children go to school?*, showed that they were trying to reconcile home and school beliefs on this subject. Most children were confident in explaining why they went to school: it was *either* in order to play, *or* to meet the convenience of adults. These latter responses, which suggest a negative rather than a positive rationale for attending school, echo the kinds of persuasion overheard from mothers: 'If you're not ill, you have to go'; 'If your mum has to go to the post office, you have to go', and in Kelly's case, 'Because your mum's had enough of you.' None of the Bangladeshi children offered this type of response; their mothers had made it clear (to me and presumably to their children) that they would prefer to keep their 4-year-olds at home with them. Most Anglo children, on the other hand, seem familiar with the cultural assumption that adults have jobs of their own to get on with, so that it is appropriate for their children to be out of the way once they reach school age. Although these children certainly enjoyed school, they also recognized the existence of a social order which required them to be separated from their mothers.

In December, I was surprised to note that only Abu Bokkar, Amadur and Mohammed, the three children observed to be *least* involved in the learning curriculum of the classroom, named curriculum skills (reading and writing) as reasons for going to school. These three, at this point in the year, still offered their parents' version of the reasons children go to school: to study and learn. When asked again in April all three offered 'play' as their rationale: they had managed to unlearn their parents' lessons, and acquire the message of the classroom pedagogy. But crucially they had only acquired the overt Reception message, rather than its hidden agenda: the obligation to *play*, rather than an expectation of *learning through play*. While the children whose mothers are aware of this underlying subtext (such as Joshua, Katy, and Troy) receive reinforcement and scaffolding for their play accomplishments at home, those whose parents are ignorant or sceptical about the subtext appear to have no inkling that they are 'learning' from their play in school. In April, consequently, Joshua asserts that you go to school to 'learn things', and Sonia and Katy that you 'work', while most children still cite 'playing' or the obligations of the social order. Khiernssa alone seems, against the evidence of her actual school experience, to have constructed her own theory:

> [Children go to school] because they want to be busy doing work, because their teacher is going to say, Good boy, and Good girl; I know that because I know everything because I am a good girl!

In April, after two terms of school, nine of the children cited 'playing' as 'the most important thing you do at school', while seven mentioned 'work' (Khiernssa and Abdul Rahman), 'worksheet' (Joshua), 'read' (Jemma and Kelly), 'write' (Mohammed) or 'count' (Tuhura) in their response. But when I asked them to tell me something they were 'really good at, at school', many still cited aspects of the social order: 'the register, answering the register' (Cameron); 'washing my hands at dinner time' (Tuhura); 'not playing with the doors because it's dangerous' (Troy); 'sitting down properly while I'm eating my lunch' (Kelly); 'wearing your coat' (Rufia); 'tidying up' (Sonia). Such responses give few indications about children's progress in learning. By Easter, Troy was continuing to race ahead of the class in most curriculum areas, although he suggests that the most important thing to do at school is 'sticking'. And Mohammed, who thought he had 'learned to read, all by myself', and said the 'most important thing' was 'writing', is revealed in field notes and diaries to have almost dropped out of the classroom curriculum altogether.

It was not clear from these responses that any child had consciously identified the intentions of their parents in sending them to school, or of their teachers in planning the curriculum and the classroom environment, but Troy perhaps came closest to cracking the code. Asked to explain *why* children have, in his words, '*got* to go to school', he replied, 'They've got to do busy things and choosing and eating all your dinner up.' In this neat summary, the social capital of appropriate classroom behaviour (choosing, and eating your dinner) is joined with the cultural capital of appropriate learning behaviour (being busy) to produce a model for learning in Reception.

Case study: Abu Bokkar's changing fortunes

Abu Bokkar, in his family's eyes, was a 'little prince': 'We call him that because he's smart, he's very clever.' His home advantages appear to be considerable: he has a family loyal to the school and staff, a mother who dotes on him and a father with high status in the community and an informed interest in education. He hears English spoken at home, and experiences family study sessions (including letter and number tuition) around the dining table. His front door is opposite Khiernssa's and the two families walk to and from school together. What goes wrong when he starts school?

Field notes suggest that his experience of transition was mixed:

Day 1: A little shy, but smiling and joined in quite well – painting, home corner, water, car track; after some difficulty learned to play simple computer game, matching shapes, and having learned it had several more tries (after getting rid of Tuhura who was interfering and doing it wrong). Says little: is watchful though smiling.

Day 2: A more difficult afternoon – tried to join in with Rufia and Khiernssa, by poking or pushing them or the things they were playing with; they got very annoyed with him but he couldn't be persuaded to stop. Got no satisfaction from what he was doing, e.g. refused to paint but leaned against painting table, getting in the way of other children.

As the weeks went on, Bokkar gradually discovered ways to integrate himself: by half-term he had formed a tight-knit group with Amadur and Mohammed (not the friends his father would have chosen for him) and occasionally Abdul Rahman. This particular in-group, referred to by staff as the Three (or Four) Musketeers, did not support him in accessing the curriculum, and during the period of systematic observation he was markedly uninvolved in learning activities. He was frequently recorded in observations as 'passive', 'uninterested', 'idle', 'desultory', 'wandering', and there were few occasions when he seemed to be occupied with acquiring knowledge or skills. His greatest effort and ingenuity was some-times directed at evading the curriculum: the observation records include long periods in the toilets or looking through children's lunchboxes, and several episodes where he disrupted other children's activities. His six 'interactions with an adult' included asking to go to the toilet, and being asked to take a plate to the sink. But they also include some dialogue with Becky, in a bilingual group activity which went wrong because Mrs Khan was called away. This runs as follows:

18.11.97: Becky conducts group activity on bread and toast
 1 Abu Bokkar sits quietly as Becky explains task; Mrs K called away.
 2 AB and others wait while Becky tries to recall Mrs K.
 3 AB talking to others, waiting . . .
 4 Becky asks questions; AB doesn't respond.
 5 She asks him by name; he tries to respond (not shy).
 6 Tells Amadur what question is, then chats with him.
 7 Told to 'feel' bread and pats it: non-plussed!
 8 Mucking about with Amadur, not listening to Becky.
 9 Bored, looks round room, grinning.
10 Addressed by name, and answers.
11 Plays with bread and chats to Amadur.
12 Looks around, watches other children in room.
13 Giggles and plays at poking with Amadur.
14 Quite interested when toast pops up; says it is hot.
15 Returns to blank staring around room.
[Systematic observation records]

This carefully planned activity proved unprofitable for all its participants.
  Bokkar achieved low Baseline scores for both Core Skills and Personal/Social development, and his behaviour in the classroom did not identify him as a promising pupil. In consequence, it required an intervention from his mother to bring about a significant change in his behaviour,

and the way it was perceived by staff. Rahena approached me one day in November, to ask me to ask Mrs Goode if Bokkar could be given a book bag to take home. In Mrs Goode's view he showed no sign of being 'interested' or 'ready', but she agreed to the request. As if awakened to the purposes of school, Bokkar became almost overnight an enthusiastic 'reader':

> *Much more motivated now: looks at books, concentrates well with Sally, asks to change his book!*
>
> [Field notes, 26.11.97]

The increased contact with adults which resulted marked the beginning of an upward trend in his school career which persisted after the Christmas holidays, when he began to make new friendships and find new routes to involvement.

Summary: starting school

When the children's experiences of starting school are compared, a number of features emerge. First, it is clear from their earliest days in the classroom that those with mainstream pre-school experiences and 'school-like' homes can access many of the toys, games and tasks on offer far more easily than children from ethnic minority or 'marginal' backgrounds; and that these tasks, in this pedagogy, are the principal vehicle for learning. Second, it was evident that the exchange of information between the two settings of home and school was full and friendly for some children's mothers (Katy, Cameron), awkward for others (Jason and Sonia, Jemma) and non-existent for Bangladeshi mothers; such exchanges are also important for children's early learning, and are discussed at greater length in Chapter 6. Third, the Baseline assessments of children were unfair to children outside the mainstream; in consequence, there was a risk of children being seen, wrongly, as unprepared and unready for school learning. Structural aspects of the school organization (such as the large class, and the inadequate provision of bilingual support) prevented these early differentials in children's access to knowledge from being addressed, except in the area of social behaviour, where all children received explicit training.

When children's social and cultural capital was deployed in the classroom, the preparation some had received at home bore little resemblance to the curriculum or pedagogy of the school. For some children, their primary habitus, and the knowledge they had acquired in their communities, were unhelpful in the classroom, and 'learning to be a pupil' meant learning to be someone different altogether. The discontinuity experienced by such children early in the year created patterns and expectations for their progress throughout Reception. Children who were slow to display their dispositions and skills – who did not appear 'ready to read' or 'motivated to learn' in their first weeks at school – could find themselves excluded early in their school lives from understanding the discourse, and accessing the curriculum. In consequence they were at risk of just, in Mr Ali's words, 'passing the time' at school. Significant change, as Abu Bokkar's story demonstrates, may require an intervention of the kind made on his behalf by Rahena. Only in this way are assumptions disrupted, and expectations – those of the staff, and Abu Bokkar's of himself – overturned.

The influential role of parents in shaping their children's classroom experience is discussed next.

6

LINKING HOME AND SCHOOL: LEARNING TO BE A PARENT

Being a parent

When you take a child into your class, how conscious are you of the family's influence on the child's learning?
I'm conscious of the fact that I assess what the parents' expectations of school and their learning are, in terms of the difference, and also what input they expect to have . . . because some parents send their children to school to be educated, and they then pick them up and take them home, other parents have a different view . . . so without judging I say to the parents, look, we've got to work together on this, there's got to be some give and take . . . But the other thing is, because I've been here so long I know a lot of the families, and that makes a difference.

[Interview with Mrs Goode, March/April]

At the same time as the 16 children were learning to be a pupil, many of their parents were learning, in a new sense, to be a 'parent' – a school parent, that is to say, a role that, despite Mrs Goode's inclusive perspective, carries some quite specific expectations, which the school ethos does not address.

The wide variation in parents' own early experiences, which made such a difference to the ways they prepared their children for school, is very evident when they bring their child to the classroom for the first time. This chapter suggests that the role of parent (an 'unconscious' and 'natural' condition) has to be learned afresh by each family as their children enter and progress through the education system. The pedagogic discourse of schools includes parents in its sphere of influence, and its expectations of parents, as of children, may be more or less visible, more or less explicit, and thus more or less difficult to learn.

This chapter looks in turn at the ways parents view their own role and their relationship with the school, and the ways schools conceptualize their relationship with families. Theoretical models of home–school links help explain the many forms of parental involvement in children's development and learning. The ways in which these aspects are realized, in policy and in practice, at All Saints', are discussed, with special reference to the home–school reading scheme. Finally, the chapter describes the contrasting experiences of two parents whose background situates them *inside* and *outside* the school's pedagogic discourse, and sets out the need to re-vision parental roles and relationships. But we begin with Tuhura's family.

Case study: Tuhura's parents

Tuhura's father works in a restaurant 50 miles away, and is rarely seen at school or on my visits, but her mother Jamila manages the household confidently in his absence. When Tuhura starts school, Jamila becomes a 'Reception parent' for the third time: Tuhura's brother Abdul Rakib is starting Year 2, and her sister Tahmina is now in Year 1. (Baby Asim, who is 1 year old, starred with Jamila in a health authority advertising campaign – 'Breast is best' – when he was newborn, and the family display the photograph from the local paper proudly on the mantelpiece.) So Jamila can be considered quite an experienced parent within both the school and the local community.

Jamila is socially aspiring within her community, and has taken pains to accumulate social and cultural capital for her children. She has brought them up to speak 'good Bengali, not Sylheti dialect', as Mrs Khan confirms, and to use the correct respectful forms for addressing elders and betters; and rather than send the children to mosque school, she pays the imam to teach her children at home for three hours on Sunday, when he also eats with the family, a further source of pride to her. The children learn three writing systems at home, and study the Qur'an and say prayers together every evening, as well as getting out their school books and looking at them together.

One aspect of Tuhura's early experience is problematic for her subsequent school career. As Jamila explains, 'something *happened to her*' in Bangladesh, when she was little; it seems she suffered some mild affliction which relatives there regarded as having a supernatural aspect, and which has marked Tuhura as 'special' within the extended family. For this reason she is regarded as a 'little princess', to be indulged and deferred to more than other children – Jamila describes how Tuhura even 'sits on the toilet like a princess' and 'afterwards calls out to Tahmina to come and flush, and Tahmina does'. Her indolence at home is viewed with some pride:

> She spends a lot of time sitting down nicely, she doesn't bother to play with her brother and sister . . . Tahmina looks after the baby, but the baby will look after Tuhura before she looks after him!

On arrival at school, Jamila's status and confidence visibly diminish. Like other Bangladeshi mothers she stands silently inside the classroom door before backing out, still anxiously checking that Tuhura is settled. She rarely makes contact with staff, but sometimes asks me for my opinion, or for information. When late in the first term Tuhura is given a book bag, Jamila never writes in the reading folder. When letters and forms are sent home, she rarely responds, and Mrs Khan has to be instructed to obtain her signature. Above all, she is unpunctual, and keeps her children at home for reasons unacceptable to the school, including, unforgivably, when trips and outings come round – thus denying them the opportunity of unlicensed fun and excitement which is a special part of the school's pedagogy.

The staff find it hard to sympathize with Jamila's point of view – her wish to keep her children near her, her fears for their health and safety, and her failure to recognize the value of the Reception curriculum and ethos. At one time Mrs Khan reports that Jamila has discovered that Tuhura *does not have to come to school yet* (because she is still only 4) and is considering keeping her at home for another year. Although this threat never materializes, Jamila's lack of appreciation is noted. Meanwhile Tuhura refuses to play outside, or play with water, because 'I get a cold . . . Mummy says'; and at Christmas Jamila flatly refuses to let her children go to the pantomime in town – a school tradition of which she remains suspicious.

As time goes on, Jamila begins to take pre-emptive action, announcing that her children are 'poorly' *before* the day of a trip, to justify keeping them home. Field notes record:

> *Jamila intercepted by Mrs Khan at Sally G's request, to explain refusal for outings, and is pressured into giving a range of excuses ('We take them there all the time, no need to go with the school . . . there are snacks, she can't eat school food . . . she won't eat her lunch or go to the toilet . . . she can't tell the teacher she wants the toilet . . . she isn't like other children, she has problems, she better stay with Mummy') – genuine anxiety evident.*

Jamila, it is clear, has been transformed from a 'good' into a 'bad' parent by her encounter with the school. But how is she to learn, without instruction, how to be a proper parent?

Perspectives on parenting

Being a parent: the home perspective

In the debate over parental interest and involvement, the most funda-mental fact is sometimes forgotten: that most families *want* the best for their children, and *do* the best they can according to their circumstances – circumstances which may however be constrained by poverty, inexperi-ence or ignorance.

Asking families about their children's learning has produced consistent responses over the decades. A high proportion of parents attempt to teach their children basic literacy and numeracy content before school, support their children with reading and spelling tasks brought home from school, and encourage them to practise their reading, writing and arithmetic at home (Plowden 1967; Tizard *et al.* 1988; Chavkin and Williams 1993). A good many parents, including those with poor school experiences and memories themselves, feel inadequate to offer such help (Joly 1986; Moles 1993), and many of these are shy or anxious when on school premises or in conversation with teachers (Reay 1998). The majority of parents, especially from low-income and minority groups, 'trust' pro-fessional educators and assume they know what is best (Pratt 1994; Holden *et al.* 1996).

The options open to parents from any class or cultural background to display their 'interest' or to become 'involved' depend crucially on whether 'involvement' is viewed as support for children's *learning*, or support for their *schooling*. The former, naturally, includes all the ways in which parents attempt to teach their children at home, before or during their school attendance. The latter includes only those practices which are undertaken on school premises, or at the request of teachers. A study of inner-city schools (Siraj-Blatchford and Brooker 1998) found that only about one in ten parents were willing or able to participate directly in their children's schooling, while almost all were involved in their learning at home.

Government initiatives to transform parents into educational consumers appear to have had little impact on parents' own sense of an appropriate relationship with their children's schools (Hughes *et al.* 1994). While privileged parents continue to exercise their social and cultural capital in their dealings with professional educators (Lareau 1987; Vincent 1996; Reay 1998), the majority of low-income families, most of the time, support their children's schools. African-Caribbean parents in the UK, and African-American parents in the US, alert to the school practices which have contributed to low achievement for their children, are the only significant groups to have taken a stand against the status quo (Reeves and Chevannes 1988; Harry *et al.* 1996).

Meanwhile, parents are aware that their own abilities as parents are being judged from the day their child starts school – by other parents as well as by school staff. The effort to present a child in new clothes and shoes (whether school uniform or fashion garments, Start-Rite shoes or

Spice Girls sandals), and with a well-scrubbed face and school haircut, is the outward sign of this awareness, but parents know too that the behaviour and ability their child displays in the classroom reflects directly on their own reputation as good parents (Vincent 1996; Connolly 1998).

The views of All Saints' parents

Most parents in the study were clear about their own roles and responsibilities towards their children, including their duty to prepare them for school in ways which would give them a good start: all expressed strong views on the importance of education for their children's future. Most families believed that parental input into their children's learning had an influence on their academic success, and judged their own performance accordingly. Anglo parents were particularly concerned to stress that they had made the effort, even if their children had not acquired the desired knowledge. As Kath said of the twins,

> We did the ABC on a video, they liked that better than books – I did all that with them, I *have* tried . . . they *should* know some letters, we've looked at little dictionaries and different letters, Sonia more than Jason . . .

Alison could not conceal her annoyance with Cameron, who 'just doesn't make the effort, he doesn't want to know' despite her energetic and ingenious efforts to teach him with educational toys and videos. Like other Anglo mothers, she suspected that her child was deliberately evading and subverting her intentions in this respect, and would only 'learn' when no adults were watching.

Such a notion did not present itself to the Bangladeshi parents, who assumed that their children, on the whole, learned anything their parents taught them. Most families, as described earlier, had invested considerable time and effort in their children's early education. Even those (like Amadur's and Mohammed's) who were conscious of failing in this expectation had prepared their children for school by telling them how to behave; like other families, they emphasized submission to the teacher, and studying:

> We told him, be good, sit down and study: don't do anything naughty!
>
> (Asima)

> We told him he would study reading and writing, and he must behave.
>
> (Shazna)

Since educational achievement is seen as all-important, many parents admit that they are anxious for their Reception children to stop playing and start learning. Some Anglo parents, although reluctant to find fault with the school, admit their concern that their children may be sacrificing learning for playing. Even Kath, by no means a pushy parent, observes that 'the school does its best, but I think they may not learn as much as we did when we went to school'. Many Bangladeshi parents, seeing no benefit in playing except that their children are happy, are frustrated by their inability to force the pace: Minara insists to me, 'You have to teach Khiernssa, she has to be better than my other two . . . we want her to work hard at school, every day, Monday to Friday.' Other parents remark that they did not expect their children to be playing, and can only hope that they will learn, 'little by little'. None of the Bangladeshi parents has attempted to communicate this view to Mrs Goode. But they are in consequence rather weakly motivated in bringing their children to school every day, and in all weathers.

This did not mean that any parents were dissatisfied with the level of involvement offered to them by the school. Few attended the September induction evening, at which Mrs Goode described the school's views on children's learning, and all the parents when interviewed affirmed that they would feel able to approach her if they had any queries. In fact several remarked on how easy she was to talk to:

> I'd definitely speak to Sally Goode, no problem . . . I think the school's very approachable from that point of view, all of them, to be honest, in the school, are very approachable.

This is Katy's mum, a privileged insider, but many mothers said they *would* speak to Mrs Goode if they had a problem, although they had not done so to date. Bangladeshi mothers added that they would be more likely to ask Mrs Khan first. No mothers would refer a problem to Becky: Becky presents herself as a resource for children, rather than as a resource for parents, and all parents seem to have sensed this.

Parents, in other words, seem to accept the school's arrangements with good grace: as Rahena put it, 'I am not shy: if I can't explain any problem about my children, the problem will be my problem.' In the event, of course, she chose to make her intervention on Abu Bokkar's behalf through me.

Being a parent: the school perspective

In recent years, research suggests, teachers are more understanding of parents' personal perspectives and social circumstances than they were when the profession reported to the Plowden committee in the 1960s (Plowden 1967; Jowett *et al.* 1991; Hughes *et al.* 1994). Parents are now widely recognized as their children's first educators. Still the gulf between the two groups – one composed of individuals who *whatever* their own class or ethnic background have acquired mainstream beliefs and values in the process of becoming professionals; one composed of the huge heterogeneity of social identities which the UK increasingly contains – persists, despite the investment of time, effort and good will at every level. Since parental 'interest' and 'involvement' is only visible, in most educational settings, when parents are on school premises – helping in classrooms, or with routine chores or fund-raising, attending meetings – a real effort of will is required for teachers to conceive of the mountain of *invisible* investment made by parents, in comparison with the visible molehill. Ethnographic studies (Vincent 1996; Huss-Keeler 1997) support the findings of larger surveys, that teachers are frequently unaware of the efforts made by parents to teach their children at home; and that parents who fail to keep school appointments and attend school functions are viewed as less supportive of their children, as well as less supportive of the school (Jowett *et al.* 1991; Siraj-Blatchford and Brooker 1998).

While some sympathy is shown for minority parents' difficulty in accessing the language and curriculum of the school, the rich contribution of children's own culture to their development is rarely recognized, other than the token recognition of inclusion in a multicultural curriculum plan. (In the case of white working-class families, even this token is unlikely: few teachers will muster the same enthusiasm for parents' skills in darts or snooker that they express for their ability to create *mendhi* patterns or Chinese calligraphy.) Where parental teaching methods are known to feature 'old-fashioned' rote learning, most teachers face the difficult task of questioning or abandoning their own hard-won professional knowledge if they are to entertain parental beliefs and practices. But it is common for parental teaching which does not equate with the school's methods to remain hidden from view – a form of cultural capital which gets stuck at the boundary between home and school (Huss-Keeler 1997; Reay 1998).

The role of a successful parent, we might conclude, consists first in offering the child a school-like curriculum and pedagogy at home, then in bringing her or him to school regularly and punctually, and finally in supporting the school and teacher, as well as the child, in the classroom. For as Vincent points out (1996), teachers only welcome the involvement of parents who support and agree with them, not those who reject or contest school policies and practices, or undermine the authority of the professionals.

The views of All Saints' staff

The All Saints' ethos is one which overtly welcomes parents as individuals and includes them as partner-educators. Teachers are enjoined to 'ensure that the school's "Open Door" policy is fully implemented, that parents are made to feel important and welcome visitors, and that they are listened to and their views receive a positive response'. But teachers are humans with their own personal history and ideology, so this is not as easy as it sounds. While Mrs Goode aimed, as she said, to 'work with' families in the ways they taught their children at home, in the majority of cases no dialogue existed from which she could learn what *was* going on at home. So even this inclusive and non-judgemental approach did not enable her to work with parents whose practices differed from her own, while Becky's wholehearted endorsement of the school's pedagogy (and her less sympathetic stance towards parents) would not admit diverse views about teaching and learning. Mrs Khan, as we saw, was torn between faith in the traditions in which she was raised, loyalty to her employers, and a generous affection for all the All Saints' families, whatever their background.

On a practical level it was not easy for parents' views to be 'listened to'. The school did not make provision for home visiting, which Mrs Goode in any case disapproved of, believing it to be an intrusion into the private lives of families; and no individual parents' appointments were offered before the child started school, or during their first term – not in fact until the end of the school year, after written reports had been distributed. Only those parents with the linguistic and social skills to engage Mrs Goode in conversation at the start or end of the day were able to share information about their child, or to find out more about the classroom. Perhaps this is why Mrs Goode is unaware of the families' high expectations for their children, and feels that '. . . we need to, as we do with lots of our families, we need to encourage them to know that we think, that it's a good thing, education! – but that would apply to all the families in my opinion'.

If All Saints' staff express a negative view of parents, it is almost invariably on the grounds of their failure to bring their children to school regularly and punctually. This well-founded frustration is supported by the data for the children's attendance in Reception, which correlates almost perfectly with their levels of achievement. Regular attenders are children from well-organized, coping families who are able to provide high levels of support for their children at home as well as ensure that they gain the maximum access to the curriculum. These children are doubly advantaged and make good progess in school: they include Troy (with 99 per cent attendance), and Katy and Joshua, who achieved 96 per cent and 91 per cent despite bad bouts of chicken pox. Families who are struggling to manage their social and financial problems, or to adapt to life in the UK, have more difficulty in getting their children to school, as well as having fewer resources with which to support them at home. Their children include Jemma (84 per cent attendance, but 35 late marks), Amadur (69 per cent, 42 late marks) and Mohammed (56 per cent, 27 late marks), all of whom made slow progress over the year. Most teachers, even if they recognize the underlying causes of this pattern, are not able to think constructively about remedying it. Instead they feel irritation for the parents, who are seen as spoiling their child's chances of benefiting from the opportunities provided for them.

Understanding home–school relations: the role of theory

To improve the ways in which homes and schools work together, we need to look beyond empirical description and towards theoretical models which can both explain existing practices and suggest how they may be modified. Models of home–school relations range from the large-scale macro-level explanations derived from the theories of Bernstein and Bronfenbrenner to the more pragmatic and evidence-based descriptions of empirical researchers (Epstein and Dauber 1991; Jowett *et al.* 1991). The former offer society-wide explanations for the local variability in home–school relations, and expound principles on which the practical understandings and recommendations of empirical studies may be based.

Macro-theories: Bernstein and Bronfenbrenner

Both these theorists affirm the centrality of children's early experiences in the home to their long-term outcomes, at the same time as they recognize that it is the larger mechanisms which connect homes with other settings experienced by the child which influence subsequent development. For Bernstein, the boundaries between homes and schools, teachers and parents – the linguistic, social and cultural barriers created by the pedagogic discourse – exclude some parents and children from participating fully in the official education system. Paradoxically, those educational settings which appear most accessible and inclusive to families from all backgrounds may be those in which it is hardest for children and parents to discover and enact the rules. Invisible boundaries are the hardest to surmount, because those they exclude have first to become aware of them. Parents who are welcomed with genuine warmth into a setting like All Saints'; who encounter Mrs Mason's openness, the school's affirmative policies, and Mrs Goode's enthusiastic commitment to every child in her care, may assume that their children have every chance to make progress without institutional hindrance. But the barriers which impede parental access, and children's progress, are aspects of the invisible structure of the setting, as we have seen. The 'rules' underlying the pedagogic discourse, and the official curriculum, incorporate knowledge and beliefs constructed at a broader societal level, and can only be challenged by those who have identified them. Mothers like Jamila can neither engage in dialogue with the school, since none is available, nor comply with the unspoken expectations for 'good parents'.

Bronfenbrenner's account of the essential links between the micro-systems experienced by the developing child has been described earlier. It identifies both the similarities, or regularities, between the settings within a system, and the crucial significance of multiple and bidirectional connections between settings. Where parents are unable to accompany the child into a new setting, and exchange information with the new caregivers, and where the child experiences no continuity of experience between the activities and values of different settings, the development of the child is likely to be slower than where links and continuities are strong. Young children starting school offer an exemplary case for Bronfenbrenner's argument; and the children starting school at All

Saints' are a living demonstration of his propositions. Children whose home and school experiences overlap to a significant extent, and whose parents are present in the classroom, and engaged in continual exchanges with the staff, experience few setbacks in their developmental path. Those with wholly different experiences of home and school, whose parents are not comfortable in the classroom, and not able to engage the staff in dialogue, find many obstacles in the way of their continuing development.

Micro-models from empirical research: Epstein

Research on parental involvement in their children's education (both *learning* and *schooling*) has generated a range of terms for the roles and relationships available to parents in the last half-century (Bastiani 1993; Crozier 2000). In the UK, legislation and government reports have identified parents as 'problems', 'partners', 'participants', 'consumers' and 'collaborators' in their child's education through the school years. Most of the definitions and typologies offered have focused, understandably, on the contributions of parents and teachers to children's learning of academic knowledge – the knowledge which eventually gains them qualifications and entry to the worlds of higher education, training and employment. The focus of a significant body of research, for instance, has been on the effectiveness of home–school reading schemes (Hannon 1987; Wolfendale and Topping 1996). Since literacy is widely recognized as the key to children's academic progress in all areas, this focus is important (and is taken up below, in the discussion of the All Saints' scheme). But for the youngest children in particular, the most helpful models are those which allow consideration of the whole range of the child's, and family's, experience of the move from home to school. One such model is offered by Joyce Epstein (1987), who suggests a typology of forms of parental involvement which is helpful in describing the experiences of parents at All Saints'.

Epstein depicts the relationships between homes and schools spatially and temporally, as spheres whose degree of similarity, and degree of overlap, ebbs and flows dynamically over the years in which a child attends school. For any individual family, the overlap between home and school (in beliefs, practices and experiences) may be almost perfect, or almost non-existent. But for many families, there will be times in their children's school careers when the two spheres come closer, or pull apart. Where a high level of overlap exists, Epstein suggests, children experience 'family-like schools' and 'school-like families': these fortunate children find the same kinds of rules and expectations operate in both settings. But for many children of course the reverse is true, and the rules and expectations of the home are quite at odds with those encountered at school. The solution to this mismatch, Epstein insists, *must* be seen as the responsibility of teachers; and in a series of related studies (Epstein and Dauber 1991) she demonstrates the processes involved, and their consequences for families and children.

Epstein's starting point (1987) was an inclusive typology of the ways in which parents may be involved in their children's development and learning. She defines five types of involvement:

- *Type 1:* Parents' basic obligations in caring for their children in the pre-school and early school years.
- *Type 2:* Basic obligations of schools to communicate with parents about their child.
- *Type 3:* Parental support for children's learning, on school premises and under school direction.
- *Type 4:* Parental support for children's learning in the home.
- *Type 5:* Parental involvement in school organizations, leadership or governance.

These five types of involvement provide a framework for discussing the different levels of involvement of the All Saints' families.

Pedagogic discourse and parental involvement at all saints'

Using Epstein's typology we can compare the ways in which the All Saints' parents are involved in their children's development and learning with the ways in which the school would implicitly like them to be involved.

Type 1: Parental practices at home: explicit and implicit rules

All the parents provided basic care for their children: they housed and fed, bathed and clothed them, and endeavoured to teach them age-appropriate behaviour and self-care routines, as well as early learning appropriate to their future school career.

Mrs Goode and her colleagues were careful not to 'pry' into children's home lives, or to criticize the practices of their families, but when some families' 'inappropriate' practices came to their attention it was hard for them to refrain from critical comment. The main occasions for disapproval are those familiar to Early Years teachers: clothing, shoes and personal hygiene; daily routines, diet and bedtimes. The ethos of the school carries strong but implicit expectations in these areas, which relatively few of the All Saints' parents met. There was no need for prying questions for many of these irregularities to be evident: children like Jemma, who enters the classroom half an hour after the start of school, finishing the remains of a packet of crisps and a bottle of fizzy drink, have clearly not experienced the desirable morning routines of a family breakfast and a well-timed departure for school.

Jemma's family failed most of the school's implicit expectations for parenting. Her attendance and punctuality were poor, and the reasons for both exacerbated the family's low status in the school. They included recurrent outbreaks of head-lice and diarrhoea; lack of money for the meter, or for breakfast; and problems with the police and social services, usually brought on by the teenage daughters. Jemma's physical appearance was unhealthy (pale skin and dark marks under her eyes) and her clothing often unsuitable for school (worn-out old jumpers or skimpy fashion tops; thin sandals or plastic 'jellies' which made her feet sore). Her packed lunch was remarked on, sometimes indiscreetly, by the meals supervisors (it contained crisps and snacks but no sandwiches or fruit). Since her book bag was soon declared to be 'lost', it was assumed that no one read with her at home, and that the family's life was disorderly (the first of these was not true).

There can be no doubt that June knew she was regarded as a bad parent. She was immensely shy and embarrassed on school premises: although she came to talk to me regularly, it took months for her to decide she was ready to be interviewed. She had taken to communicating with Mrs Goode through me ('Can you just ask her, like, if I can take Jem early, only I've got an appointment'; 'Can you give her this for me, only I know it's late'). Becky assured me that she 'never comes up the school, never, hasn't come once' for a parent interview.

Other families ranged along the continuum of desirable or disapproved practices. The Bangladeshi children's lack of a regular bedtime, and tendency to poor time keeping, was accepted but lamented. Their clothes – Tuhura's satin crinolines, Rufia's threadbare cast-offs, and the boys' lack of underpants – were also the cause of raised eyebrows, and those who brought packed lunches had also failed to observe the guidelines on healthy eating. Asima caused astonishment when she arrived at school at lunchtime with food for Amadur: an enormous fresh cream doughnut on one occasion, and on another a freshly cooked dish of chips, with a bottle of ketchup to put on them. These lunches, evidence of his mother's devotion, were evidence too of a lack of conventional healthcare information, or input from school.

Poor provision of healthcare guidance was responsible for other irregularities in parenting which came to the school's attention. Khiernssa's continued reliance on large baby-bottles of milk for sustenance may have contributed to her fragility and susceptibility to infection, and was of course not regarded as age-appropriate. But most conspicuous in this respect was the discovery that Mohammed (then aged 5) was coming to school in disposable nappies: his mother, who had been introduced to them on her arrival in England, had not been told that children are to be trained to manage without them. The family was assigned a health visitor and interpreter at this point so that Mohammed could be trained, and return to school, but they chose to take him to Bangladesh instead. He did not reappear at school until two months later.

In these forms of involvement as in many others, the exemplary families were those with the most middle-class and teacher-like behaviours – Troy's, Katy's, Joshua's and Cameron's. Their children came to school well-fed, well-clothed and well-rested, as well as regularly and punctually.

Type 2: Channels of communication

There was really only one way for most parents to communicate with the All Saints' staff, and it was a deceptively difficult one: to 'catch' Mrs Goode during the twenty minutes or so when she was available to chat at the start of the day. The informality of the school ethos (the weak classification and framing of the school as an institution) implied that no barrier to communication existed, *therefore* no special arrangements needed to be made to breach it. Few letters or newsletters were sent home (and those there were, were in English): these were almost all announcements about class outings or school social events. Few letters were sent in by parents, and these were mostly the briefest of absence notes.

In any case, the school's view was, in Mrs Goode's words, that 'We greet them in the morning, and talk to them in the evening, so the informal part of that is probably the best bit, if you like, so if they've got anything to say . . .' This was easier said than done: a parent who had 'anything to say' required persistence and skill, as well as linguistic, social and cultural capital. Even Maisie, one of the most included mothers, recognized the difficulty: 'Sometimes the teachers are busy and if you have a problem you feel that you're intruding, during the day or after school, so sometimes it's easier to grab Mrs Mason.' Few of the parents would be bold enough to 'grab' the head teacher, however, although most recognize her as kind and welcoming. Though *all* the parents say they would feel free to talk to Mrs Goode if necessary (mostly with the aid of Mrs Khan, for Bengali speakers), only a minority have done so in their child's first two terms at school. Field notes show that, of this minority, a small handful take up the opportunity, day after day.

Although Maisie, Maxine and Alison all have close working relationships and frequent informal chats with Mrs Goode, it is Charlotte who contrives the most active communication, on Troy's behalf. Her list of strategies is impressive:

- She brings Troy to the induction afternoons in June, and engages Mrs Goode in lengthy conversation about the school's methods, and about Troy's achievements at nursery. [Field notes] *Seems super-keen for Troy to progress and succeed, and very anxious that his achievements will not be recognized by teachers, and the pace of his progress therefore not maximized.*
- She and Bob bring Troy to school extremely early every day (he is invariably the first in the classroom), and Charlotte uses this opportunity to continue the dialogue with staff: *[Mum always has a question or*

complaint, 'You're not to do dots for him to write his name, he has to do it without . . . He says they counted up to 10, well he can already count up to 20, only we don't want him held back by the others!']

- By December she is asking for his book bag to be 'changed' every day, rather than once or twice a week; Charlotte has supplied an exercise book in the bag so that longer comments can be written by staff and parents, and she contributes lengthy accounts of what Troy has learned at home.
- In spring, she begins to include in his folder the 'flashcards' he has learned at home, with a request that he practises them at school; out of politeness, the staff occasionally comply.
- Charlotte collects Troy's 'work' (mostly drawings) from his tray regularly, checks it and discusses it with Mrs Goode, pointing out what he can do, and what he needs to correct.
- Troy regularly brings in written accounts (by Charlotte) of the family's leisure activities (going to a christening, to play football, or to a theme park), which he is instructed to 'read to Mrs Goode' and 'tell the children about'.
- Charlotte challenges his end-of-year report, saying that it does not do justice to his abilities; Mrs Goode invites her to write a response, which is attached to the report, and the school also tests Troy on the contested items (such as counting to 100) and amends the report ready for his next teacher.

Mrs Goode certainly does not invite or welcome this demanding activity on Charlotte's part, and is only too aware of the privileges it generates for Troy. But in an informal, demand-led system she is almost powerless to regulate the growing inequality of access and opportunity which Troy, already advantaged at home, is extracting from the scarce resources of the school.

School reports provide another index of the success of home–school communication for individual families. When I asked all parents for permission to read and copy their child's report, some produced it the same day (and quoted their favourite sentences by heart); some had temporarily mislaid it (Kelly, Sonia and Jason); some had thrown it away 'because we can't understand them, what difference does it make?' (Khiernssa, Rufia); and others were not aware of having ever received one (Amadur, Mohammed). Without an explanatory dialogue, and in some cases an interpreter, the school report is a form of non-communication for families outside the pedagogic and linguistic discourse.

The consequences of parents' different levels of communication with teachers permeate their children's daily school experience. An example of the variation in staff knowledge of children's families concerns mothers' pregnancies. For *included* parents (Maxine and Alison among others), these are a source of regular interest, which is communicated to the whole class ('Not long till Katy gets a new brother or sister!'; 'Cameron's brought in a photo of his new baby in his mum's tummy!'). The child's esteem is boosted as the class is invited to take an interest in her/his family. In the case of *excluded* parents (Tuhura's, Amadur's and Abdul Rahman's) staff are quite unaware that mothers are pregnant or have given birth. Though they react with enthusiasm if told that a pupil has a new sibling, no further interest is taken, whereas the children of included parents, and their friends, are given the materials to make cards for the new baby. This differential treatment is quite unintentional.

Type 3: Parents in the classroom: insiders and outsiders

The Reception pedagogy, in particular its instructional discourse, acts to filter parental access to the school and classroom. According to Mrs Mason, 'Parents are encouraged to come and be in classrooms, to come and help, and join in or hear readers as well, but that's up to individual class teachers, they do that'. In Reception, it seems, they don't. Mrs Goode has her own explanation for the lack of parental presence in the classroom:

> It's very difficult to say to parents, we'd like you to come in and stay every morning, and stay for twenty minutes, because they've got other things to do as well . . . you do say, are you available to come in, just to 'be' or to help, and that happens, but again most of them are busy . . .

But in practice, the invisible pedagogy of the Reception class ensures that very few parents are actually suited for this role: as Bernstein succinctly observes, 'If the mother is to be helpful, she must be resocialized or kept out of the way' (1975: 128). Being 'resocialized' in this case would mean adopting the ways of behaving and conversing which Mrs Goode so skilfully demonstrates.

In the course of the year, only four mothers helped in the classroom. All four held high social capital within the school, and participated in other roles, both as 'Friends' of All Saints', and as part-time employees (meals supervisors, cleaners, literacy assistants). One of these (the school cleaner) was included in systematic observations of adult–child interactions over the year, which showed how successfully she had adapted to the discourse, giving continuous positive and personalized feedback to children. For a large number of other parents (certainly the Bangladeshi mothers, but also Kath, June and Gaynor) this acquisition of the regulative and instructional modes of the classroom would be out of the question. This unsuitability extended outside the classroom, to school outings: none of the parents except Bob (who was now the school premises manager) was invited to accompany us on any of the summer trips.

The key to parents' unsuitability as classroom helpers was certainly not their lack of academic skills: rather, it might be their too-narrow insistence on correct answers, and on copying and repetition. Where reading was concerned, Mrs Goode was aware that even some of the parents with whom she was most friendly were in the habit of 'testing' their child on the words, rather than creatively constructing text with them: in consequence any parent who offered to read with children at school would need retraining. Even traditional forms of classroom help such as sewing with children could not be entrusted to parents, who would teach and enforce conventional skills rather than allowing messy, 'creative' sewing (I was allowed to sew with the children, whereas Mrs Khan was barred from this activity, as she exhorted the children to sew in a straight line or, worse, unpicked their stitches and did it for them). Despite Mrs Goode's large class and heavy workload, she preferred to restrict the adults in the classroom to a trained and trusted few, who would operate the pedagogy according to instructions.

> *Would it help, with this large class, to have more adults around . . . ?*
> Oh no, because it has training implications . . . It's got to be adults who like children, who understand them, and who fit into the regime that is already established within here, and who will have expectations so that it's consistent for the child . . .

Few of the parents could meet these requirements. The rules of the pedagogy, though invisible, were very strict.

Type 4: Parental support at home: learning to read

Almost all the parents supported their children's learning at home: both the 'school' curriculum and a home curriculum which varied with parents' interests, and ranged from detailed knowledge of Play Stations and Star Trek, model railways and Heavy Metal (Jemma, Joshua, Katy and Kelly) to early stages in learning the Qur'an. The only form of parental support which received acknowledgement from the school, however, was help with reading; and the only way this could happen was if parents participated actively in the home–school reading scheme.

The 'Reading Curriculum Policy' at All Saints' does not refer to the role of parents and other family members in children's literacy learning. Nevertheless the school sends books home in a 'book bag', and offers advice to parents on a sheet entitled 'Helping Your Child to Read'. The advice covers only the social and pastoral aspects of reading at home ('Find a quiet part of your home'; 'Give regular praise and encouragement'; 'Don't be anxious or worried or angry') rather than the techniques recommended for teaching reading. Parents who are anxious about their child's acquisition of this key skill are not made more informed by the leaflet.

The rationale for the absence of instructional advice is implied in the school's policy statement that 'The approach used to teach reading at All Saints' is very much an individual, child-centred one . . . Therefore no one approach will suit all children.' The ideal course, therefore, would be for Mrs Goode to speak to families individually about their child's needs and learning style. Since this is impractical, she writes to them in a friendly and individualized way via the home–school reading record, a photocopied sheet which travels to and from school in the book bag. Her messages skilfully combine encouragement and specific advice:

Time for Dinner	Rufia is making good progress with her book skills. Please help Rufia to point to all 'the' words in the book, so she begins to focus on words.
Huggles Breakfast	I am trying to encourage Kelly to slow down and begin to follow individual words with her finger.
Little Rabbit FooFoo	A story to read to Kelly: she is very good at joining in with the repetition.

The subtle differentiation of this child-centred and child-friendly approach, however, has an additional dimension. Not only is it personalized with respect to children, but with respect to parents. Thus Charlotte, predictably, is offered particularly detailed, fine-tuned information and guidance:

The Storm	Troy quickly recognized the pattern of text, and after we had shared the story together he was able to follow each word as we read. This book introduces new vocabulary: 'look', 'at'. Troy is also becoming confident at using the pictures to help him with unfamiliar words – this is important and should be encouraged.

The only other parent in the group to write on the home–school record was Alison. The majority of parents, therefore, gave no sign that they were reading or responding to Mrs Goode's thoughtful comments. Though most assured me they 'did try to find the time' to read their children's books at home, they were not necessarily aware of the dialogue that was supposed to take place in the reading folder. (It was only in our April interview with Jamila that she learned from Mrs Khan that she could write a comment in Bengali if she preferred.)

The most damaging aspect of this situation for the children was that parental 'demand' (based on their social and cultural competence in the school context) also regulates their child's access to reading in the classroom, since a child whose book bag is not returned regularly receives a smaller share of Mrs Goode's and Becky's time. Class reading records for the year showed that some children 'read' with Mrs Goode or Becky much more frequently than others. Mohammed's total number of sessions for the year was six: in addition to having poor attendance, he lost his book bag early on, and so dropped to the lowest level of provision –

occasional input from me or from Mrs Khan. Once again, the children who were most advantaged in their home learning were rewarded for it by additional access to learning at school; but in this case the extent of their home learning was judged by their parents' ability to participate (without adequate explanation or instruction) in the reading scheme.

Towards the end of the year, Mrs Goode asked me to read regularly with a group of children who 'ought to be reading by now, but they get no support at home'. To my surprise the group included Khiernssa and Abdul Rahman (of whom this could not be said) as well as Kelly (for whom it was possibly true).

Type 5: Leadership and governance

Within the group at All Saints', some parents had more access to power and influence than others, through their formal or informal roles within the school community. These parents are familiar to the reader by now: Maisie, whose active membership of the 'Friends of All Saints' conferred entry to classrooms and the staffroom with her raffle tickets and disco plans, and made Joshua familiar with the out-of-school activities of teachers; Maxine, whose role in the playgroup and in planning an after-school club required frequent meetings with staff, while Katy listened or amused herself nearby; and Bob, whose appointment as school premises manager made him both a school governor and an important member of the planning group for school functions. The 'leadership' role did not so much transform the relationship these parents had with the school, as enhance and consolidate an existing good relation. But their children enjoyed multiple links between their home and school settings because of these additional roles.

Case studies: schooled and unschooled parents

Asima and Amadur

Much of Amadur and Asima's early school experience has already been sketched: the mysteries which the Reception class presented to Amadur are matched by those encountered by his mother as a UK parent. Her own education was of a high quality: although she left school early she was tutored at home, and is knowledgeable about Bengali novelists and poets as well as about traditional embroidery. But she has no idea how old she is, or her date of birth, and has not brought Amadur up to know any of the things that children are assessed on when they start school.

Though Asima and her husband prepared Amadur for 'study' in his pre-school years, they were always fearful that his reckless disobedience would spoil his school career; at home Amadur climbs on the furniture and writes on the walls of the sparsely furnished house, and deploys his excess energy in fighting with his young brother, while his parents plead with him to obey. There are no extended family or community links for them to call on, and they receive no support from official agencies. When interviewed Asima was weak and tired from coping with three children while expecting her fourth. But she and her husband attempt to bring Amadur to school on time, and are always there to collect him.

One wonders whose job it is to support Amadur's family in their parenting. Not, evidently, the school's: the Open Door policy does not provide any structures which can support Asima and her husband in Epstein's 'five types' of involvement – with information about health, nutrition and behaviour management; about the availability and bene-fits of pre-school provision; about the curriculum and pedagogy of the classroom; and about the school's expectations of parents. (During her April interview, Asima is embarrassed to learn from us that she was ex-pected to return the book Amadur brought home, so that he could change it for another one. The book has long since been lost or scribbled on.) Nor can it enable any exchange of information between home and school to take place, since this is expected to occur naturally, as if between friends. Mrs Khan attempts to be a friend to families like Amadur's, but she is only timetabled for such tasks for a few hours a week, and cannot be available whenever she is needed.

In the absence of any guidance on child development and learning, or community support, Asima creates her own theories. In April she tell us that Amadur's unchecked television viewing (the only form of behaviour management she has to hand) has destroyed his other faculties, and caused him to forget everything he has learned at school; that he no longer even knows how to write his name. I was able to point out that he had written his name beautifully on a picture he had just coloured while we talked, but she could hardly believe it. Yet Amadur's non-school entry assessments (the British Ability Scales) disclosed high levels of cognitive development and potential, and his classroom behaviour, recorded in field notes throughout the year, displays high levels of curiosity, persistence and ingenuity. The failure to involve his parents amounts to a failure to involve Amadur himself in his own education.

Maxine and Katy

Amadur's case shows what can go wrong when parents are not closely involved with practitioners in their child's development; Katy's case suggests how involvement can overcome the problems which can arise in any family.

Although Maxine is by many indicators an 'ideal-type' parent at All Saints', her children's school careers do not run smoothly. Katy's older brother Charlie has been a slow learner and a difficult pupil, and Maxine has been required to consult his teachers regularly and work with them closely on learning goals and behaviour strategies. When Katy starts school, aged 4 years 3 months, she is difficult and anti-social: Maxine has given birth to an unplanned and unexpected baby in the summer, and Katy is suffering from a congenital problem in her knee which makes walking painful; her father is also unwell, and an aunt is terminally ill, so the family is stressed and anxious. Katy's early behaviour in the classroom reflects these difficulties: she is obstinate and rude to adults, and defiant in her relations with children. Her Baseline scores are quite low, in part because she refuses to cooperate with assessment activities.

Fortunately for Katy, Maxine is able to discuss all these symptoms with Mrs Goode, and establish a relaxed understanding of the difficulties Katy is experiencing. Katy is given plenty of opportunities to become involved, and is shown a great deal of friendly interest by staff: both Mrs Goode and Becky chat to her about her brother, her baby and her dog, and rapidly establish an easygoing relationship which accommodates Katy's 'difficult days'. At home and in the play schemes she organizes, Maxine continues to offer a range of educational play opportunities, with an emphasis on literacy and creativity. Katy and Charlie read their school books together (and return their book bags regularly), draw and 'make things' together, and spend their free time with cousins and relatives in the farmland on the edge of town. Their family routines – mealtimes, play-times, story times, bathtimes, bedtimes – have a regularity which mirrors the regularities of classroom life.

Although Maxine, like other Anglo parents, is looking forward to the time when the children start to 'learn a bit more', for the time being she supports the school's play pedagogy and encourages Katy in the appropriate dispositions, helping her to make independent choices, to plan and persist with activities, and to review them in conversation. She displays an intimate knowledge of what Katy is capable of – which letters she can write, which numbers she misses out when counting – which is at one with the individualized learning fostered in the classroom. With the coordinated efforts of her family and teachers, Katy makes rapid progress in every aspect of her development over the course of the year.

Summary: re-visioning home–school partnerships

Parents, like children, have to be socialized over time and through appropriate mediating strategies into the pedagogy of their child's school and classroom. If they are not, they may never be able to provide appropriate support for their children's school learning. Worse, their children may be disadvantaged in the classroom, as teachers fine-tune their provision for individual children in relation to unconscious assumptions and expectations. But becoming a parent, like becoming a pupil, involves acquiring the recognition and realization rules of the classroom discourse – a task achievable for some parents but problematic for others. Like their children, the All Saints' parents were offered little explicit instruction in what was expected of them. Those who acquired the rules shared certain advantages: some personal experience of liberal–progressive schooling; a good face-to-face relationship with the school staff; the confidence to feel at ease on the school premises; and for the favoured minority, some training in play provision.

In order to overturn prevailing models of parental involvement, with their heavy emphasis on what parents can do for schools, an alternative model is required – one which weighs the needs and strengths of parents in order to assess not only the contribution they can make to their child's schooling, but also the contribution the school can make to the family. One such model is offered by Hornby (2000), who envisages a form of home–school link which offers a role for every family – from those with the most needs, to those with the greatest strengths – rather than just for the favoured minority whose own culture and practices accord with those of the school.

I return to this model, and discuss the ways in which schools can work with *all* parents, for the benefit of *all* children, in Chapter 8. For this is what an Open Door policy fails to do. It is not explicit about the ways in which parents can engage with the beliefs and practices which underpin, and flow from, the pedagogic discourse of the school. An Open Door offers a deceptive lack of resistance; it leaves parents uncertain whether they are inside, outside or on the margins of the school community.

Before returning to this issue, we consider, in Chapter 7, the children's progress in Reception, and the outcomes of their first year in school.

7

OUTCOMES: CHILDREN'S PROGRESS AND ACHIEVEMENTS

Khiernssa is an enthusiastic and lively girl who settled quickly and confidently into the school routine. She enjoys all aspects of school life and happily participates in a wide range of activities. Khiernssa can independently direct and maintain her own activity and will concentrate and persevere at a task. She is also becoming more willing to face a challenge.

[Report to parents, July 1998]

Introduction

How are we to assess the progress the children made in Reception? The official version is conveyed in the end-of-year reports which are sent to parents to inform them of their child's achievements, and passed to the Year 1 teacher to assist her in planning for the coming year. Khiernssa's report, quoted above, gives clear signals to both parents and staff of a successful year completed, and a bright future predicted.

Reports like these are the outcome of ongoing records and observations of children's performance during the year; like all such assessments, they contain both a subjective element (deriving from the teacher) and a structural bias (deriving from the values and culture of the school). So it is important to recognize that any account of children's outcomes at the end of Reception must be ambiguous. It reflects, not just the child's actual learning, but also the attributes which are valued in the school culture, and the methods by which these are evaluated. This caution applies too to my own assessments of the children, and to those made by their parents. Evaluation is integral to the pedagogic practices of both homes and schools, and parents, as well as being alert to the school's assessments, carry out their own continuous, common-sense assessments, from their children's early infancy.

Before describing the All Saints' children's outcomes, this chapter discusses the different ways in which the families and the school assessed them. In the case of the school, it shows that early and ongoing assessments of the children have direct effects on their experience in the classroom – on their levels of curriculum access, and adult support. The chapter goes on to discuss three aspects of the progress made by individual children – their cognitive gains, their social development, and their acquisition of learning dispositions. It argues that, in addition to the general structural influences which are known to shape children's outcomes, some specific *local* influences are taking effect as the children adjust to the culture of the classroom, and attempt to behave as the new setting requires.

A complex combination of factors underlies each of these aspects. These include: the cultural and social capital the children have managed to transfer from home to school; the primary habitus they have acquired during their early years; and their acquisition of what Bernstein calls the 'recognition and realization rules' of the pedagogic discourse of the classroom. Since the pedagogic discourse is vague and implicit, weakly classified and framed, these rules can be extremely difficult for some children to acquire. To take each aspect in turn:

- Children's cognitive gains (the knowledge and skills they are seen to possess at the end of the year) are influenced by both the cultural capital they have brought from home and the curriculum access and adult support they have been offered in the classroom. The latter depends to a large extent on their knowledge of the rules of the *instructional discourse* (the ways to learn in school): both the recognition rules which enable them to identify the discourse, and the realization rules which enable them to participate in it fully.
- Children's social development (their approximation to the school's idea of a pupil) depends both on the social capital they arrive with, and on their acquisition of the rules of the *regulative discourse* (the ways to behave in school). Individual children's adaptation to school is visible in certain desirable attributes which emerge from all the evaluations made of them.
- Children's learning dispositions are seen in the development of a school-like habitus, which enables them to develop appropriate and positive attitudes towards the kinds of learning offered by the school. The degree to which this is achievable for any individual child depends on the relation between the primary habitus acquired in the home, and the school's unspoken requirements.

Before considering these aspects we review the development over the year of Joshua, who emerges, like Khiernssa, as a highly successful pupil and learner.

Case study: Joshua

Despite being only just 4 years old, Joshua started school with many advantages. The youngest child of a playgroup worker, he had been prepared for school in ways wholly consistent with school practices. Maisie supports the child-centred pedagogy of Reception, saying 'It's easy to say it's just like nursery, but then they're learning there too.' There are minimal boundaries between Joshua's family and his teachers, and between his pre-school and school experience.

Joshua is a confident conversationalist, and on entry already had an affectionate relationship with Mrs Goode and Becky. He could easily access the regulative and instructional rules of the classroom, and he displayed a practical mastery of all the main curriculum activities. He excelled at puzzles and pattern making, construction toys and computer programs, and all kinds of imaginative play; he loved writing, reading and drawing, and was familiar with sorting, matching and counting tasks. Joshua therefore made a smooth transition from the curriculum *and* pedagogy of his home and playgroup to those of the school.

Joshua's wholesome and 'child-like' quality, which particularly endeared him to adults, set him apart from some of his more streetwise peers. Confronted with a new activity, he characteristically stood apart to observe other children's behaviour first, but approached an adult when he felt ready to join in, and negotiated his turn. Though relaxed and chatty with adults, he would walk away from the arguments and disputes that arose during children's play. Despite his age, he was awarded very high ratings by the staff on the Baseline assessment of Personal and Social Development (on a 1 to 5 scale, he was rated 5,4,3,5,5,4 on the subscales). His 'Core Skills' Baseline of 18 was also high, compared with a class mean score of 12.7.

During his first term, Joshua was consistently highly involved and committed to tasks; systematic observations record him as high in adult interactions (27, mean 11.8) but low in child interactions (28, mean 42.2). He was subsequently allocated to 'top' maths and writing groups, and then to the summer term literacy group. He was offered 21 reading sessions during the year, and Maisie received detailed feedback on his home–school reading record.

We Like Animals Joshua and I did a lot of word matching with this book – he is able to focus on individual words and is ready to establish a sight vocabulary of familiar common words.

(Written by Mrs Goode)

The Bath Joshua enjoyed this book and quickly became independent. He was able to find all the <u>in</u> and <u>went</u> words.

(Written by Becky)

One field note gives an indication of his 'special relationship':

J sits at Sally's feet throughout register, acting as her little pet and helper, either holding out the right colour pens for her, or hiding them to tease her; maintains an affectionate 1:1 relationship with her, within the large group: she responds, accepting the intimacy.

Joshua knows such strategies are acceptable because he understands the rules governing classroom behaviour. His interview responses show the degree to which he has acquired the *underlying* messages of the weak-framed regulative and instructional discourse of the classroom: by his second interview, he knows that children go to school 'because they need to learn things', and names the most important thing he has to do as 'stay with the lines on the worksheet'.

In evaluating her children's learning, Maisie to a great extent shares the school's perspective – she values the child's effort, and the *processes* of learning, rather than simply judging the *product*. At home, she reports, Joshua's big sisters tend to reinforce this stance:

The trouble was, with him, if he said 'red triangle' and it was a yellow circle, we did react differently with him being the youngest . . . the girls just said, 'Ah, isn't he sweet, he's really trying'!

Once Joshua starts school, she monitors his progress with pleasure: 'His writing's often back to front, but from the point of view that he's actually writing now, whereas he didn't used to be interested, only in drawing and crosses and squiggles . . .'

Joshua makes good all-round progress over the year: in July, when he is reassessed against the Baseline descriptors, his total score is second only to Troy's, and observations show him to be an ideal-type pupil. His school report describes his progress in all aspects of the curriculum as 'good' or 'excellent', and depicts Joshua as 'cooperative and willing', 'gentle and sensitive', and as able to engage in the classroom ethos: 'Joshua has a developing sense of humour and fun, and enjoys playing tricks, especially on the adults in the class!' It is clear that he is viewed as a pleasure to teach.

Evaluations

How families evaluate

Conversations with parents throughout the year confirmed that all of them, like the teachers, were making continuous evaluations of their child's knowledge and skills. What and how they assessed, however, was quite various: the wide variety of pedagogic practices adopted by families and teachers generates an equally wide range of evaluative practices.

All the parents assessed their children on certain common items – reading and writing, counting and adding – but beyond these core skills there was little consensus. Many Anglo parents took considerable interest in their children's drawing, at home and at school, as well as the other 'creative' products they brought home: Charlotte had 'kept every drawing [Troy's] done since he was a baby'; Maisie had kept Joshua's mother's day gift on display on the mantelpiece; Kath describes Jason spending a whole Sunday reproducing a drawing he had seen of a country church.

Bangladeshi parents seemed less interested in their children's creative talents (Charlotte reported with disbelief seeing an 'Indian' mother throw her child's pictures in the bin). Instead, they were unanimous in prioritizing their child's second-language acquisition; mothers with little English themselves took especial pride in their child's progress:

He's improved a lot. When the doctor was checking him, he gave all the answers in English.

(Rahena, of Abu Bokkar)

He speaks English to his mum. She is glad he speaks English even though she doesn't understand; they laugh about it together.

(Shazna, of Mohammed)

Tuhura's mother was particularly impressed with her:

She learned to speak English with a full sentence, clearly . . . every new word she learns, she comes home and tells me, 'we learned that new word' . . . long, long words: 'happy-mother's-day'.

(Jamila)

In language, as in other curriculum areas, the Bangladeshi parents are only guessing at their child's actual achievements. When asked if they are satisfied with their child's progress they are unable to be specific: they seem resigned to being excluded from their children's schooling, and have no information with which to monitor their progress. Though they express faith in the children's abilities, and trust in their teachers, they seem also to recognize their own powerlessness. Rufia's father is forthright in describing his non-involved stance:

Your child has been at school for nearly two terms now. Do you feel she has changed much since starting?
I couldn't see any change.
Are you pleased with the progress she has made?
She learned some English; and I don't know whatever you are teaching her, but anything you are teaching her she learns; we don't notice what she is learning.

The possibility of a pedagogy in which no one is 'teaching' his child is not one he can entertain.

Interviews conducted after the children had been at school for six months highlighted other group differences in family priorities. The majority of Anglo parents, when asked to describe their children's progress, commented on their social development:

He's a lot more outgoing; his confidence, he's asserting himself more.

(Alison, of Cameron)

He's got a lot more confident in himself, talking to people – he's no different otherwise.

(Kath, of Jason)

Definitely she's matured a lot, the baby side is definitely going.

(Maxine, of Katy)

Bangladeshi parents, however, took the question to refer to their child's academic progress:

Yes, he's learned a lot . . . when he comes home he talks to his brothers and sisters in English, and he can read books, and copy writing.

(Rahena, of Abu Bokkar)

He's more interested in pens and pencils and studying at home.

(Sabina, of Abdul Rahman)

Yes, she is speaking English and doing some reading and writing as well.

(Minara, of Khiernssa)

Paradoxically, these families' evaluations are not informed by knowledge either of their children's progress, or of the way it is evaluated in the classroom.

Some Anglo parents, when asked about academic skills, seem well informed about the school's evaluative criteria, as well as confident in their own evaluations. All of them have acquired some of the terms employed in the evaluative discourse of the school; in reading and writing, for instance:

Concepts about print:
Before he didn't point to words at all, he was trying to say what the story was but he didn't realize it was the words that said it.

(Alison, of Cameron)

Phonics and phonemes:
Sometimes he guesses, he does look at the pictures a lot . . . I always have to say, what letter does that begin with?

(Charlotte, of Troy)

She's mostly doing letters and seeing what words begin with that letter; we have to write them all down and she copies.

(Kath, of Sonia)

Letter orientation:
She'll try and copy things down but she gets some letters back to front.

(Gaynor, of Kelly)

Most Anglo parents were better informed than the Bangladeshi families as to their own child's progress in literacy. For all parents, however, the criterion for 'good' writing is neatness and correct letter formation, rather than content or originality. Related to this is the belief common to all the parents that children learn by *copying*: every parent refers to their child as 'copying under' their mother's writing, 'copying out' reading books, or learning through copying at school. The word is not one Mrs Goode uses to describe how children learn: while she looks for originality and creativity, and values divergent, individual 'products', the majority of parents appear to value conformity and 'normality' in their children's work. As a result, they often encourage at home efforts which would be deplored by the school (copying pages of writing or spellings, copying or tracing pictures from comics).

Two aspects of the parents' backgrounds influence this preference: for most Anglo parents, there is a social class inheritance of beliefs and practices emphasizing conformity (discussed for instance by the Newsons, 1968, 1976). For Bangladeshi parents, there are much broader cultural assumptions, embodied in the parents' own early learning experiences (Dwivedi 1996; Bhatti 1999): these may include valuing conformity and community interests over divergence and individual interests. Mrs Khan, whose efforts at didactic instruction include teaching the children to 'draw properly', values a product which all the families aspire to for their children, although it prompts disapproval in the classroom. In this respect, the home and school may be working towards conflicting goals.

How the school evaluates

Although central government at this time was insisting that children's attainments should be evaluated according to a 'performance' model (Bernstein 1996: 57), the All Saints' Reception classroom still adhered to the 'competence' model traditionally preferred by Early Years educators (Drummond and Nutbrown 1996). This mode of evaluation is characterized, in Bernstein's terms, by 'what is *present* in the acquirer's product' (1996: 59): it gives credit for the child's accomplishments rather than indicating those which are lacking; it focuses on processes rather than products; and it employs criteria which are 'multiple, diffuse, and not easily subject to apparent precise measurement' (Bernstein 1975: 130) – and thereby not transparent to the majority of parents. Such evaluations, which describe the 'whole child', give great power to the teacher, who holds the key to what is assessed, and how.

There were many forms of ongoing assessment in Mrs Goode's class: brief notes on book-sharing sessions constituted a reading record;

occasional notes on maths concepts updated the maths records; children's worksheets and tracings were filed and collated; individual outcomes for group activities were monitored; and some written observations were made, principally of children with specific social or educational needs. The records of all these evaluations indicate high levels of expertise on both Mrs Goode's and Becky's parts: they were both supportive and personal, providing information which was specialized to the child, rather than norm- or criterion-referenced. Most observations discussed social and cognitive aspects, including motivation, and described children's enjoyment of the activity as well as their developing skills.

The school assessed the children on a range of skills far broader than those prioritized by parents, or included in the Baseline. Mrs Goode is true to the principles of her nursery training, and her observations record such items as 'cutting in a straight line/round a shape'; 'throwing a ball at a target'; 'balancing along a low beam'; 'exploring properties of sand' – as well as skills such as identifying letters, words, or numbers. In consequence, the end-of-year reports, rather than emphasizing the core skills prioritized by parents, present a broad picture of the 'whole child'. Overall, cognitive outcomes receive less emphasis than social attributes: the reports praise children as 'happy and cheerful . . . rarely seen without a smile on his face' (Abu Bokkar); as having 'a sense of fun', 'a mischievous sense of humour' (Cameron); as 'gentle and friendly' (Jemma) and as sympathetic, confident, cooperative, caring and independent (Katy). None of these children (whose numerical skills, for instance, consist of 'counting to four' or 'understanding numbers to seven') is described as making disappointing academic progress.

These positive depictions of children, which reflect Mrs Goode's broad view of their development, may mislead some parents as to their children's actual gains. In particular, parents such as Tuhura's and Abu Bokkar's, whose high expectations for their children are founded in academic achievement, may be unaware of their child's relatively low performance until it is made 'official' (at end of Key Stage). In this group, Charlotte was the only mother to query the assessments cited in the report, on the basis of Troy's 'performance' at home, and the teaching she herself had provided.

Most parents accepted the professional judgement of their children's teachers without question, and expressed themselves pleased with the report (Joshua's mother was tearful with pride). Parents with limited English, however, could only access the school's information, spoken or written, through an interpreter, and several ignored or mislaid the reports as soon as they received them. Only Abu Bokkar's father, having monitored the evaluations of his older children, expressed scepticism about the report.

Allocating children: the effects of school evaluations in Reception

Mrs Goode was committed to providing an environment which allowed every child to develop in every aspect. She recognized that individual children have very different needs, and that some children could benefit from extra nurturing, or subtle 'social engineering', while others needed additional support for their listening or language skills, or their physical strength and coordination. Her observations took note of all these concerns, and her planning showed how she tried to make time and space for individual needs.

Although Mrs Goode genuinely de-emphasized the 'core skills', seeing them as only a small part of the curriculum for this age group, the multiple top-down and outside-in pressures from government and society obliged her, as the year went on, to focus much of her provision on literacy and numeracy. In consequence, the ongoing assessments made in the classroom resulted in the children being grouped for tuition in these key skills. Inevitably, some children were assigned to more cognitively demanding activities (phonics, written maths) which were postponed for others until they appeared to be ready. But such 'specialization of knowledge to different groups' (Bernstein 1999), on the basis of early observations, also became the means of perpetuating differential rates of learning: a child was less likely to make progress in phonics if he or she was not in the phonics group.

The selection and grouping of children was influenced by several different, overt and covert, pressures. By Christmas certain groupings were explicit, and built in to the curriculum planning: both writing books and maths books were stored in separate piles so that children at different levels of skill could be seated and instructed together. Mrs Goode had specific criteria – their number concepts, their pencil skills – for allocating children to these groups.

During the spring term, children were grouped for one of three types of writing activity: emergent writing, in which the child's unaided letter strings were discussed with an adult and a note made of the child's writing intentions and strategies; dictation to an adult, followed by copying under; or dictation which the child was not required to copy. The allocation to groups did not always conform to the children's actual needs or intentions. The 'top group', as Becky called them, received lengthy input and discussion: they were asked to think about what they wanted to say, think about what the first word sounded like, and think about what the first letter might be. The middle and lower groups, after an initial discussion to elicit their 'sentence', were not invited to think any more about the writing process. One day's observations suggest the different levels of instruction received by different children:

Groups discussing town carnival with Cathy (p/t assistant), ready to write about it:

Troy: writes letter string, says he wants to put 'the sun came out for the carnival'; talks about the /s/ and the /f/, knows how to write /the/, writes /k/ for carnival. Writes 3 sentences altogether, thinks about words and sounds separately.

Joshua: chats about carnival, writes strings of /m/ and /y/, dictates 'the police were there at the carnival', copies it beautifully in large perfect letters.

Cathy has written sentence for **Rufia** and told her to write under. Rufia writes 'over' instead (incorrect letter formation), Cathy tells her again to write under but she writes her own letter string instead; later opts to do more writing, asks me to guess what it says; keeps on and on writing, while I sit and watch: 'These are my numbers, one of them is a 2' etc.

Tuhura: discusses carnival with Cathy; asked to suggest sentence, offers 'Teletubbies'. Draws a TV, colours it in and eventually starts to write her own letter strings, occupies herself happily for long period, unobserved by staff.

[Field notes]

The summer term phonics groups were similarly stratified, so that the same children, each week, were offered an afternoon of either programmed instruction or free play and singing. (The differential access to books and reading, based on teacher evaluation of children's 'interest' and parental demand, has been described earlier.)

While the constitution of these groups was open to discussion, that of the 'spontaneous' groupings was unconscious and for that reason perhaps more insidious. As Becky reported, 'It's just as it comes', but careful monitoring suggested that it was the same children who 'came' repeatedly. Without conscious intention, and in response no doubt to the pressures of getting groups 'done', the children who were chosen first were those who would pick up a new activity quickly, be amenable to instruction, be pleasant to interact with, and produce a product which could be used as a template for subsequent groups' efforts ('Let's look at the one Joshua did! Do you see how he's stuck all these bits down carefully?'). The exception to this rule was the attention given to children identified as having special needs (none of the case study group), who were given planned and targeted tuition for a few minutes every day or two. Thus the more middling and unremarkable children settled into a hierarchy – of teacher attention, and curriculum access – which soon came to seem entirely normal and natural, as well as being matched to children's level of demand: if children like Troy or Kelly asked repeatedly to be chosen for a group, they were likely to be selected quickly; those like Jemma or Tuhura, Jason or Mohammed, who did not demand to be included, were frequently left till last, squeezed in to the final group of the day. The constant pressure to 'deliver' the planned curriculum made any other course of action unrealistic.

Thus it was that evaluations of the 'whole child' – not simply their cognitive abilities and current skills – came to perpetuate the stratification of knowledge in the classroom. Amadur, whose entry assessments on the British Ability Scales were remarkably high, and whose curiosity and persistence might have marked him out as a successful learner, possessed none of the qualities which could guarantee him high levels of adult attention and curriculum access: he could not chat or discuss (in English), rarely made eye contact with adults, failed to understand the rules and routines of the classroom, almost never 'asked' to be included, was not easy to teach and *was*, frequently, easy to ignore. In addition, his poor attendance and punctuality meant that he often missed activities, and was therefore less well prepared for the follow-up. It was understandable, though regrettable, that he was so often ignored when groups were picked, and by the summer term was increasingly left to his own devices.

For the Bangladeshi children in particular, school policies served to reinforce all the other institutional pressures which produced this pattern. The extra help and support which Mrs Khan should have given them was frequently timetabled for the first half hour of the day, when the rest of the school was in Assembly. At this time, she was instructed to take her group of Bangladeshi children to complete an activity while Mrs Goode took the register session. This practice generated a range of outcomes, all unacceptable: either the children were absent (and missed the input anyway), or were late (and missed the essential introduction to the activity), or were present (and missed the class session which introduced the day's activities). For the rest of the day, these children – unless, like Khiernssa and Rufia and Abdul Rahman, they were highly motivated – were often left to support each other. Nothing that Mrs Goode could devise could make much difference to their situation.

Outcomes

At the end of the year, the children were not formally assessed by the school, and the information on their record cards and in their reports was often vague and imprecise. In order to construct more systematic evidence on their progress over the year, I reassessed the children using the Baseline descriptors and the Social Behaviour Inventory. These outcomes, inevitably, reflect my own subjective interpretation of the assessments. I made a conscientious effort, however, both to *look* for evidence of each of the descriptors, and to *record* only those aspects of each child's knowledge, skills and behaviour which I had observed. In this section, this information is combined with the evidence of school records and reports to present a picture of the children's outcomes, in each of the aspects already described.

Table 7.1 Group means for Sept / July Baseline scores, and progress during Reception

Group	September mean	July mean	Mean progress
Anglo children	14.9	26.5	11.6
Bangladeshi children	7.7	22.8	15.1
Whole group	11.5	24.8	13.3

Table 7.2 Children's individual gains in core skills, from September to July

	September score	Gain	July score
Troy	26	+9	35
Kelly	19	+9	28
Joshua	18	+13	31
Jason	14	+10	24
Sonia	13	+13	26
Jemma	11	+13	24
Abdul Rahman	11	+15	26
Katy	10	+16	26
Khiernssa	10	+18	28
Rufia	9	+17	26
Tuhura	9	+13	22
Cameron	8	+11	19
Abu Bokkar	8	+13	21
Mohammed	4	+15	19
Amadur	3	+15	18

(July mean score: 24.9; median score: 26)

Cognitive progress: children's gains in 'school knowledge'

When I reassessed the Baseline Core Skills in July, the bilingual children as a group had begun to make up their earlier disadvantage: as Table 7.1 shows, they had made greater progress over the year, from their lower starting point, than the monolingual group. Most had probably been under-assessed on entry, so the large gain in descriptors achieved in July (which includes a large gain in Speaking and Listening descriptors) may exaggerate their actual progress.

There was very little variation in the progress of boys and girls: the two groups had similar means on entry, but the girls made slightly more progress. Individual children's gains, shown in Table 7.2, indicate the movement within and across groups: the maximum possible score was 41 points.

Though each individual has made different gains, some patterns emerge:

- The three (Anglo) 'high scorers', who are still achieving well, are joined by Khiernssa, who has made the greatest overall gain of any child in the group.
- The four children who share the July median score of 26 have all made good progress, and Rufia and Katy have 'caught up' particularly well.
- The four children just below the median have made reasonable progress but seem unlikely at present to catch up with the median group.
- The three boys with scores below 20 are making insufficient progress to lift themselves from their low ranking: Amadur and Mohammed's apparently large gains build on extremely low entry assessments, while Cameron's modest progress was from a modest starting point.

By the end of Reception, the scores of the Anglo and Bangladeshi *groups*, though still divergent, are more integrated and overlapping than in September; there is relatively little sign of advantage due to gender or age. Although the Bangladeshi children have made more progress as a group, their initial disadvantage in the assessments seems to have evolved into a two-tier condition, in which some children are catching up with monolingual children while others are falling further behind. Despite the tendency of scores to close up over the year, in July Troy was still achieving twice as many items as Amadur.

Social development: becoming a successful pupil

Just as the school curriculum and 'official' assessments are the ultimate yardstick for children's cognitive gains, so assessments of their social development must reflect the ways in which they are viewed in the classroom. They are thus inextricably linked with the regulative discourse of the school. Possession of social capital for the 4-year-old in Reception means being a successful pupil, a well-adapted member of the class – in other words, possessing the recognition and realization rules of the *regulative discourse*. Several forms of evidence reveal the school's view of children's social development: the Personal and Social Development Baseline and the Social Behaviour Inventory (completed during their first term), and their end-of-year reports.

When evidence from all three sources is combined, three distinct clusters of personal characteristics emerge which define the qualities of a successful pupil. The three clusters have been described in earlier studies (Hogan *et al.* 1992; Melhuish *et al.* 2001) as 'compliant', 'prosocial' and 'independent' behaviour. The forms of words, and kinds of qualities, associated with each of these essential attributes are suggested here:

Source of description	'Compliant'	'Prosocial'	'Independent'
Baseline scales for Personal and Social Development	Behaviour	Relationships Cooperation	Initiative Independence
Social Behaviour Inventory items	Compliance	Sociability	Confidence
School reports (typical phrases)	Eager to please Helpful Responsible Responsive	Relates confidently Cooperative Collaborative Sensitive Caring	Confident Independent

Since the regulative discourse of the classroom is defined by Mrs Goode, it is above all her view of children's behaviour which defines their success as pupils. The children's reports indicate that, as with cognitive progress, the 'high scorers' on entry continued to perform well by these criteria, while some lower scorers gained ground, and the truly disadvantaged minority continued to lag behind in some or all respects. But my own observations suggested that some children's failure to observe the rules was more easily tolerated than others.

Although the children varied so much in their acquisition of desirable attributes, some children's status was consistent and unambiguous. Troy, for instance, achieved high ratings on the Baseline in October (*Initiative: 4, Relationships: 4, Cooperation: 4, Involvement: 4, Independence: 5, Behaviour: 4*) and the highest of any child on the Social Behaviour Inventory. His end-of-year report reaffirms these positive behaviours. Mrs Goode describes him as 'cooperative' and 'confident'; 'independent and can direct and maintain his own activity'; he can 'negotiate with his peers . . . cooperate . . . work collaboratively'; he is 'sensitive towards the feelings and moods of others and can be very caring and understanding towards them'. There is no hint of the wariness and watchfulness, or spiteful and sneering behaviour towards other children, which was sometimes recorded in Troy's observation notes. His 'deviance' (Waksler 1991) is overlooked or forgiven because he is in the main a highly regarded child. Troy's report contains more praise than any other (though it must be remembered that perhaps even more than others it was written with his mother in mind). A Year 1 teacher, reading the report, would hold high expectations of him.

Children who have made large social gains from a low Baseline include Abu Bokkar, Rufia and Katy. All three are praised in their reports on all three behaviour clusters. Their growth in confidence and social success is easy to detect:

> **Abu Bokkar:** *Always eager to please . . . independently directs and maintains his own activity . . . relates confidently to others . . . independent and assertive . . .*

Abu Bokkar, after a difficult first term in his social relationships, had made a best friend – an English boy who joined the class after Christmas – and had been tutored by this newcomer in a manner which brought success and satisfaction to both of them.

> **Katy:** *Her confidence has grown . . . more independence . . . cooperative . . . understanding of the needs of others . . . helpful, and responds to responsibility.*

Katy, whose unhappy and rather bad-tempered start to the year has been described, had flourished with the support of both friends and teachers. When the children became full-time pupils she was reunited with Barry, her best friend from playgroup, and in the course of the year established affectionate relationships with all the classroom adults too: her early difficulties seemed by July to have been a mere blip in Katy's generally favoured existence, although they might not have been resolved without close home–school communications.

> **Rufia:** *Cooperative and helpful . . . friendly and sociable . . . more independent . . . her confidence and social skills have developed.*

Rufia's initial low ratings are hard to explain unless by shyness. The role she quickly adopted as guide, friend and interpreter for Khiernssa enabled both girls to share their understanding of school behaviour and expectations: both frequently referred to things they knew about school because 'my sister told me', and both were emphatically encouraged by their fathers to take up learning opportunities. Once established in the classroom, Rufia applied all the responsible skills she had learned at home (organizing, tidying, looking out for others) and became an ideal pupil.

Most conspicuous for their failure to meet classroom requirements (according to their school reports) are Amadur, Mohammed and Tuhura. By the end of Reception, Amadur is viewed as neither compliant nor prosocial; Mohammed as neither compliant nor confident; while Tuhura is not prosocial, and her 'compliance' (as we see below) is viewed negatively. By comparison, Kelly's lack of compliance, and Jason's lack of sociability, seem partially 'forgiven', or mitigated by other aspects of their behaviour. None of these children, however, starts Year 1 as a successful pupil.

Learning dispositions: evaluating the secondary habitus

Children's changing habitus is an important aspect of their Reception experience, and an important indicator of their future school success. Since symbolic capital – both social and cultural – needs in Bourdieu's account to be 'invested' in order to achieve returns, the habitus which influences what the children *do* with their assets both contributes to their outcomes, and exists as an outcome in itself. It shapes their learning in Reception, and constructs the attitudes and aspirations they take with them into their National Curriculum years. Classroom observations of the children, like their end-of-year reports, suggest that some of them are able to make much more effective use of their capital than others.

On entry, the children displayed distinctly different dispositions, resulting from the wide range of family experiences and cultural influences present in their early years. Once settled in the classroom, their changing habitus was identified as the 'system of dispositions towards learning' they displayed in their interactions with the curriculum. In order to analyse the observational and other evidence of dispositions, the small group of attributes which seemed to be most frequently associated with learning were again identified. Since, for most children, being a good 'pupil' was an essential precondition for being a good 'learner', the three attributes associated with the pupil role – prosocial, compliant and independent behaviours – played an important part in this identification. Once in school, the dispositions towards learning which count are those appropriate to the classroom: having a strong disposition towards rote learning at the dining table, or watching alphabet videos, will not necessarily help the child to become a successful, active learner in Reception. To these characteristics was added the last of the Baseline descriptors, 'Involvement', an attribute frequently associated with early learning (Pascal and Bertram 1997; Siraj-Blatchford 1999).

These four desirable attributes embody the pedagogy of the classroom. In this particular setting, learning is consequent on children's independence (or confidence), their social relationships ('the lynchpin', as Mrs Goode says), their willingness to do as they are 'asked', and their ability to sustain or maintain an activity that they have chosen. In order to learn, we might say, the child must: choose activities, sustain them, interact with others, *and* conform to the implicit behavioural expectations of the setting. These four attributes are therefore the indicators of children's individual learning dispositions in school, and their relationship with early learning can be seen when we consider how such behaviour *looks,* and what might be its prerequisites.

Compliance	The child is settled, adapted and self-regulating; takes responsibility for self and environment; responds well to adult regulation.
[Prerequisite]	*Child feels 'at home' and accepted in classroom, and understands the rules and requirements.*
Prosociality	Child interacts with peers and adults, cooperates and collaborates, integrates self into activities and relationships, initiates and sustains conversations.
[Prerequisite]	*Child feels secure in relations with adults and peers.*

Independence Child selects and sustains a range of activities without adult direction, manages own learning, is purposeful and committed.

[Prerequisite] *Child feels secure and knowledgeable about her/his own abilities and about classroom activities and expectations.*

Involvement Child is absorbed and focused on activities for lengthy periods, is committed and curious, is not easily distracted.

[Prerequisite] *Child has been motivated to participate and is secure in own abilities or supported by more experienced others.*

Three critical factors emerge from these descriptions: the high level of interdependence between the conditions that are needed for each; the crucial importance to all of them of the child's confidence and self-esteem; and the significance of the adult's role in fostering such feelings. Together they make possible a description of individual children's strengths and weaknesses in developing a habitus conducive to school, rather than home, learning.

Children's individual habitus

Over the year, all the children were observed to display the characteristics needed for classroom learning, but the frequency of such observations varied dramatically from child to child and from month to month. Some children whose family practices bore no resemblance to classroom expectations were noticeably handicapped in the early months of school: children whose home concepts of time and space were fluid (Abu Bokkar, Amadur, Mohammed) spent many weeks lost and unfocused, unable to detect the implicit instructional discourse within the weak-framed regulative discourse. Some children (Tuhura, Jason, Amadur), in the course of following up the activities which motivated them – nursing dolls, building towers, or pouring water for long hours, became *less* involved in learning the skills of the official curriculum as the year proceeded.

There is clearly something wrong when children who are confident and competent learners at home become poor learners in the classroom. When this happens it seems clear too that additional support from school staff is needed. As the systematic observations revealed, however, it was precisely these children – children seen by the school as lacking some of the attributes necessary for learning (such as Tuhura and Jason) – who enjoyed the *least* support from adults, either in social or in instructional interactions. The children (such as Katy and Joshua) who received the highest levels of support were those who needed it the least. Some children who exhibited, in different ways, high levels of resilience and self-direction acquired from home (such as Kelly and Rufia) were able to become involved in activities without strong adult support. Others, including Abu Bokkar and Jemma, eventually became involved through the catalyst of a well-adapted 'best friend'. But the needs of the more undemanding children, who would have benefited from adult support (including the twins, Abdul Rahman, and Cameron), tended to be overlooked. In this classroom, the adults' capacity for attending to individual children's needs was severely constrained, both by the inappropriate class size and by the determination to offer every child literally hundreds of different curriculum experiences.

Two examples may suggest the different routes by which children can adapt to classroom learning. Both these children were developing a school-like habitus by the end of Reception.

Jemma's home environment was quite unlike the school setting. In her first term, her mother's and sisters' efforts at pre-school preparation (letters, numbers, colours, stories, writing her name) bore no fruit in the classroom: Jemma was recorded as mute or monosyllabic, vague and unfocused, solitary and flitting. She engaged in only the simplest forms of repetitive play. Jemma's integration into classroom learning took many months to achieve: it was only in the summer term, when she acquired a special friend, that she became purposeful and involved. Afeera was a shy but self-possessed little girl from a rather middle-class Pakistani home; though unobtrusive in the classroom, she knew all the rules of the discourse, and inducted Jemma into long sessions of concentrated playing. In her last months in Reception, Jemma's engagement with activities was prolonged, and she began to make rapid progress in learning to read and write.

Troy, with the advantages of high-quality, 'school-like' pre-school learning, appeared able to invest his curriculum knowledge to the full in the classroom. But this apparent mastery masked another kind of difficulty. Troy's anxiety and insecurity, visible in his wariness and isolation for much of his first term, was only slowly overcome. Mrs Goode's skilful nurturing, and high levels of attentiveness towards him, allowed him gradually to relax his guard. In November, observations record him as 'watchful' and 'uninvolved', as well as 'committed' and 'animated'; but in the spring term he is more often relaxed and unself-conscious, and in the summer has begun to pursue his own interests (manufacturing complicated artefacts from card and sellotape) with pleasure, *at the same time* as acquiring, with great rapidity, the literacy skills of which he had been so suspicious in his early months at school.

The classroom offered certain quite specific *ways* of learning to children, and an important aspect of acquiring a school-like habitus is adapting to these ways. While both Jemma and Troy did manage to adapt to the school pedagogy, other children were less successful. Children, like Amadur and Tuhura, who have to *un*learn their home concept in order to acquire the learning behaviours approved in school require explicit and expert support during this period of readjustment. There were times when they, and some other children who had the largest adjustment to make (to become compliant, prosocial, independent, and involved), appeared to have given up trying to understand what was expected of them, and turned to other ways of passing the time.

Acquiring a school-like habitus: more than just involvement

Some of the children's school reports, despite the positive construction Mrs Goode put on their behaviour, revealed their failure to meet the criteria for being an ideal-type pupil – criteria derived more from their adaptation to the regulative (social) than to the instructional (cognitive) discourse. Some children came to school from a home culture so dissimilar to the culture of the classroom that they faced huge obstacles in acquiring a 'school-like' habitus. Others, who appeared to have received more 'appropriate' training in their pre-school years, still experienced enormous difficulties in acquiring the necessary rules for being a Reception pupil. The experiences of two such pupils – Kelly and Tuhura – suggest the different ways that the pedagogic discourse could work to exclude pupils.

Kelly

Kelly's Baseline scores gave her a good start in Reception, and she displayed high levels of motivation and involvement in her chosen activities throughout the school year. She deliberately set herself tasks (doing a jigsaw puzzle with the pieces turned upside down; guessing shapes with her eyes shut) which would challenge her, and experienced mistakes and mishaps as a spur to try again and get things right. By July, however, she had made only moderate gains in cognitive skills and she never became a successful pupil. Her social behaviour, which was fairly unacceptable on entry, deteriorated as the year went on, and by July it was clear that her lack of compliance and low level of prosocial behaviour contributed to a negative view of her. Her report comments:

> [Compliance] . . . is not always prepared to cooperate . . . determined and on occasions defiant . . . able to listen to instructions when she chooses to . . .
>
> [Prosociality] . . . finds it hard to listen to the contributions of others . . . does need to learn to compromise . . .
>
> [Independence] . . . finds it difficult to direct and maintain her activities independently

Kelly was sent for time out, mostly for interrupting during register sessions, more than any other child except for a boy with serious behaviour problems; the experience did not seem to bring about any improvement in her behaviour. Though noisy and boisterous, she generally appeared to have some purposeful project in mind (as when, in her very first week, she persuaded a boy to trash the home corner with her so that they could set about sorting and rearranging it from scratch). Despite enlisting other mature girls as her nominal friends ('We're the Spice Girls!'), she preferred the activities of boys to her girlfriends' choices of drawing and colouring, tidying up, and wiping down tables.

In systematic observations, Kelly was continually active and engaged. She sustained her chosen activities for long periods, and had high levels of interaction with other children (72 intervals from 90). This contrasted with a low level of adult interaction: Kelly approached classroom adults for assistance or information rather than for social purposes. In this large class, the staff found her high-octane egoism disruptive and annoying: field notes refer to 'difficult' days, interspersed with periods of successful and prosocial behaviour.

> *18.11.97: a difficult day for Kelly – not helped by being cooped up indoors because of heavy rain – she was wild and wilful; sent out of the room at register time for rudeness and interruptions; later insinuated herself into a group of 4 at the community blocks and managed to take over, risking everyone else's life and limb as she created stunts, pulled away supporting planks, etc.; hurt by a falling brick, she howled piteously then recovered fast and manipulated Fatima and Toni into competing for her friendship . . .*

Kelly's most challenging behaviour occurred on days which began with scenes between her and Gaynor – in interview, she claimed that children go to school 'because their mum's had enough of them at home'. Her home experience had taught her to anticipate conflict rather than negotiation with adults, and so 'learning to be a pupil' meant learning to recognize a very different regulative discourse. In her self-assessment, she completed the sentence *I want to learn to* with 'be good in this class and in Year 1'. For all her confidence and outgoing behaviour, she was aware that she had failed to form the good relationships with staff which would ensure her success at school.

Though able to access the instructional discourse (she had attended nursery for a year before school, and was experienced in many classroom activities), she was constantly impeded by her battle with the regulative discourse. Her unwillingness to accede to the implicit rule – that children do as they are asked, because the adults who do the asking are always reasonable, and always right – was not easily forgiven, and she went into Year 1 with a poor reputation as a pupil.

Tuhura

What was it about Tuhura that made her behaviour so unsympathetic to the staff at All Saints'? This docile, placid child had been extensively prepared for school by her mother, and had visited the classroom frequently with her brother and sister; she settled in to school calmly and got on with the business of playing, especially in the home corner and in drawing and painting activities; she made every effort to speak English, and seemed well disposed towards the classroom adults. Yet her report depicts her as an unsatisfactory pupil:

> [Social] Tuhura finds it hard to become involved in an activity unless encouraged to do so by an adult . . . [she]will often observe activities or walk about without any real participation. When playing with her friends [she] is compliant and does not assert herself – on occasion the behaviour of others has upset her and she cries easily . . .

> [Cognitive] She is not always willing to become engaged and explore for herself . . . [she] has a good concentration span for a very limited range of activities.

Observations show Tuhura as generally a very busy and happy girl in the classroom. She applies her home learning whenever possible – by copy-writing beautifully, drawing and colouring carefully – and obeys her parents' instructions to sit quietly and wait for the teacher to tell her what to do. Above all, she uses the home corner and dolls to do what she has learned best: rocking babies, and stirring saucepans thoughtfully while carefully regulating the gas (she was the only child in the class to adjust the cotton-reel knob on the cooker while cooking, and turn it off before removing a saucepan).

This well-adapted behaviour, however, did not make Tuhura the kind of pupil the pedagogy requires (or the kind of child the school culture approves): she displayed low levels of energy, and disliked physical activity. She was above all passive: willing to learn, but expecting to be taught, to be told what to do, to be directed to activities. Her passivity – the product of her status and position in her own family, as well as of cultural expectations – made it very difficult for the staff to implement their own pedagogy with her, and their frustration sometimes showed. Tuhura was unable to adapt to the pedagogic discourse of the classroom alone; and Jamila was unable to instruct her.

Summary: accessing learning in the classroom

Children's progress throughout the Reception year shows the influence both of their pre-school experiences and of their continuing participation in two settings – two *microsystems* in a *mesosystem*, in Bronfenbrenner's terms. All the children continued to carry with them the beliefs and values of their parents, at the same time as they were subject to the beliefs and expectations of their teachers. Since parents and teachers rarely had the chance to share their views, some children were living in two worlds, with few links between them. These 4- and 5-year-olds showed enormous skills and powers of adaptation in managing this feat to the extent that they did.

The better children are adapted to the classroom, the more learning they can access: some of the All Saints' children went from strength to strength. These children, however, were succeeding at the expense of others whose own access to learning was diminishing as the year went on – children for whom the recognition and realization rules of the discourse were just too mysterious to access. Once their early assessments had taken place, such children were at risk of progressive exclusion from the activities, and the adult support, needed for academic learning.

UNDERSTANDING OUTCOMES; CHANGING PRACTICE

(8)

The past and the future

This final chapter serves two purposes. The first part pulls together and reviews the explanations for children's variable experience and progress which have emerged from the All Saints' case studies. In particular, it draws attention to the links between the micro effects of children's daily experiences at home and in the classroom, and the macro effects of structural inequalities and cultural difference. It shows that the distribution of power in society reaches out to influence the distribution of opportunities to groups and individuals; but also that the individual agency of children and families is evident, in the ways they seize or ignore such opportunities.

'Understanding the world', as we know, is only the beginning; the important thing is, where change is needed, to change our world. All Early Years practitioners share 'desired outcomes' for the children in their care: they hope to produce children with the dispositions, as well as the knowledge and skills, to become competent and confident learners. At the same time many realize that, despite their best efforts, children continue to be offered unequal chances. The second part of this chapter suggests ways of thinking about and changing practice which may contribute to better outcomes for all children.

Understanding outcomes: winners and losers

At the start of the twenty-first century, the winners and losers in education are identified increasingly early – at the age of 3, according to evidence from large-scale research (Melhuish *et al.* 2001). The All Saints' children's stories have shown some of the ways this early stratification comes about, and some of the ways it is contested by individuals. None of the children's school careers was 'determined' by their early experiences in the home, any more than the early experiences of their parents had 'determined' the ways they raised their children. But certain structural and cultural factors limited the options open to them – the range within which their individual agency could be exercised. These factors derive from the familiar triumvirate of race, sex and social class, which continues to distribute power and opportunities unequally to different social groups. These 'structural' variables subsume cultural variables: the reason that a working-class or a Bangladeshi cultural identity has little value within the national culture, and the culture of schools, is that these groups are without power in society. Unless we keep in mind the influence of these macro structures, and the ways in which they underpin the small details of children's daily lives, we are left with a bunch of 'explanations' for success or failure which do not hang together.

The following brief summary attempts to distinguish the workings of 'structure' and 'culture' in the lives of the All Saints' children.

Structural effects

Class and capital

In this group, the families experiencing greatest financial hardship (Jemma's and Amadur's) are also the most stressed in their day-to-day lives, and the most marginalized in their communities. The mothers (June and Asima) are the least resilient and most 'defeated' in their outlook, and would need persuading that their children have any chance of escaping from the cycle of problems they themselves experience. Poverty and stress are associated with frequent ill-health, poor attendance and poor punctuality in both families; both mothers express feelings of guilt over their perceived failure as parents, and avoid contact with the school.

All the families worried about job security, serious health problems and financial difficulties at some point during their child's first year in school. There is a close match between stress of this kind and the children's levels of attendance and lateness. The families with fewer problems simply got their children to school more often, and on time. While poor attendance (commonest among the Bangladeshi children) has a direct effect on the amount of education a child can receive, lateness (which is much more evenly spread across the groups) has the effect rather of disorienting the child, making it difficult for her or him to settle into an already busy classroom, and less likely that s/he would be 'picked' for adult-directed activities.

The relatively more 'middle-class' children (Katy, Joshua, Troy, Cameron) appeared physically healthier and better nourished than the children of families under severe stress, and did not suffer from coughs and colds. Like Kelly, who had similarly robust health, all had attended pre-school provision, where they may have acquired some immunity to minor infections, and all lived in relatively uncrowded conditions. Over-crowded housing and the absence of safe outdoor play spaces may have contributed to other children's lack of robustness, and low energy levels.

Race and ethnicity

Three of the Anglo children (Troy, Cameron and Kelly) were of dual English/African-Caribbean heritage. At the age of 4, none of them seemed particularly conscious of their heritage, and their mothers, who were alert to potential problems, were not aware of them having encountered racism. All Saints' has a substantial number of mixed-parentage families, and these three children seemed wholly assimilated within the classroom: to all intents and purposes, they were members of the majority community in the school.

Bangladeshi children have a very different experience of school. Though explicitly welcomed by the official ethos and policies, they are frequently marginalized by their differences from majority children – differences of language, behaviour and expectations. The exclusion of Bangladeshi parents is a form of institutional racism – a disadvantage built in to the school's policies and practices – of which teachers seem wholly unaware. Genuine problems of communication, and inadequate levels of bilingual support (not of the school's making) multiply the effects of other forms of 'difference'. Bangladeshi mothers' *and* fathers' effusive gratitude for my attempts to greet them and inquire after their families threw into relief the embarrassment and insecurity they were experiencing at being invis-ible to school staff.

The gesture of giving Mrs Khan responsibility for the needs of Bangladeshi parents, which helped to justify the inattention of mainstream staff, was a limited and double-edged benefit. Mrs Khan too was marginalized in the school community. She was unable to answer parents' queries except of the most trivial kind, unable to represent the aims and methods of the school, and unqualified to give advice on children's learning or other difficulties: the advice she gave was often at odds with that of the school, as when she informed me that she had told Amadur's mother 'If he's naughty, beat him and threaten him with a policeman.' Though she was valued by both parents and staff, she lacked power and authority. The help that she *could* have given the children in their early months in school – both language and emotional support – was impeded by the school practice of allocating her to the whole class in rotation, rather than directing her towards the Bangladeshi children in particular.

Bangladeshi parents' ignorance about school practices was matched by the school's ignorance of their home practices. Assumptions that most parents were not able to support their children's learning, or did not 'bother' to send their children to school regularly, or did not allow or encourage them to participate in certain ways, became taken-for-granted knowledge which located the blame for children's poor progress, or attendance, or participation, within the families or within Islamic culture.

Interactions with gender and family structure

Sex and gender influences were not evident in the children's overall attainments on entry, but the girls in this group made more progress than the boys over the year. All parents of girls, when asked if they felt boys and girls should receive the same educational opportunities, emphatically agreed:

> In this day and age? Definitely!
>
> (Maxine)

> It's not true that girls are more clever or boys are more clever, but they are sometimes different with their cleverness; we want our girls to learn like boys, same education – Layla can tell Salek things that he doesn't know.
>
> (Minara)

> Girls are cleverer than boys, but I think my little boy will be a bit clever – we've got the same priorities.
>
> (Jamila)

Nevertheless, there were indications that the upbringing and expectations of Bangladeshi girls had shaped their attitudes as well as their entry attainments. Baseline and BAS assessments suggested a limited experience of spatial and logical activities (bricks, construction, puzzles) as well as of exploratory and messy activities. All the Bangladeshi girls preferred to avoid traditional boys' activities, and activities where boys were the majority, whereas the Anglo girls mixed with boys and girls fairly equally, and enjoyed construction and logical and mathematical tasks. Boys in the group were as likely as girls to be found drawing, writing, reading, threading beads, and 'cooking' or dressing up in the home corner, though the playground behaviour of both sexes was much more gendered.

One way in which gender differences took effect was through the work of siblings. Here, the experience of the All Saints' families suggests that the disadvantage sometimes associated with membership of large families may be turned to advantage. Among Bangladeshi families this was undoubtedly the case: children with teenage siblings had benefited from their fluency in English, as well as from their attentiveness in playing with them, reading to them, and passing on what they had learned at school. Both brothers and sisters had been expected by their parents to teach and care for the little ones. The children who were *least* well prepared for school were those without this input from siblings, while those in large families appeared to receive plentiful attention from their parents.

When families were coping well, Reception children seemed to thrive on the additional care of siblings. Only when the family was in difficulties, or the older children were themselves causing concern, did the 4-year-olds appear to lose out: this was the case with Jemma's teenage sisters, who both became pregnant during the year, and the twins' older brothers, who were in trouble with the police. The differences between Sonia's and Jason's experiences, at home and at school, suggest an accumulation of effects. Sonia, who was effectively parented and tutored by her older sister, also displayed prosocial and compliant attributes in school, and made close relationships with her peers and with Becky. Jason, who shared a room with his wayward older brothers, and stayed up late with them in the evenings, became steadily more isolated: at school, he was regarded as unsocial, and received little individual attention.

An equally important aspect of family structure is extended-family support, which sometimes plays a decisive role in enabling parents to cope in times of difficulty. Most socially disadvantaged families are likely to require outside support from time to time, and there was a real difference between those who were isolated and helpless at times of crisis, and those who could call on the support of grandparents and other relatives. The assurance of family or community support is a form of social capital which strengthens the family habitus, and consequently the child's.

Cultures and pedagogies

Parental experiences and ethnotheories

The effects of parental educational experience prove more complex than large-scale studies indicate. Importantly, it is the quality rather than the quantity of mothers' experience of schooling which influences their understanding of education for their child. Many Bangladeshi mothers express positive views of the teaching they received and of their own success as pupils, and have correspondingly high expectations for their children's school success. The Anglo mothers describe less successful school experiences, and are considerably more cautious in anticipating success for their children. Children's dispositions towards learning bear the imprint of their parents' experiences and expectations, and the Bangladeshi children could be advantaged by their families' strong orientation towards learning. This advantage is outweighed, however, by aspects of the children's early preparation, which turns out to be poorly matched to the school's pedagogic discourse.

Beliefs about play are a major aspect of cultural difference in the parents' views of childhood. Most Anglo families, at some level, approve of play as the *modus vivendi* for young children, and the medium for learning. The Bangladeshi families, however, assume their children will spend their time at home apprenticed to adults, observing and participating in family activities: they regard their play as a passing phenomenon to be indulged rather than encouraged. When Bangladeshi parents consciously prepare their children for school they expect them to be motivated, not by fun or pleasure, but by an awareness of their duty to work hard and learn. Anglo parents, with their rather half-hearted acceptance of the pedagogy of play, attempt to sneak in instruction without their children noticing. But they generally provide the kinds of educational games, toys and tapes their children will encounter in the classroom.

Beliefs about the value of independence and autonomy in childhood are also strongly evident. None of the Bangladeshi families appear to have in mind any developmental 'milestones' for their children: they are not anxious for their child to become independent at an early age, and see no need for children to 'make choices', or take the initiative, as the Reception pedagogy requires. Anglo parents' views are closer to those of the children's teachers in this matter: for them all, starting school is the start of being a 'big' boy or girl, as many mothers (including Alison) make clear to their children:

> That's what makes me mad; [Cameron] can do it but he doesn't want to, he's so stubborn. In the mornings he makes us late, he says '4 boys can't do their own shoes', '4 boys don't do their own trousers' so I say '4 boys won't go to school then!'

Bangladeshi mothers, by contrast, seem happy for their children to remain dependent and cared for. Many would rock and cradle their 4-year-olds on their knees while talking to me, and questioned the need for them to start school at such a tender age.

The groups' home pedagogies are additionally informed by their concept of an 'intelligent' child: the Sylheti families' image is of a child who 'listens', passively, whereas Anglo parents perceive intelligence more actively as 'how they do things', 'the way they talk to you'. Children's behaviour in the classroom reflects such beliefs, which are not equally compatible with the beliefs of teachers.

Home language and literacy

All the mothers described their children as fluent speakers of their first language, although both monolingual and bilingual children were sometimes silent or monosyllabic in the classroom. The bilingual children experienced varying degrees of disadvantage in starting school through the medium of an additional language. Children with siblings in their teens had heard both English and Sylheti from an early age, and were able to acquire conversational fluency in English quite rapidly. Those who had not were in differing degrees denied access to aspects of the curriculum, and of the pedagogic discourse. Both their sense of security and self-esteem, and their cognitive learning, must have suffered in consequence. The Bangladeshi children's communication difficulties at school may have been enhanced by the parental instruction to 'keep quiet and listen': Anglo parents were far more likely to have told their children to 'speak up', 'tell the teacher' and so on, in keeping with the high priority they gave to 'speaking confidently' as part of children's preparation for school.

All the families in the study engaged in some regular household 'literacy events', but the frequency of these, and their relationship to the official literacy practices of the dominant culture and the school, showed huge variation. The children whose homes contained the least print, and the fewest mark-making materials, also had the least access to environmental print in the shops and streets, and may have received their largest 'print' input from their constant TV viewing.

School culture

For the majority of children in the class, the 'school effects' of the Reception year were overwhelmingly positive: children made good gains in knowledge and skills, and many developed positive and enthusiastic attitudes towards school and learning. But the Reception experience was not equally favourable for all the children. The school ethos, and the pedagogic discourse of the classroom, worked to differentiate and stratify children in ways which reinforced the inequalities they displayed on entry.

From the children's point of view, the relation of their symbolic (social and cultural) capital to their progress in Reception can be understood through the following formulations: once the children start school,

- *social capital*, to be effective, requires possession of the recognition and realization rules of the *regulative* discourse;
- *cultural capital*, to be effective, requires possession of the recognition and realization rules of the *instructional* discourse.

The social and cultural capital of children's family and community environments, rich and relevant as it may be within these settings, has little transfer value unless the above conditions are met. The language and literacy practices of the home; the child's preparation for school learning; local cultural knowledge acquired in the community; knowledge of the mainstream mass culture which holds sway outside the school walls – none of these are 'useful knowledge' for children unless they can negotiate their incorporation into the classroom. Some children managed this effectively, and their home practices and home news – Troy's 'flashcards', Kelly's performance of Spice Girls numbers, Cameron's new baby – became a part of *all* the children's school knowledge and experience. For many children, however, their home learning was left outside the classroom.

As we have seen, this was not because the staff were ignorant of the effects of social disadvantage, of racial and cultural discrimination, of discontinuities between school and home, or of differences between families. It was rather because they genuinely believed that the solution to these inequalities lay in creating 'a good Early Years environment', which would allow all children to follow their own interests and discover their own motivation and learning style. Such environments, though theoretically 'inclusive', are founded in an *exclusive* western view of childhood, and a specifically western view of learning, which for some children creates a barrier to learning in the classroom. They operate a strong though invisible pedagogic discourse whose rules are not taught, but must be learned by children and their families before they can begin to make progress.

The child who lacks the appropriate rules has difficulty in transferring capital from home to school, and in transforming the habitus acquired in the home into a secondary habitus fitted to the practices of the school. In consequence she or he may be allocated both to a restricted curriculum, and to a restricted range of relationships with school adults. Once such differentiation has occurred, the child's chances of accelerated progress and a steep learning curve may progressively diminish.

Boundary effects

The implications for children's learning of boundaries between home and school have been discussed at some length. The boundaries take many forms, and their effect tends to be cumulative: children who are disadvantaged through *one* form of boundary maintenance (such as transfer of information about the child from home to school) tend to be disadvantaged in other respects (such as frequency of home–school reading activity). Children whose parents and siblings, home culture and history accompany them (physically or symbolically) to school build up a secure and reciprocal relationship with school adults which is the basis for rapid development and progress, and for the multiplication of home–school connections. Children who are cut off from their home and family background when they start school have less chance of creating all the links necessary for such relationships, or of fully assimilating the school ethos.

The effect of the school ethos in excluding some parents through including others is to deprive certain children of the constant attention and access which other children regard as a right. Included parents demand that their children are regularly read to, included in new activities, and given help with academic and social difficulties as they arise. The children of these parents are themselves demanding, and get to be chosen and included first in new groups and activities. Excluded parents make few or no demands of teachers, and their children follow suit: most Bangladeshi children, like their parents, were never seen to demand attention, help or inclusion. At group times they sat quietly listening, or whiled away the time in covert communication with each other. Jemma, similarly, whose mother avoided communication with staff and made no requests or demands on Jemma's behalf, remained for many months a passive recipient of whatever attention was available to her after other children's more vocal needs had been met.

I have tried to indicate that most participating parents have done everything in their power to promote their children's learning. Some of them, however, have very little power, and their economic, social and cultural capital is inadequate or inappropriate to the task. All Saints' staff are aware of parents' circumstances, and aim to accommodate the very different kinds of knowledge and skills which children bring with them to school, through providing an environment that benefits all children. The children's experiences and outcomes show that this is not enough. Without wishing to, the school continues to distribute knowledge unequally to children from different backgrounds, offering its scarce resources to those who demand them most vociferously (children and parents), rather than to those in greatest need. Individual children's ability to acquire the recognition and realization rules of the pedagogic discourse, and so access new knowledge and skills, continues to depend on the relationship between their family and their school. Thus hidden differences in children's early cultural learning at home become visible differences in their ability to access the culture, and the knowledge, of the classroom.

Changing practice: looking forwards

The All Saints' study is already history. As the new century began, a new Foundation Stage curriculum was launched for 3- to 5-year-olds, and new policies were in place, designed to reduce educational failure and social exclusion through strategies for improving schools, and reducing child poverty. The steady reduction in class sizes in Early Years classrooms meant that adult–child ratios like those at All Saints' were no longer permitted. The impact of measures such as Sure Start, and the expansion of childcare and tax credits, on the long-term outcomes of children from poorer communities will take some time to show. Meanwhile, Reception classes continue to welcome thousands of new 4-year-olds every year, and more of them, every year, are from poor and minority backgrounds. Whatever government is able to accomplish in the longer term, the challenge for practitioners is immediate, and recurrent.

Twenty-first century policy in the UK conspicuously fails to understand, and accommodate, culture. Party political wrangles over *multi*culturalism only scratch the surface of the daily experience of children from all the different class and cultural backgrounds which the UK, like all advanced industrial societies, contains: food and festivals are still the defining characteristics of culture in this particular discourse. It remains, as it always has, for practitioners to be in advance of policy makers – both better informed, and more thoughtful. The following sections indicate some priorities, and some strategies, for cultural inclusiveness.

I have chosen to highlight three aspects of Early Years education which might become more inclusive: the processes of pedagogy, the understanding of culture, and the involvement of parents. But all of these are obviously interlinked: listening to parents (unless they are just like ourselves) compels us to examine our beliefs and pedagogy, and question some aspects of the culture created in our classrooms; reflecting on pedagogy compels us to examine its cultural underpinnings, and relate these to the culture of parents. All of these aspects are closely linked too to the persistently reflective style of most Early Years teachers. For change to occur, however, that reflectiveness must extend to recognizing the impact of the distribution of power at a wider, societal, level on the ways in which schools make learning available to children.

The role of practitioners

Practitioners in Early Years settings, like all educators, face ever-increasing pressures, and ever-increasing levels of public accountability. In addition to managing classrooms, they now have to manage budgets, curriculum requirements and policy changes, and cope with the scrutiny of the government inspection service. In the face of these pressures, it may seem unreasonable to suggest additional priorities and challenges to current practice. But the reality, as many teachers have found, is that efforts to work *with* the culture of pupils, and *with* their families, in their education, have the effect of reducing the stress of classroom life, as well as of improving children's short- and long-term outcomes.

Reflecting on pedagogy

Teachers, like everyone else, are shaped by the cultural contexts of their personal and professional biographies. For many, the taken-for-granted beliefs acquired in their professional training and working contexts, which derive from the 'ideological tradition' identified by Bennett and colleagues (1997), have set firm boundaries for their views of child development and learning. In the western industrialized world it has until recently been hard to step outside the narrow cultural perspective of the 'play pedagogy'.

That step has become possible in part through the voicing of ethnic minority parents' oppositional views. African-Caribbean parents in the UK, like African-American parents (Delpit 1990; Harry *et al.* 1996) have articulated their demands that their children should be *taught* (and taught to behave) rather than left to learn, and self-regulate. They have argued that the relative under-achievement of their children is the direct consequence of teachers' failure to teach them, as well as of the climate of under-expectation and institutional racism in schools. It is not necessary to agree with these parents to recognize the disturbing truth which underlies their claim: that in matters of pedagogy Early Years practitioners have been overwhelmingly culture-blind. Our conviction that our own understanding of children's development and learning – whether Piagetian or Vygotskyan – is universally acceptable, and appropriate, demonstrates an astounding ethnocentricity. Logically it implies (as Mrs Khan understood, in her apologetic defence of 'our system') that cultures which differ from our own in their fundamental educational and developmental beliefs produce children and adults who are inferior in their education and development. Unless we are willing to make that claim, it seems clear that we must open our minds to other views of pedagogy.

The broader and more diverse perspective which results from recent challenges to universalist notions (Mallory and New 1994) may not require a radical change in current practice, but does require a fuller awareness of that practice and its consequences. As Wood and Attfield argue (1996: 54), 'We cannot assume that playing leads to learning or that play is the only valuable means of learning in early childhood' – but we often do. What is more, in making that assumption we may be making a self-fulfilling, reality-defining prophecy: for as Bruner demonstrates, 'If it is held widely enough to be possible that man *can* learn from experience, then we arrange our conduct and our institutions in such a way that it is *necessary* that he learn from experience' (1986: 138). In so doing – in constructing classrooms where it is necessary to behave in certain prescribed ways in order to access knowledge – we are making it harder for some children to learn.

Re-examining beliefs and practices may require practitioners to question many cherished terms and concepts – such as 'freedom to choose', for instance. Bennett and colleagues point out:

> There is an assumption that when children make their own choices, learning becomes a much more powerful activity. But in reality this is dependent on the range of choices available, the amount of interaction with more knowledgeable others (including peers and adults), the provision of supportive resources and the potential for activity to be connected with worthwhile learning.
>
> (1997: 13)

Providers of a child-centred and play-based pedagogy need to ask how well it meets conditions like these, and how well such provision meets the needs of children from different backgrounds. The 'ideological tradition', which assumes that it is natural for children to choose, play and display intrinsic motivation to explore, may pathologize children whose early socialization has taught them to stand back and observe, or to join with adults in their activities. In such circumstances it is clear that practitioners have a duty to explain, to both children and families, how and why they expect their learning to come about. (If play is to be the medium of instruction, such explicitness must extend to the pedagogy of play. If freedom and independence are the school's markers for a 'learner', these concepts too must be made explicit.)

But first we should consider (without fearing a return to direct instruction or 'rote learning') whether the pedagogy of child-initiated free-flow play, which derives from the Piagetian as well as the 'ideological' tradition, is the best way to bring about learning in young children. We might start by revisiting Vygotsky (1978), whose work challenged but did not topple the pre-eminence of Piaget ('the towering Jean Piaget', as Bruner calls him, 1996: xiii) in Early Years pedagogy. We should remind ourselves that Vygotsky's account of 'learning through play' offers a theory of instruction which, seeing learning as co-constructed by the participants of an activity, names the 'more experienced other', whether child or adult, an *instructor*. 'Instruction' is essential in Vygotsky's vision because worthwhile learning is that which precedes, and leads, development, rather than that which follows development. Accordingly, instead of waiting for children to demonstrate their 'readiness' to learn, we make it our job to bring them to that point: 'the idea of "readiness" is a mischievous half-truth', in Bruner's words, 'largely because it turns out that one *teaches* readiness or provides opportunities for its nurture, and does not simply wait for it' (1966: 29). Motivation, similarly, need not come from the child, in a spontaneous flowering of curiosity, but can be supplied by the instructor – the child's learning partner. For while both Vygotsky and Bruner recognize the contribution made by innate curiosity to exploration and learning, neither assumes that curiosity alone can drive learning. If it did, the child's learning would be at the level of her or his development, instead of ahead of it; and the child would lack the 'tools' (such as language, symbols and skills) to move forward. In any case, as Bruner suggests, 'we get interested in what we get good at. In general, it is difficult to sustain interest in an activity unless one achieves some degree of competence' (1966: 118). The child who fails to 'get good at' something – reading, catching, block building – will soon lose any motivation she or he may have felt.

The 'demand-learning' model, which waits for the child to display motivation, is seen from the perspective of other pedagogies, including those of many non-western cultures, as an abnegation of the teacher's duty to teach – to motivate the child by instruction, in its broadest sense. Because instruction rarely, in Vygotsky's view, takes the form of explicit face-to-face transmission: more often it takes the form of the co-construction of meanings which occurs when two or more individuals (of whom one is 'more experienced') share an activity, or perform a task together. This task, in fact, is quite likely to be a playful one: for Vygotsky, play is 'the leading source of development in the pre-school years' (1976: 537), the means of handing over to children the 'cultural tools' they will need for subsequent learning.

Research has shown us that play has many purposes, and that learning is often accomplished through play (and not just among the playful young). On the whole, too, it confirms Vygotsky's supposition that the most effective learning takes place when children's play is supported by adult conversation and participation (Sylva *et al.* 1980; Hutt *et al.* 1989). If the different kinds of learning which can result from different kinds of play, and the supportive role of adults and 'more experienced' peers, are explained to parents, they may be less distressed by their children's reports that they 'play all day' at school. But before such exchanges take place, practitioners must be honest about the range of play experiences they make available. This includes being prepared to admit that not all of children's playful activities are educative, though they may have plenty of other benefits. Parents are happy to know that their children are happy; but when they see their child, every day, wandering to the same activity – the sand, the water tray or the Lego – they may be sceptical about the relationship of play and learning. (If they happen to see them throwing the sand and water, or fighting with Lego guns, they may be still more reluctant to submit their child to this type of educational setting.) These same parents may be content to observe their child counting cups of water, or balancing scoops of sand, with an adult; or working on tasks, such as jigsaws or mosaics, which have a demonstrable 'right' outcome. This form of play can be recognized as 'instruction' by parents from all backgrounds.

A theory of play must explicitly include a theory of instruction: it must show that play activities are, in Wood and Attfield's term (1996), not only 'hands-on' but also 'brain-on'. Only in this way can we ensure that children are able to access knowledge and skills through their play, and that parents are able to see that this is so. Without interaction, with more experienced peers or with adults, children may be left at their current stage of development; or, when they construct new knowledge through solitary (Piagetian) exploration, may lack the opportunity to represent it, to themselves or others, through the cultural tool of language.

Multiculturalism or culture creation?

What has 'including culture' to do with 'multiculturalism'? It depends, of course, on the way we define culture – whether as a collection of artefacts, beliefs and practices characteristic of a particular group, or as a way of life which we continually remake for ourselves, as individuals, families, communities and societies. The first definition was applied, with limited success, in the multicultural policies of the 1970s and 1980s. Schools and teachers were assessed as multicultural on the basis of their books and posters, their multi-ethnic dolls and home corner paraphernalia, and their teaching about faiths and festivals. Much of this work was enjoyable and informative for children, and gratifying for parents who felt that their way of life was becoming more visible within the classroom – even if their gifts and goodwill were rather taken for granted by schools.

But it is questionable whether it brought real improvements in the academic progress and life chances of the children whose culture was celebrated. Being admired for your use of chopsticks, or your Bhangra dancing, may have a limited impact on your reading and writing skills; some teachers will remember with embarrassment the days when African-Caribbean children were praised for their athleticism or their sense of rhythm.

Nor was this version of multiculturalism without problems for home–school relations. On the one hand it alienated some white working-class parents, whose own already tenuous relationship with their children's schools seemed further threatened by poorly presented school policies, and curricula which appeared to be substituting Diwali for Christmas. On the other hand, minority parents who were developing an increasingly sophisticated understanding of their children's school careers were not impressed by the time spent on celebrations, preferring their children to spend more time on basic skills. The increasingly restrictive National Curriculum, during the 1990s, further marginalized the teaching of non-British cultures.

If we turn to other conceptions of culture – those of Vygotsky and Bruner, and also of Bernstein – we are presented with a different task: the task of developing a pedagogy which is culturally inclusive at a more fundamental level. Such a pedagogy engages with children, not on the basis of specific cultural practices (food, faith and festivals; texts, scripts and artefacts) but on the basis of a shared experience of learning – what Bruner famously calls 'joint culture creation': 'It is not just that the child must make his knowledge his own [*sic*], but that he must make it his own in a community of those who share his sense of belonging to a culture' (1986: 127). From this perspective, the fact that teachers and their children come from increasingly diverse backgrounds is no obstacle to sharing the activity of learning.

The theory of instruction Bruner proposes says nothing about class or ethnic culture. Instead it describes the *processes* of education as 'culture making'. The culture that is made and shared is a 'microculture' or 'sub-community' (1996: 21), derived from classroom practices which ensure a common focus of attention: pupil and instructor attending jointly to the activity at hand. Bruner's concept extends, through every level of education, the concept of 'joint involvement episodes', the term used by Schaffer (1992) to describe the ways in which babies and their caregivers develop a shared focus on an object or activity outside their mutual relationship.

As children grow older, such episodes are facilitated by, and themselves facilitate, the development of linguistic skills, both as spoken language and as thought. An example from my field notes – a day trip which included a visit to a children's zoo – illustrates the opportunities for learning which become possible when such a shared focus is momentarily created:

Stopped to feed the ducks with Amadur – new experience for him: throwing bread and having them respond brings him to peak of excitement; listens to my comments about ducks ('He's a big boy' etc.) and his own language flows, 'Hello big boy, come here big boy'; points to other waterfowl to learn from me if they are ducks, and tries to memorize 'coots' and 'moorhens'. When we moved on to the caged birds he was enthralled, called me back constantly so we stayed behind while he talked and pointed ceaselessly, 'Look Mrs Brooker look Mrs Brooker, all of them big, all of them daddy, all of them blue, one two three four five blue, this one baby, this one yellow, one two three four yellow.'

This was the most vivid learning experience I observed for Amadur in the whole year, and was the occasion when he chose to speak more English than at any other time. It was a rare moment in which Amadur could control the agenda, and identify himself as a *learner*. The significance of this experience was evident when we met up with other groups for lunch: Amadur sought out Mohammed, took him to one side and stood recounting the incident to him, with all the passion his facial expressions and hand gestures could communicate (and with key English words incorporated in the flow of Sylheti). As Vygotsky and others have shown, once you have learned something you are able to instruct others; and at this point Amadur was, in relation to Mohammed, an expert. The incident demonstrates, graphically, the benefits of a few minutes spent with a child in constructing a shared focus – in effect, a shared agenda and experience of learning – in comparison with the months given over to experiencing the packed Reception curriculum. This experience of 'joint culture creation' can be contrasted with the common scenario of schooling: one in which children are 'busy' at a succession of activities, and their teacher tells them they are 'having fun' (while telling herself, and their parents, that they are learning).

Although school outings, as the All Saints' staff recognized, offer particularly good opportunities for incidents like this, they can happen at any time. What is needed is for adults to make themselves available to children; to be as alert to the focus of children's interests as good caregivers are to the direction of a baby's gaze. (Mrs Goode's insistence on 'constant input, constant stimulation' from adults accompanying school trips was understandable, but it risked initiating another familiar scenario, in which adults talk too much and listen too little.) In the classroom, Amadur developed a method for enlisting adult support for his learning, by transporting objects to an adult and signalling his wish to know what they were called, or how they worked, and he consistently reported his findings ('that mummy lion, that daddy lion') to Mohammed, as on this occasion. But most of the time the adults were too busy 'getting through groups' to be approached.

To return, finally, to Bernstein on this issue: his famous aphorism, 'If the culture of the teacher is to become part of the consciousness of the child, then the culture of the child must first be in the consciousness of the teacher' (1970: 31), points to a similar understanding of culture. Bernstein was concerned to remedy the educational under-achievement of children from low-income groups, *not* by adopting a curriculum which included working-class cultural practices, but by recognizing and engaging with the language and the perspectives which children from different backgrounds bring to school with them. Unless school adults are alert to children's own ways of seeing and understanding and representing the world to themselves, it is unlikely that the child will ever manage to identify with the school's, and teacher's, ways of seeing.

Building connections

In recent years, work with practitioners on the relationship of play and learning (Bennett *et al.* 1997; Anning and Edwards 1999) has offered many examples of more effective ways of working with young children. Few parents will be aware of this new and fuller understanding of the play pedagogy. The All Saints' parents are probably not untypical in their view of their children's classroom activities: like the participants in Tizard and colleagues' (1981) study, they see children filling bottles with water and emptying them, while their teachers see children working on volume and capacity. But as with pedagogy, so with parental involvement: school practices, which seem normal and natural to those inside the school culture, can only be changed through a process of reflection, and an honest scrutiny of the effects of those practices. Since staff at All Saints' are unaware of the extent of the barriers between the culture of the school and the cultures of children's homes, they believe it is possible for all parents, if they are interested, to participate in their children's schooling. Mothers like June and Gaynor, who are uncomfortable on school premises, are deemed to have opted out. Families like Khiernssa's and Tuhura's who do not communicate via the 'book bag' are deemed to give no support. Meanwhile, Tizard and colleagues suggest, 'an "open" policy is probably an excellent way, whether intentional or not, to forestall parental criticisms' (1981: 69).

In order to rethink home–school relations, schools have to take at least three steps. The first is to set aside, at least temporarily, the possible benefits of parental involvement to the *school* (classroom help, library work, fund-raising activities) and consider instead the probable benefits for children and families. The second step is to make a deliberate effort, at whole-school level, to raise staff awareness of the range of roles undertaken, and the range of contributions made by families in their children's development. Staff who believe, as Becky did, that some parents 'haven't done much' for their children need the opportunity to reflect with colleagues on the range of cultural knowledge, as well as physical skills, which all children have acquired before they come to school. The third step is to devise, again at whole-school level, strategies for supporting those roles, and benefiting from those contributions.

To identify parental roles, we may wish to return to Epstein's typology of parental involvement (1987), which recognizes the multi-level and many-faceted nature of parenting. Transforming this recognition into a restructured school policy requires a more reciprocal understanding of home–school links, such as that proposed by Hornby (2000). Hornby's model offers two equal zones of parent involvement. One of these depicts the various needs of parents: *communication* from the school (needed by all parents), *liaison* with staff (needed by many parents), *education* (needed by some parents), and *support* (needed by a minority). The other zone sets out parents' strengths. These include: *knowledge* of their own child (true of all parents), *collaboration* in teaching (most parents), providing *resources* for the school (some parents) and, for a minority, a role in *policy making*. In such a model, every adult in the child's two environments is recognized as having a role, and as contributing in important ways to the child's learning. A school whose home–school policy is built on such an inclusive framework is able to demonstrate to parents the importance of their varied roles, and the value of all their contributions. It thus has a basis for developing appropriate relationships with parents from all backgrounds, in all phases of their child's involvement in education.

Home–school policies, as all teachers know, quickly founder when a minority, or even majority, of parents, fail to respond to the school's invitation to participate. Here again, Epstein's work is particularly helpful in reporting strategies which have been shown to be effective with 'uninvolved' families. Much of the success of home–school links rests on the quality of *Type 2* involvement: communication between parents and families about the child, and about the curriculum. For this Epstein suggests multiple strategies – not one quick-fix solution, but a battery of methods for establishing and maintaining communication with all the parents whose children attend school in disadvantaged communities. All of them – handbooks, videotapes, audiotapes, translations, early morning meetings, twilight meetings, interpreters, phone-ins, home visits, year-group meetings – require additional time, effort and resources from teachers. Each and any of these strategies may only include two or three additional parents; but every new parent who becomes involved strengthens the teacher's hand, enhances her confidence in working with the child, and contributes to 'making sense' for the child. Epstein's review of research (1996) concludes that teachers' attitudes are crucially important to the success of such strategies, and that, when teachers are proactive in involving parents, children become more involved in their learning, and parents believe them to be better teachers.

Epstein, like other researchers in the field (Bastiani 1993), prefers 'partnership' as the term for family–school relationships. The difficulty with this term should be evident: partners enjoy equal power and status in their relationship, and parents and teachers, in many cases, do not.

Here again the power differential between professionals (with some allegiance to the middle-class mainstream in society) and parents from poor and minority communities has to be confronted. Sharing points of view, and recognizing differences, is never going to be easy when it involves the powerful giving away some of their power to the less powerful. Early Years practitioners, however, have a better chance than most educators, because there are more frequent opportunities for exchange between those who share the care of the youngest children. It is up to schools as a whole, as well as individual practitioners, to ensure that the opportunities are offered to, and taken up by, all parents.

Teachers and children learning cultures

While academic research has a role to play in improving understanding, and changing practice, the most effective way forward may be research by practitioners – either in collaboration with external projects, or independently. Practitioner research – particularly action research – can effect more rapid improvements, because it cuts out the intermediate stages (publication, dissemination, teacher training) between understanding and changing practice. Projects which work within institutions, and with practitioners, such as the Effective Early Learning Project (Pascal and Bertram 1995) enable teachers' habits of reflection and self-appraisal to effect improvements in the quality of children's learning from an early stage of the school's involvement. Once again, the evidence is that Early Years practitioners voluntarily undertake additional 'workloads' if they see them as instrumental in improving their own practice, and their children's experience.

Equally valuable, however, is the 'local' research knowledge gained through reflective sharing within an early childhood setting. Few education systems make provision for such extended sharing by practitioners (Reggio Emilia in Italy, and Te Whariki in New Zealand are well-known exceptions). But where staff prioritize such reflective activities, the effort is rewarded, both in the new knowledge and insights made available to adults, and (in the Reggio and the High/Scope models) in the insights children acquire into their own learning.

Recruiting children as co-investigators enhances both children's metacognitive powers, and their power and status within the learning community. Clark and Moss (2001) offer a methodology for inviting children as young as 3 and 4 to express their views on their educational setting. As a class teacher (Brooker 1996) I found that the time spent in explicitly consulting children about their learning in Reception – in listening to, scribing and discussing children's points of view – was repaid in many ways: in the rapid rise in metacognition among the children, in the resolution of misunderstandings, and in the relaxation of pressures in the classroom. Handing over decision-making powers to children, even decisions about their curriculum and pedagogy, proved to be far less risky than I had feared. Vivian Paley's work (1984, 1993) offers the best, and best-known, example of the benefits over time of negotiations with children on the rules governing their classroom behaviour, as well as on issues arising from their shared and individual experiences.

Schools and pre-schools have to set their own priorities, in a climate in which the existing, statutory, burden on teachers can already seem overwhelming. Those who choose to prioritize, for instance, improved communication with parents, and a broadening of the school culture, can hope to be repaid in many ways: with relationships which are more relaxed and less stressful, with children who are more receptive, and with outcomes which offer children better chances in life. Empowering parents and children may mean disempowering (to some extent) the professionals who work with them, but this can be a liberating, rather than a threatening, experience. The 'power' over parents and children which a teacher relinquishes proves to be no longer necessary when hierarchical relationships are replaced by relationships of exchange and cooperation.

The 'Open Door' that is needed in schools, then, is one through which multiple forms of communication can occur: between home and school, parent and teacher, teacher and child. As these first, structural, barriers are removed, the process of sharing cultures becomes increasingly possible – even 'normal' and 'natural'. But schools and teachers will only succeed in creating shared understandings, a jointly owned culture, and a continuity of experience for children by seeing their role as working with families and communities, rather than simply with children. In doing so, they will open their own minds to an infinitely broader range of learning cultures.

APPENDIX

Though essentially ethnographic, the All Saints' study used a range of methods to create data on the home and school experiences of the children involved. These are summarized below.

Access to All Saints' Primary (January–July 1997)
For two terms I 'volunteered' in the Reception and Key Stage 1 classrooms once a week, becoming familiar with the staff and the school's ethos and organization at the same time as becoming a familiar face to some of the parents and children. For a few weeks I was also employed as a Section 11 teacher working with Bangladeshi pupils in Key Stage 1 and 2.

Access to families (June–September 1997)
As the September Reception roll began to take shape, a tentative selection of case study children was made, and their families were approached. Anglo families were contacted at school or in the nearby playgroup because I was able to introduce myself. Bangladeshi families were contacted through home visits with Mrs Khan, who interpreted.

Field notes (September 1997–July 1998)
Informal observations were made from the moment children started arriving in the classroom, until they had been collected, from one to four days a week, all year. One day each week I was 'fully participant' (taking responsibility for activities with the children) and wrote notes as and when possible, with the full knowledge of the children (who were very used to being observed by all classroom adults).

Entry assessments (September–October 1997)
LEA Baselines (with the whole class) and research assessments (with the case study children and any others who demanded to have a go) were undertaken, and behavioural assessments completed.

Parent interviews (September–October 1997, March–April 1998)
Taped semi-structured discussions lasting about 90 minutes were conducted with all parents. The first sequence used Mrs Khan to interpret for Bangladeshi families. She was not available for the second sequence, which relied instead on the efforts of fathers, grandfathers, teenage siblings and aunties to communicate with Bangladeshi mothers.

Daily diaries
Parents completed an account of their child's previous day at home, with prompts from me ('What time did he wake up? Did he do anything before he had his breakfast? What was he doing while you were doing the washing?' and so on). I kept diaries of each child's day at school about once a term.

Parent questionnaires
All parents in the class were asked to complete a questionnaire (in English and/or Bengali; unaided, or with my help) which briefly covered the topics discussed in the parent interviews. The 35 completed questionnaires enabled more general findings about the children and families in the class to be used as a context for the case study children.

Systematic observation (November, February, June)
After initial piloting, timed and pre-coded observations were made in these three months of children's behaviour, children's take-up of core curriculum activities, and child–adult interactions.

Child interviews (December, March–April)
Children were invited to sit and talk to me quite formally, to tell me 'things about school that teachers are not sure about'. Mrs Khan interpreted for the Bangladeshi children. All responses were taped but also written down so that the process was transparent to the children.

Document analysis (January–March 1998)
Ofsted reports, school policies and curriculum plans, and 'letters home' were scrutinized.

Analysis of children's products and ongoing records (September 1997–July 1998)
Children's drawing and writing samples were collected regularly while working with them, and pages from their maths and writing books were photocopied. Reading and maths records and home–school reading sheets were also photocopied.

Staff interviews (March–April 1998)
Lengthy taped discussions were held with all the staff working in the classroom, and the head teacher. Some interviews carried over to a second session.

End-of-year assessments (July 1998)
Children were reassessed on the Baseline and the Social Behaviour inventory, and completed a self-assessment sheet with their teacher. Reports to parents were scrutinized.

Debriefings with parents (July–August 1998)
Parents were asked for their response to their child's report, and their view of the child's year, and thanked for their participation (all received packs of photos of their child, taken during the year). They were asked if they had any questions for me, but the only question really was 'Will you write a book/will my child be in it?'

GLOSSARY OF
THEORETICAL TERMS

Note: BB: Basil Bernstein; PB: Pierre Bourdieu

Capital (PB)
Capital of all kinds derives its power from its exchange value – what it can 'buy' for its owner. While the power of **economic capital** is universally acknowledged, Bourdieu emphasizes the equally potent forms of **symbolic capital**:
Cultural capital refers to not only the 'knowledge' acquired through schooling, but also the other forms of knowledge and skills, and ways of being and behaving, which confer status and privilege in society. These might include membership of elite organizations, possession of artistic talents, experience of foreign travel, or simply information about the school system and how to make the best use of it. Cultural capital also includes the accomplishments of families, especially mothers, in the early education of their children, 'the domestic transmission of cultural capital' (Bourdieu 1997: 48).
Social capital combines both the individual's own status and esteem (in his or her local community or the broader society) and the reflected esteem of others in the individual's social network. Parents, for instance, gain social capital through their own occupations (such as doctor or lawyer) or through connections with people like these, on whom they can call for information, recommendations or references. Such networks enable the individual to enjoy, vicariously, the esteem which belongs to others.

Classification and framing (BB)
Classification describes the strength of the boundaries between aspects of a setting. It may refer to the strict boundaries between school subjects in traditional school, or the tolerance of 'non-school' forms of dress, language and behaviour by pupils. Where clear demarcation exists – between home and school, boys and girls, parents and teachers, English and Maths – classification is said to be strong.

Where boundaries are blurred, as in open-plan schools with an integrated day, classification is said to be weak.

Framing describes the strength of the rules which operate within the classifications. These may govern relationships and behaviour, styles of learning, or educational aims and objectives. Within a strongly classified 'lesson' (such as the new Numeracy Hour), the framing of classroom behaviour and activities may be weak (children chatting and circulating, choosing maths games, listening to tapes of number rhymes) or strong (children under direct instruction from a teacher or engaged in narrowly-defined tasks).

Field (PB)

Fields are locations in which capital is acquired and evaluated, and power is contested. The child's earliest field is the home or immediate locality, where s/he acquires and learns her/his position within that field. The *capital* acquired in this setting is then transferred to the new 'field of education', in which it may be evaluated as legitimate (useful knowledge and skills for school) or illegitimate (knowledge and skills which serve no useful function in school). But each field is viewed as a 'site of struggle': in the case of schools, children struggle to achieve recognition, and qualifications, which they can take with them into the fields of adult life.

Habitus (PB)

Habitus is the 'system of dispositions' acquired by the child in her/his earliest years in the home (the **primary habitus**) and transformed through successive experiences in new fields into a **secondary habitus** (adapted to the requirements of schooling) and tertiary or subsequent habituses adapted to further training and employment. Though unique to the individual, any child's primary habitus will be shaped by the collective habitus of her/his family, including the experience of membership of a particular social class or cultural group. In the field of education, the habitus is specifically a 'system of dispositions towards learning', which includes the child's motivation, self-concept, confidence, learning styles and expectations of success.

Knowledge (local and official) (BB)

Bernstein's terms for what Bourdieu might call cultural capital. **Local knowledge** refers to the knowledge and skills which are acquired in the home, and are necessary and appropriate within that context. It includes family, community and perhaps religious beliefs and practices.

Official knowledge is the knowledge and skills required for school success. These may or may not coincide with the learning acquired in the home. Without them the child will not make good progress in the school system.

Pedagogic discourse (BB)

Pedagogic discourse describes the entire process of bringing about learning in a setting. A number of subordinate terms, together with *classification* and *framing*, enable a more finely-tuned description of the pedagogy:

The **instructional discourse (ID)** contains the rules for how to *learn* in a classroom, but these rules (about 'work' and 'play', asking and answering questions. filling in work-sheets) are always and importantly embedded in the **regulative discourse (RD)**, which contains the rules for how to *behave* in a classroom. The regulative discourse is therefore the most important aspect of the pedagogic discourse as a whole: it defines the approved ways of being a *pupil*, which need to be adopted before that pupil can become a successful *learner*.

Recognition rules and **realization rules** play an important part in the child's acquisition of the discourse of the setting. With their help, the child is able first to make sense of (*recognize*) the way learning is enacted in the classroom, and then to act appropriately as a learner (*realize* the discourse). In practice, this might mean that the child first identifies 'what the teacher is on about' when s/he asks questions, and then works out how to produce approved answers to such questions.

Strategies (PB)

Though not used as a technical term, **strategies** are an important aspect of Bourdieu's account of educational and social processes because his use of the term explicitly rejects Bernstein's reliance on **rules** of various kinds. For Bourdieu, the lives of individuals and families are constituted of their selection of strategies from a range of options. The particular range available to a child or family will be constrained and limited (by the habitus, as well as by structural conditions in the family's circumstances), but choices are always available, and such choices allow members of disadvantaged communities to break out of the expectations society holds for them.

REFERENCES

Anning, A. and Edwards, A. (1999) *Promoting Children's Learning from Birth to Five: Developing the New Early Years Professional.* Buckingham: Open University Press.

Ball, S. (1981) *Beachside Comprehensive.* Cambridge: Cambridge University Press.

Barrett, G. (1986) *Starting School: An Evaluation of the Experience.* London: AMMA.

Bastiani, J. (1993) Parents as partners, in P. Munn (ed.) *Parents and Schools: Customers, Managers or Partners?* London: Routledge.

Bennett, N., Wood, L. and Rogers, S. (1997) *Teaching Through Play.* Buckingham: Open University Press.

Bernstein, B. (1970) Education cannot compensate for society, *New Society,* 26 February.

Bernstein, B. (1971) *Class, Codes and Control, Volume 1: Theoretical Studies Towards a Sociology of Language.* London: Routledge and Kegan Paul.

Bernstein, B. (1975) *Class, Codes and Control, Volume 3: Towards a Theory of Educational Transmissions.* London: Routledge and Kegan Paul.

Bernstein, B. (1990) *Class, Codes and Control, Volume 4: The Structuring of Pedagogic Discourse.* London: Routledge.

Bernstein, B. (1996) *Pedagogy, Symbolic Control and Identity.* London: Taylor & Francis.

Bernstein, B. (1999) Verbatim record of seminar presentations, Institute of Education.

Bernstein, B. and Young, D. (1973) Social class differences in conceptions of the uses of toys, in *Class, Codes and Control, Volume 2.* London: Routledge and Kegan Paul.

Berthoud, R. (1998) *Incomes of Ethnic Minorities.* Colchester: Institute for Social and Economic Research.

Bhatti, G. (1999) *Asian Children at Home and School: An Ethnographic Study.* London: Routledge.

Biggs, A. and Edwards, V. (1992) 'I treat them all the same': Teacher–pupil talk in multiethnic classrooms, *Language and Education*, 5 (3): 161–76.

Blatchford, P., Burke, J., Farquhar, C., Plewis, I. and Tizard, B. (1989) Teacher expectations in infant school: associations with attainment and progress, curriculum coverage and classroom interaction, *British Journal of Educational Psychology*, 59: 19–30.

Bourdieu, P. (1990a) *The Logic of Practice*. Cambridge: Polity.

Bourdieu, P. (1990b) *In Other Words: Essays Toward a Reflexive Sociology*. Cambridge: Polity.

Bourdieu, P. (1997) The forms of capital, in A. Halsey, H. Lauder, P. Brown and A. Wells (eds) *Education, Culture, Economy, and Society*. Oxford: Oxford University Press.

Bourdieu, P. and Passeron, J-C. (1977) *Reproduction in Education, Culture and Society*, London: Sage.

Boyle, M. and Woods, P. (1998) Becoming a proper pupil: bilingual children's experience of starting school, *Studies in Educational Ethnography*, 1: 93–113.

Bronfenbrenner, U. (1979) *The Ecology of Human Development*. Cambridge, MA: Harvard University Press.

Brooker, L. (1996) 'Why do children go to school?': consulting children in the Reception class', *Early Years*, 17 (1): 12–16.

Bruner, J. (1966) *Towards a Theory of Instruction*. Cambridge, MA: Harvard University Press.

Bruner, J. (1986) *Actual Minds, Possible Worlds*. Cambridge, MA: Harvard University Press.

Bruner, J. (1996) *The Culture of Education*. Cambridge, MA: Harvard University Press.

Bryant, P., Bradley, L., Maclean, M. and Crossland, J. (1989) Nursery rhymes, phonological skills and reading, *Journal of Child Language*, 16: 407–28.

Byrne, B. and Fielding-Barnsley, R. (1995) Evaluation of a program to teach phonemic awareness to young children: a 2- and 3-year follow-up and a new preschool trial, *Journal of Educational Psychology*, 87: 488–503.

Chavkin, N. and Williams, D. (1993) Minority parents and the elementary school: attitudes and practices, in N. Chavkin (ed.) *Families and Schools in a Pluralistic Society*. Albany, NY: SUNY Press.

Clark, A. and Moss, P. (2001) *Listening to Young Children: The Mosaic Approach*. London: National Children's Bureau.

Coles, G. (1998) *Reading Lessons: The Debate over Literacy*. New York, NY: Hill and Wang.

Connolly, P. (1998) *Racism, Gender Identities and Young Children: Social Relations in a Multi-Ethnic Inner-City Primary School*. London: Routledge.

Crozier, G. (2000) *Parents and Schools: Partners or Protagonists?* Stoke on Trent: Trentham Books.

Cummins, J. (1989) *Empowering Minority Students*. Sacramento, CA: California Association for Bilingual Education.

Delpit, L. (1990) The silenced dialogue: power and pedagogy in educating other people's children, in N. Hidalgo, C. McDowell, C. and E. Siddle (eds) *Facing Racism in Education*, Cambridge, MA: Harvard University Press.

DES (Department of Education and Science) (1988) *Education Reform Act*. London: HMSO.

Drummond, M-J and Nutbrown, C. (1996) Observing and assessing young children, in G. Pugh (ed.) *Contemporary Issues in the Early Years*. London: Paul Chapman.

Drury, R. (1997) Two sisters at school: issues for educators of young bilingual children, in E. Gregory (ed.) *One Child, Many Worlds: Early Learning in Multicultural Communities*. London: David Fulton.

Dwivedi, K. (1996) Race and the children's perspective, in R. Davie and D. Galloway (eds) *Listening to Children in Education*. London: David Fulton Publishers.

Elliott, C. (1996) *British Ability Scales II*. Windsor: NFER-NELSON.

Emblen, V. (1988) Asian children in schools, in D. Pimm (ed.) *Mathematics, Teachers and Children*. London: Hodder and Stoughton.

Epstein, J. (1987) Towards a theory of family–school connections: teacher practices and parent involvement, in K. Hurrelman, F. Kaufmann and F. Losel (eds) *Social Intervention: Potential and Constraints*. New York, NY: DeGruyter.

Epstein, J. (1996) Perspectives and previews on research and policy for school, family and community partnerships, in A. Booth and J. Dunn (eds) *Family–School Links: How Do They Affect Educational Outcomes?* Mahwah, NJ: Lawrence Erlbaum.

Epstein, J. and Dauber, S. (1991) School programs and teacher practices of parent involvement in inner-city elementary and middle schools, *Elementary School Journal*, 91: 289–303.

Fetterman, D. (1989) *Ethnography Step by Step*. Newbury Park, CA: Sage.

Gewirtz, S., Ball, S. and Bowe, R. (1994) Parents, privilege and the education market-place, *Research Papers in Education*, 9 (1): 3–29.

Gillborn, D. and Gipps, C. (1996) *Recent Research on the Achievement of Ethnic Minority Pupils*. London: HMSO.

Gregory, E. (1993) What counts as reading in the Early Years classroom?, *British Journal of Educational Psychology*, 63: 214–30.

Gregory, E. (ed.) (1997) *One Child, Many Worlds: Early Learning in Multicultural Communities*. London: David Fulton.

Gregory, E. and Biarnes, J. (1994) Tony and Jean-Francois: looking for sense in the strangeness of school, in H. Dombey and M.M. Spencer (eds) *First Steps Together*. Stoke-on-Trent: Trentham.

Gregory, E. and Williams, A. (1998) Family literacy history and children's learning strategies at home and at school: perspectives from ethnology and ethnomethodology, in G. Walford and A. Massey (eds) *Studies in Educational Ethnography: Children Learning in Context*. London: Jai Press.

Hannon, P. (1987) A study of the effects of parental involvement in the teaching of reading on children's reading test performance, *British Journal of Educational Psychology*, 57: 56–72.

Harry, B., Allen, M. and McLaughlin, M. (1996) 'Old fashioned good teachers': African American parents' views of effective early instruction, *Learning Disabilities Research and Practice*, 11 (3): 193–201.

Harste, J., Woodward, V. and Burke, C. (1984) *Language Stories and Literacy Lessons*. New York, NY: Academic Press.

Heath, S.B. (1982) What no bedtime story means: narrative skills at home and school, *Language in Society*, 11: 49–76.

Heath, S.B. (1983) *Ways With Words: Language, Life and Work in Communities and Classrooms*. Cambridge: Cambridge University Press.

Heath, S.B. (1986) Questioning at home and school, in M. Hammersley (ed.) *Case Studies in Classroom Research*. Milton Keynes: Open University Press.

Hogan, A., Scott, K. and Bauer, E. (1992) The Adaptive Social Behaviour Inventory: a new assessment of social competence in high-risk 3 year olds, *Journal of Psychological Educational Assessment*, 10: 230–9.

Holden, C., Hughes, M. and Desforges, C. (1996) Equally informed? Ethnic minority parents, schools and assessment, *Multicultural Teaching*, 14 (3): 16–20.

Hornby, G. (2000) *Improving Parental Involvement*. London: Cassell.

Howarth, C., Kenway, P., Palmer, G. and Street, C. (1998) *Monitoring Poverty and Social Exclusion: Labour's Inheritance*. York: Joseph Rowntree Foundation.

Hughes, M., Wikely, F. and Nash, T. (1994) *Parents and their Children's Schools*. Oxford: Blackwell.

Huss-Keeler, R. (1997) Teacher perception of ethnic and linguistic minority parent involvement and its relationship to children's language and literacy learning: a case study, *Teaching and Teacher Education*, 13 (2): 171–82.

Hutt, S., Tyler, S., Hutt, C. and Christopherson, H. (1989) *Play, Exploration and Learning: A Natural History of the Preschool*. London: Routledge.

ILEA (Inner London Education Authority) (1981) *Race, Sex and Class*. London: ILEA Research and Statistics Branch.

Jackson, B. (1979) *Starting School*. London: Croom Helm.

James, A. (1998) Play in childhood: an anthropological perspective, *Child Psychological and Psychiatric Review*, 3 (3): 104–9.

Joly, D. (1986) *The Opinions of Mirpuri Parents in Saltley, Birmingham, About Their Children's Schooling*. Warwick: Centre for Research in Ethnic Relations.

Jowett, S., Baginsky, M. and MacNeil, M. (1991) *Building Bridges: Parental Involvement in Schools*. Slough: NFER-NELSON.

Lareau, A. (1987) Social class differences in family–school relationships: the importance of cultural capital, *Sociology of Education*, 60: 73–85.

Levine, J. (1996) *Developing Pedagogies in the Multilingual Classroom*. Stoke-on-Trent: Trentham Books.

Lightfoot, C. and Valsiner, J. (1992) Parental belief systems under the influence: social guidance of the construction of personal cultures, in I. Sigel *et al.* (eds) *Parental Belief Systems: The Psychological Consequences for Children*. Hillsdale, NJ: Lawrence Erlbaum.

Lubeck, S. (1985) *Sandbox Society*. London: Falmer.

Luke, A. and Cale, J. (1997) Learning through difference: cultural practices in early childhood language socialisation, in E. Gregory (ed.) *One Child, Many Worlds: Early Learning in Multicultural Communities*. London: David Fulton.

Macleod, F. (1985) *Parents in Partnership: Involving Muslim Parents in their Children's Education*. Coventry: CEDC.

Mallory, B. and New, R. (eds) (1994) *Diversity and Developmentally Appropriate Practices*. New York, NY: Teachers College Press.

Melhuish, E., Sylva, K., Sammons, P., Siraj-Blatchford, I. and Taggart, B. (2001) *The Effective Provision of Pre-School Education (EPPE) Project, Technical Paper 7: Social/Behavioural and Cognitive Development at 3–4 years in Relation to Family Background*. London: University of London Institute of Education.

Merton, R. (1972) Insiders and outsiders, a chapter in the sociology of knowledge, reproduced in W. Sollors (ed.) *Theories of Ethnicity: A Classical Reader*. Basingstoke: Macmillan.

Moles, O. (1993) Collaboration between schools and disadvantaged parents: obstacles and openings, in N. Chavkin (ed.) *Families and Schools in a Pluralistic Society*. Albany, NY: SUNY Press.

Mortimore, P., Sammons, P., Stoll, L. and Ecob, R. (1988) *School Matters: The Junior Years*. Wells: Open Books.

Newson, E. and Newson, J. (1963) *Infant Care in an Urban Community*. London: Allen & Unwin.

Newson, E. and Newson, J. (1968) *Four Years Old in an Urban Community*. London: Allen & Unwin.

Newson, E. and Newson, J. (1976) *Seven Years Old in the Home Environment*. Harmondsworth: Penguin.

Ogilvy, C., Boath, E., Cheyne, W., Jahoda, G. and Schaffer, R. (1990) Staff attitudes and perceptions in multi-cultural nursery schools, *Early Child Development and Care*, 64: 1–13.

Osborn, A. and Milbank, J. (1987) *The Effects of Early Education: A Report from the Child Health and Education Study*. Oxford: Oxford University Press.

Paley, V. (1984) *Boys and Girls: Superheroes in the Doll Corner*. Chicago, IL: University of Chicago Press.

Paley, V. (1993) *You Can't Say You Can't Play*. Cambridge, MA: Harvard University Press.

Pascal, C. and Bertram, A. (1995) *Evaluating and Developing Quality in Early Childhood Settings: A Professional Development Programme*. Worcester: Amber Publishing.

Pascal, C. and Bertram, A. (1997) *Effective Early Learning: Case Studies in Improvement*. London: Hodder and Stoughton.

Plowden Committee (1967) *Children and their Primary Schools*. London: HMSO.

Pollard, A., with Filer, A. (1996) *The Social World of Children's Learning: Case Studies of Pupils from Four to Seven*. London: Cassell.

Pollard, A. and Filer, A. (1999) *The Social World of Pupil Career*. London: Cassell.

Pollard, A., Broadfoot, P., Croll, P., Osborn, M. and Abbott, D. (1994) *Changing English Primary Schools? The Impact of the Education Reform Act at Key Stage One*. London: Cassell.

Power, S. (1998) Researching the 'Pastoral' and the 'Academic': An Ethnographic Exploration of Bernstein's Sociology of the Curriculum, in G. Walford (ed.) *Doing Research about Education*. London: Falmer.

Pratt, S. (1994) The educational experiences, views and aspirations of ethnic minority mothers under 30, *Multicultural Teaching*, 12 (2): 29–32.

Rampton Committee (1981) *West Indian Children in Our Schools: Interim Report of the Committee of Inquiry*. London: HMSO.

Rashid, N. and Gregory, E. (1997) Learning to read, reading to learn: the importance of siblings in the language development of young bilingual children, in E. Gregory (ed.) *One Child, Many Worlds: Early Learning in Multicultural Communities*. London: David Fulton.

Reay, D. (1998) *Class Work: Mothers' Involvement in their Children's Primary Schools*. London: UCL Press.

Reeves, F. and Chevannes, M. (1988) The ideological construction of black underachievement, in M. Woodhead and A. McGrath (eds) *Family, School and Society*. London: Hodder and Stoughton.

Rist, R. (1970) Student social class and teacher expectation: the self-fulfilling prophecy in ghetto education, *Harvard Educational Review*, 40 (3): 411–51.

Rogers, C. (1989) Early admission, early labelling, in C. Desforges (ed.) *Early Childhood Education*. Edinburgh: Scottish Academic Press.

Rogoff, B. (1990) *Apprenticeship in Thinking: Cognitive Development in Social Context*. New York, NY: Oxford University Press.

Rutter, M. and Madge, N. (1976) *Cycles of Disadvantage.* London: Heinemann.

SCAA (School Curriculum and Assessment Authority) (1996) *Desirable Outcomes for Children's Learning.* London: HMSO.

Schaffer, R. (1992) Joint involvement episodes as contexts for cognitive development, in H. McGurk (ed.) *Childhood and Social Development: Contemporary Perspectives.* Hove: Lawrence Erlbaum.

Sharp, R. and Green, A. (1975) *Education and Social Control. A Study in Progressive Primary Education.* London: Routledge and Kegan Paul.

Siraj-Blatchford, I. (1994) *Praxis Makes Perfect.* Ticknall: Education Now Books.

Siraj-Blatchford, I. (1999) Early childhood pedagogy: practice, principles, and research, in P. Mortimore (ed.) *Understanding Pedagogy and its Impact on Learning.* London: Paul Chapman.

Siraj-Blatchford, I. and Brooker, L. (1998) *Parent Involvement Project in One LEA: Final Report.* London: Institute of Education.

Stevenson, H., Chen, C. and Uttal, D. (1990) Beliefs and achievement: a study of black, white and Hispanic children, *Child Development*, 61: 508–23.

Strand, S. (1999a) Pupil background and Baseline assessment results at age 4, *Journal of Research in Reading*, 22 (1): 14–26.

Strand, S. (1999b) Ethnic group, sex and economic disadvantage: associations with pupils' educational progress from Baseline to the end of Key Stage 1, *British Educational Research* Journal, 25 (2): 179–202.

Stuart, M. (1995) Prediction and qualitative assessment of 5 and 6 year old children's reading: a longitudinal study, *British Journal of Educational Psychology*, 65: 287–96.

Stuart, M., Dixon, M. and Quinlan, P. (1998) Learning to read at home and at school, *British Journal of Educational Psychology*, 68: 3–14.

Swann Committee (1985) *Education for All.* London: HMSO.

Sylva, K., Roy, C. and Painter, M. (1980) *Childwatching at Playgroup and Nursery School.* London: Grant McIntyre.

Taylor, D. and Dorsey-Gaines, C. (1993) *Growing Up Literate: Learning from Inner-city Families.* Portsmouth, NH: Heinemann.

Teale, W. (1986) Home background and young children's literacy development, in W. Teale, and E. Sulzby (eds) *Emergent Literacy: Writing and Reading.* Norwood, NJ: Ablex.

Tizard, B., Mortimore, J. and Burchell, B. (1981) *Involving Parents in Infant and Nursery Schools.* London: Grant McIntyre.

Tizard, B. and Hughes, M. (1984) *Young Children Learning.* London: Fontana.

Tizard, B., Blatchford, P., Burke, J., Farquhar, C. and Plewis, I. (1988) *Young Children at School in the Inner City.* London: Laurence Erlbaum.

Tomlinson, S. (1984) *Home and School in Multicultural Britain.* London: Batsford.

Vincent, C. (1996) *Parents and Teachers: Power and Participation.* London: Falmer.

Volk, D. (1998) Siblings as teachers: co-constructing activity settings in a Puerto Rican home, *Studies in Educational Ethnography*, 1: 69–91.

Vygotsky, L. (1976) Play and its role in the mental development of the child, in J. Bruner, A. Jolly and K. Sylva (eds) *Play: Its Role in Development and Evolution.* Harmondsworth: Penguin.

Vygotsky, L. (1978) *Mind in Society: The Development of Higher Psychological Processes.* Cambridge, MA: Harvard University Press.

Wade, B. and Moore, M. (1993) *Bookstart in Birmingham.* London: Book Trust.

Waksler, F. (1991) 'Dancing when the music is over: a study of deviance in a kindergarten classroom, in F. Waksler (ed.) *Studying the Social Worlds of Children: Sociological Readings*. London: Falmer.

Waterhouse, S. (1991) *First Episodes: Pupil Careers in the Early Years of School*. London: Falmer.

Weis, L. (1992) Reflections on the researcher in a multicultural environment, in C. Grant (ed.) *Research and Multi-Cultural Education: From the Margins to the Mainstream*. London:

Wells, G. (1986) *The Meaning Makers*. London: Hodder and Stoughton.

Willes, M. (1983) *Children into Pupils*. London: Routledge and Kegan Paul.

Wolfendale, S. and Topping, K. (1996) *Family Involvement in Literacy: Effective Partnerships in Education*. London: Cassell.

Wood, E. and Attfield, J. (1996) *Play, Learning and the Early Childhood Curriculum*. London: Paul Chapman.

Woods, P., Boyle, M. and Hubbard, N. (1999) *Multicultural Children in the Early Years*. Clevedon: Multilingual Matters.

Wright, C. (1992) *Race Relations in the Primary School*. London: David Fulton.

Wright, C. (1993) Early education: multiracial primary school classrooms, in R. Gomm and P. Woods (eds) *Educational Research in Action*. London: Paul Chapman.

INDEX

PROMOTING CHILDREN'S LEARNING FROM BIRTH TO FIVE
DEVELOPING THE NEW EARLY YEARS PROFESSIONAL

Angela Anning and Anne Edwards

- What sort of literacy and numeracy curriculum experiences are best suited to the needs of very young children?
- How can early years professionals bridge the current divisions between education and care to provide an approach to young children's learning which draws on the strengths of both traditions?
- How can these professionals be supported as they develop new practices which focus on young children as learners?
- What strategies are most effective in involving parents with their children's development in literacy and mathematical thinking?

Drawing upon research carried out in a range of early years settings, Angela Anning and Anne Edwards seek to address these questions. The emphasis throughout is upon enhancing the quality of children's learning and providing support for the practitioners who work with them. The complexity of addressing the various cognitive, social, physical and emotional learning needs of young children is discussed and practical strategies to develop children's learning are explored with a particular focus on communication and mathematical thinking. Published at a time of dramatic change in pre-school provision in the UK, the book will both inform and reassure early childhood professionals. It will be important reading for managers, administrators and all professionals working in early years and family services and an accessible text for those studying for childcare and education, and teaching qualifications.

Contents
Introduction – Setting the national scene – Integration of early childhood services – The inquiring professional – Young children as learners – Language and literacy learning – How adults support children's literacy learning – Mathematical learning – How adults support children's mathematical thinking – Creating contexts for professional development in educare – Early childhood services in the new millennium – Bibliography – Author index – Subject index.

192 pp   0 335 20216 0 (Paperback)   0 335 20217 9 (Hardback)

SCHOOLING THE BOYS
MASCULINITIES AND PRIMARY EDUCATION

Christine Skelton

This book explores where masculinity is in primary schools. It has been argued by some commentators that a contributory factor to boys' underachievement is the predominance of women teachers in primary schools which has led to classroom management and teaching styles which 'favour' girls. As this book shows, primary schools produce a range of masculinities for pupils to draw on. A number of questions are raised: what are the tensions for boys between what the school expects from them as 'school pupils' and how they are drawn to behave as a 'boy'? How does a primary school produce certain masculine styles in its day-to-day routines? In what ways do girls respond to male practices and behaviours in the primary school classroom? The book aims to provide readers with an understanding of the background literature on boys and schooling, an insight into 'masculinity-making' in primary schools, and to offer strategies for developing gender-relevant programmes.

Contents
Introduction – Part one Context and theoretical perspectives – A history of boy's schooling – Theorizing masculinities – Boys and primary schooling: a feminist perspective – Part two Inside the primary classroom – Primary schools and local communities – Being a (school) boy – Male teachers and primary schools – Heterosexuality in the primary classroom – Conclusion: gender in the primary classroom – References – Index

224pp   0 335 20695 6 (Paperback)   0 335 20696 4 (Hardback)